MASS MEDIA AND
FOREIGN POLICY

MASS MEDIA AND FOREIGN POLICY

Post–Cold War Crises
in the Caribbean

Edited by Walter C. Soderlund

Westport, Connecticut
London

Library of Congress Cataloging-in-Publication Data

Soderlund, Walter C.
  Mass media and foreign policy: post–Cold War crises in the Caribbean / Walter C.
Soderlund.
      p. cm.
  Includes bibliographical references and index.
  ISBN 0–275–97785–4 (alk. paper)
    1. Caribbean Area—Press coverage—United States. 2. Caribbean Area—Politics
and government—1945– I. Nelson, R. C. (Ralph Carl), 1927– II. Briggs, E.
Donald. III. Title.
PN4888.C47 S62   2003
070.4′493249′09729—dc21   2002025309

British Library Cataloguing in Publication Data is available.

Library of Congress Catalog Card Number: 2002025309
ISBN: 0–275–97785–4

First published in 2003

Praeger Publishers, 88 Post Road West, Westport, CT 06881
An imprint of Greenwood Publishing Group, Inc.
www.praeger.com

Printed in the United States of America

The paper used in this book complies with the
Permanent Paper Standard issued by the National
Information Standards Organization (Z39.48-1984).

10 9 8 7 6 5 4 3 2 1

For Nanci

Contents

Acknowledgments

During fall 1997 I began a sabbatical leave at Florida International University in Miami and started work on organizing and editing various papers and articles I had written and cowritten over the years on the topic of media coverage of the Cold War as it unfolded in the circum-Caribbean. The book that emerged from this exercise, *Media Definitions of Cold War Reality: The Caribbean Basin, 1953–1992,* was published in November 2001.

In compiling and editing that volume, which consists largely of previously published material, I regretted the lack of an overarching research question and methods inherent in work done over fifteen years, with varying levels of funding along the way. As I got further into the project, especially the chapters on the U.S. invasion of Panama in 1989 and the Haitian election of 1990, it became clear that the Cold War was losing salience as an interpretive frame in media coverage. At this point I began to consider the possibility of extending the stream of research that had begun with the landfall of the Cold War on the Western Hemisphere in British Guiana in 1953 into the post–Cold War period. This book is the result of that research effort.

The question that I posed for the present research was, How did mainstream television news in the United States, in the period following the Cold War, interpret for their audiences a range of political/military crises that occurred in the greater Caribbean? With Communism defanged, what (if anything) would replace it as the touchstone for American foreign policy in the era of the New World Order, and how would these new policy initiatives be reported and evaluated by the nation's premier television news programs?

The three chapters dealing with Haiti were funded by the Social Sciences and Humanities Research Council of Canada (SSHRC). The University of Windsor, which throughout my career has been supportive of my work, funded the two chapters on Cuba through awards from the Humanities and Social Sciences Grant Program. At Florida International, Ivelaw Griffith, Tony Maingot, and Mark Rosenberg, in particular, were extremely helpful to me during the initial phase of this research. At the University of Windsor, Ralph Nelson, coauthor of all three chapters dealing with Haiti, and Don Briggs, who worked with me with me on the Chiapas crisis, as they have for thirty years, continued to make research an enjoyable enterprise. Secretaries Valerie Allard and Barbara Faria in Political Science helped me in countless ways and Lorraine Cantin and Lucia Brown of the Word Processing Centre did their usual exceptional job in getting my various disks and inserts turned into a coherent manuscript. My sincere thanks to all.

Because major conclusions of the research are that there was no firm compass setting for United States foreign policy toward the Caribbean region in the years after the Cold War; that the United States was extraordinarily reluctant to get involved in crises occurring there; and that, by and large, mass media supported the cautious foreign policy approach, it is not without irony that I delivered the revised draft of the concluding chapter to the Word Processing Centre at the University of Windsor on September 6, retrieving the document on September 10, 2001. Following the disastrous attacks on New York and Washington, the nature of the threat facing the United States did finally crystalize, some ten years after the end of the Cold War. The post–Cold War period ended on September 11 and a new phase in redefining the role of the United States in the world began. Clearly the role to be played by mass media in interpreting U.S. policies designed to deal with the new challenges has been, and will continue to be, an important element in their success. Hopefully the research reported in this book will allow readers to better understand the links between government and media and to evaluate critically the role played by mass media in defining the nature of the threat and the adequacy of responses to it.

Introduction

Walter C. Soderlund

Following the end of World War II, the Cold War began with events in Europe between 1946 and 1948. It ended with events in the same area of the world between 1988 and 1992. During this forty-year interval, the driving force behind U.S. foreign policy was world wide conflict with the USSR, which both sprang from and generated an ideology of virulent anti-communism, operationalized through the policy of containment. Not surprisingly, these elements also provided the key components of the frame through which media sought to understand and explain global events to their audiences as they unfolded. Indeed, domestic factors such as social and economic inequalities, racism, and political oppression, as well as international concerns such as colonialism and imperialism (regardless of their validity), tended to be submerged under the weight of Cold War preoccupations in the minds of U.S. decision makers and media observers alike (LaFeber, 1983; Schlesinger and Kinzer, 1983; Gleijeses, 1991).

With the notable exception of Cuba, the Western Hemisphere was never a major venue of U.S.–USSR confrontation, but as Ivelaw Griffith pointed out with specific reference to the Caribbean, the United States had "a low tolerance. . . for Marxist pursuits in the area" (Griffith, 1993, p. 28), and it is clear that from the time of events in British Guiana in 1953 and Guatemala in 1954 that the mass media tended, with a few notable exceptions, to interpret Western Hemispheric flare-ups in Cold War terms (i.e., the "forces of good" represented by the United States and its allies confronting the "forces of evil" represented by the USSR and its allies) (Soderlund, 2001; see also Parenti, 1986; and Herman and Chomsky, 1988).

By the late 1980s, however, there were signs that links to the Cold War were less automatic and unquestioned than had previously been the case. It was still a significant factor in the newspaper coverage of the 1989 election in El Salvador, but had diminished considerably in the same newspapers' coverage of the 1990 election in Nicaragua (Soderlund, 2001, Chapter 12). By the end of

1989, the Cold War had virtually ceased to be a factor in media explanations of the U.S. invasion of Panama (Soderlund, Wagenberg and Pemberton, 1994; see also Castañeda, 1993, pp. 250–252).

The end of communism in Eastern Europe, followed by the collapse of the Soviet Union meant, of course, that the continuation of anti-communism as a priority for the United State in Latin America lost whatever logic it might once have been argued to have (Castaneda, 1993, p. 304). It also left the media without a clear fall-back frame for the interpretation of crises erupting there. Elizabeth Hanson sums up the effects of these changes as follows:

> ...the Cold War provided a filter and a set of criteria for determining priorities in the selection of events to report... [as well]... the task of political reporting has become much more complex without the simplifying assumptions of that conflict. (Hanson, 1995, p. 351)

The question that prompted the line of research pursued in this volume, therefore, is: What interpretive frames replaced the "Communist menace" in media reporting of crisis events in the post–Cold War Caribbean Basin? With the familiar banished to the dustbin of history, in an era described by Raymond Chrétien as one in which "a single overwhelming military threat" was replaced by "a dozen subtle threats, each calling for measured military responses" (Chrétien, 1997, pp. 10–11), what explanations of conflict were U.S. media offering their audiences?

In a broad overview of post–Cold War U.S. television coverage of international events, Pippa Norris suggests that in terms of volume, running time, and placement in newscasts, international news has suffered in recent years in comparison to its domestic counterpart. After the Cold War the range of countries receiving attention in newscasts broadened, but, contrary to expectations, economic issues connected to the phenomenon of globalization did not achieve ascendancy. Rather, the dominant theme was "war, civil unrest and the military," which in fact appeared more often than during the last period of the Cold War (1973–1988) (Norris, 1995, pp. 362–366). In hindsight, considering the high level of violence experienced by the world in the early post–Cold War period, this finding is not surprising (Chopra, 1998).

The goal of this research was to determine if other interpretive frames emerged to guide U.S. audiences in their interpretation of crises occurring in the often-confusing world that emerged from the break-up of the Soviet Union, and if so, what were they. Accordingly, we undertook detailed case-study analyses of television network news coverage of seven post–Cold War crises occurring in the Caribbean Basin between 1990 and 1996: the July 1990 Jamaat-al-Muslimeen attempted coup d'etat in Trinidad and Tobago; the September 1991 Haitian military coup, which overthrew President Jean-Bernard Aristide; the unsuccessful attempt to return Aristide to Haiti in the fall of 1993; the September 1994 "invasion" that finally succeeded in restoring him to power; the New Year's Day 1994 Zapatista rebellion in Chiapas, Mexico; the Cuban "*balsero* crisis" of the summer of 1994; and the February 1996 shoot down of two Brothers to the Rescue aircraft by the Cuban air force.

In each of these seven cases videotapes of actual news stories as seen on the major evening newscasts of the ABC, CBS, and NBC networks and recorded by the Vanderbilt TV Archive provided the database for the analyses.[1] The lead author participated in the coding of all stories. For some chapters all stories were coded by both authors, while for others intercoder reliability checks were carried out on a sample of stories. With respect to story format variables (anchor, anchor-reporter, etc.), sources used in constructing the story (on-camera or quoted), item placement in the newscast, and running time, intercoder reliability fluctuated between 93 percent and 97 percent. On evaluative dimensions (stories supporting or opposing U.S. policy positions on the crises), as well as textual support or opposition to the various actors involved, intercoder reliability ranged between 84 percent and 89 percent. With respect to frames, the range of reliability scores was from 88 percent to 92 percent (Holsti, 1969, p. 140).[2]

Actual descriptive language used with respect to the major participants (the government and political leaders of the United States, the country in which the crisis took place, and any other significant participants) was recorded, collated, and distributed to six-member panels of academics in the disciplines of political science, communication studies, and Latin American and Caribbean studies. Panels were given instructions to adopt a U.S. perspective to the crisis and judge whether each descriptive word or phrase would be seen by a U.S. viewer as *positive, negative,* or *neutral/ambiguous* (see appendices to each chapter for all descriptors and panel codings). To be counted as a positive or negative descriptor, five of the six panel members had to agree that such a judgment was likely to be made by U.S. viewers. Thus, intercoder reliability for this measure was a minimum of 83 percent.

There is ample evidence that the questions posed in this research are by no means trivial. The importance of mass media in the formation of public opinion, which in turn becomes a factor in elite decision makers' consideration of appropriate foreign policies, has been well-documented by scholars (Cohen, 1963; McCombs and Shaw, 1972; Iyengar and Kinder, 1987; Rogers and Dearing, 1988; McCombs and Shaw, 1993; Rotberg and Weiss, 1996; Giffard and Rivenburgh, 2000; Rioux and Van Belle, 2001). Two relatively recent developments appear to account for the importance of mass media in foreign policy decision-making: the perceived power of public opinion to undermine elite decisions (as claimed happened in the Vietnam War) and the revolution in communication technology that brings "real time" coverage of crisis events into peoples' living rooms (thereby undermining elite autonomy) a phenomenon widely referred to as "the CNN effect" (Livingston and Eachus, 1995; Jakobsen, 1996).

Broadly, as Lance Bennett has described it, the media's role in the political system is as follows:

The first important political observation about the American mass media is that to an important extent they regulate the content of public information and communication in the U.S. political system. Mass mediated messages of reality set the limits of who in the world we think we are as a people, and what in the world we think we are doing.... This is what the mass media do; translate the complex and multi-voiced reality of our times into another, symbolic reality of simpler images and fewer voices. (1988, p. 14)

Moreover, it is now clear that, in spite of the advantage newspapers have in providing in-depth coverage of world events, it is primarily to television that the U.S. people turn for information about the world around them (Alger, 1989; Iyengar, 1991). This is especially the case for fast-breaking or crisis events (Larson, 1990), for which television news performs the critical function of alerting the population to potentially significant international occurrences (Shiras, 1996).

How a story is framed for audiences takes on considerable importance especially when, as in television news, it is necessary to present stories in an abbreviated form. As Steve Barkin has argued, TV news is obviously not fictional narrative:

It contains messages that bear some relationship to the world of events and that purport to be factual. At the same time, it is selective, incomplete, fragmentary, and reliant on a set of organizational values, narrative forms, and representational conventions that shape our understanding of that world. (1989, p. 154)

Thus, the typical news story may be seen to be composed of the following components:

- introductions and conclusions that bracket stories, relate them to other stories, and frame the report
- anchors and correspondents who act as narrators
- characters who appear within the narrative
- settings conveyed in establishing sequences
- verbal text that may or may not reinforce the visual narrative
- the use of graphic symbols and photographic techniques that, apart from their referential value, serve as aesthetic devices to convey meaning (for example, . . . intensely tight close-ups).
  (Barkin, 1989, p. 155)

Framing, according to William Gamson, is the "central organizing idea for making sense of relevant events and suggesting what is at issue" (Gamson, 1989, p. 157), and, as Robert Entman adds, can be employed to define problems, diagnose causes, offer moral judgments, and suggest remedies – all important to the way in which audiences interpret particular crisis events (Entman, 1993, p. 57; also see 1991). It has been argued that "[p]olitics is about whose views, understandings, and definitions will prevail" (Pride, 1995, p. 7); and it is in this sense, that framing provides a lens through which mass audiences form their perceptions (Iorio and Huxman, 1996).

Shanto Iyengar has distinguished between two types of framing: episodic and thematic. The difference is between events portrayed as isolated and discrete, and those seen as part of a larger and more fundamental problem (Iyengar, 1991). The Cold War was a quintessential thematic frame, providing a long-term, well-understood context for the discussion of any crisis situation. By simply invoking the familiar language of the Cold War (pro-communist, pro-Castro, Marxist, etc.), complex events instantly became clarified for audiences. As Pippa Norris explained, ". . . the Cold War frame ran like a red thread through most coverage of international news. . . . The schema simplified and prioritized coverage of international news by providing certainties about friends and enemies" (Norris, 1995, p. 359).

The seven case studies of politico-military crises examined in this book should offer ample evidence to determine whether other such threads emerged in the coverage of crises occurring after the end of the Cold War. There is no doubt that "[w]ithout the Soviet Union as a countervailing superpower, and therefore without anti-communist dogma to neatly divide the world into friends and enemies, the United States had to adjust its ideological compass" (McFadyen and LaRamée, 1995, p. 2). Our findings should indicate what new compass heading was set by the U.S. government, as well as how U.S. responses to conflict in the historically important Caribbean area were portrayed to U.S. audiences by network television news in the early years of the new era of international affairs.

NOTES

1. The author wishes to thank the Vanderbilt TV Archive for providing the video tapes of news stories on which the various analyses of media coverage in the book are based. Because the tapes were sent in unedited form, the Archive bears no responsibility for the coding or interpretations of the data reported herein.

2. The formula used to calculate intercoder reliability is $CR = \dfrac{2M}{N_1 + N_2}$.

The Jamaat-al-Muslimeen Coup in Trinidad and Tobago, 1990

Walter C. Soderlund

BACKGROUND

In the Caribbean Basin, U.S. involvement with Trinidad and Tobago (a British colony until its independence in 1962) has not been extensive, consisting primarily of investments in the oil industry and the U.S. naval base at Chaguaramas, negotiated with the British as a part of the World War II Lendlease Agreement. With respect to the former, nationalizations of the late 1960s affected mainly European companies, which facilitated the entry of U.S. companies into the oil industry (Farrell, 1983, pp.183–206). With respect to the latter, Eric Williams, an ardent nationalist, championed returning control of the Chaguaramas base to Trinidad and Tobago a number of years before independence had been achieved (Ince, 1983, pp. 275–276), and its return was negotiated successfully in 1961. Although Williams remained a strong nationalist, following the Cuban Revolution, in what Ince describes as "acquiescent behavior," he decided to align Trinidad and Tobago with the West and led the former British Caribbean colonies in their attempt to join the Organization of American States (OAS). For Trinidad and Tobago this occurred in 1967 (Ince, 1983, p. 277). In 1970, however, Williams, always his own man, "called for the reintegration of Cuba into the Western Hemisphere" (Ince, 1983, p. 283), a position that gives the United States discomfort even in the early years of the twenty-first century. In summary, it would be safe to say that during the latter decades of the Cold War, relations between Trinidad and Tobago and the United States, while proper, were not especially close.

At approximately 6:00 PM on Friday, July 27, 1990, Imam Yasin Abu Bakr (a former Trinidad policeman born Lennox Phillip and converted to Islam in the 1960s) led some 120 armed men belonging to the Jamaat-al-Muslimeen in coordinated strikes on three crucial points in Trinidad and Tobago's capital, Port of Spain: a fire-bombing of Police Headquarters (which gutted the building,

located a stone's throw from the Red House or Parliament Building), and twin
assaults on Trinidad and Tobago Television House and the Red House where
hostages, including the nation's Prime Minister A.N.R. Robinson, were taken
and held (Maynard, 1990, p. 42). In an interesting comment on the power of
mass media, Abu Bakr chose to lead the forces holding Television House,
leaving his lieutenant, Bilaal Abdullah, in charge of the political hostages and,
the negotiations that ended the coup attempt (Pantin, 1990).

Claiming his actions to be "the Will of God," at about 7:00 PM, Bakr
announced in a newscast format on T&T television that "the Government of
Trinidad and Tobago has been overthrown;" that the Prime Minister and his
Cabinet were "under arrest;" and that the army should "lay down its arms to
facilitate a peaceful transition." He also cautioned the people "not to be involved
in any looting" at the risk of severe consequences. He further proclaimed that he
"could no longer stand by while our country reached the abyss," that he had
"made a noble act on your [the people's] behalf," and that "animosity and hatred
must come to an end."[1]

Beginning within an hour of Abu Bakr's initial television broadcast, and
continuing for the following five days, 31 people were killed, another 693 were
wounded, 4,000 people were left unemployed, and property damage resulting
from looting and fires in Port of Spain reached an estimated TT$500 million
(Griffith, 1993, p. 31). According to Selwyn Ryan, the events of July 27
"marked the beginning of the most serious political crisis the country had faced
in its history as an independent nation state" (Ryan, 1991, p. 52).

In explaining why the attempted coup occurred when it did, perpetrated by a
group on the fringes of even the relatively small Muslim population in Trinidad
(estimated at 6 percent)[2] a number of diverse factors have to be considered.

First, as Ryan points out, Trinidad and Tobago has a history of "racially
inspired riots, rebellions and revolutionary movements" (1991, p. vi), and he
places the attempted coup in a chain of such violent events occurring in 1903,
1917–19, 1934, 1937, 1946–48, 1970, and 1973.

Second, at the societal level, the country was undergoing an economic crisis
triggered by a dramatic fall in oil prices in the 1980s, leading to a decline in
governmental revenues. The estimated contributions by individuals (as opposed
to industry) to the national coffers increased by 19 percent from 1982 to 1990
(Ryan, 1991, p. 18). As a consequence, in 1988 the Government had been forced
to go to the International Monetary Fund (IMF) for a loan of US$128 million.
"These loans brought on massive retrenchment, drastic increase in social
problems such as crimes, unemployment, inadequate housing facilities, and
poverty unequaled in the history of the country" (Trinidad and Tobago *Mirror*,
August 21, 1990; as quoted in Furlonge-Kelly, 1991, p. 233). Ryan points out as
well the link between "deep-seated poverty and the appeal of millenarianism" in
accounting for the coup (Ryan, 1991, p. 18).

Third, the political system itself was in a state of confusion, if not in overt
crisis. Ramesh Deosaran argued that society "had reached a state of lawlessness
and even shamelessness in public affairs such that one more deviant act, albeit a
violent one, seemed to fit into the general pattern of public misconduct"

(Deosaran, 1993, pp. 1–2). In 1986, A.N.R. Robinson had led the National Alliance for Reconstruction (NAR) to an electoral victory over the People's National Movement (PNM), the political party that had held power since independence in 1962 and had been led by Eric Williams until his death in 1981 (Grant, 1990, p. 6). The NAR government seemed fixated on investigating misdeeds and scandals of previous PNM governments and, in an act of seeming insensitivity, had just announced that TT$500,000 would be allocated to build a monument to a civil servant who died trying to bring PNM corruption to light (Deosaran, 1993, pp. 64–68). In one of his television statements to the nation, Abu Bakr mentioned this incident as the final straw leading to the coup. As argued by Mickey Matthews,

> Unmistakable by the time the young men of the Jamaat-al-Muslimeen struck, parliament was already violated and its illegality patent. Its members for the most part stood discredited, the three forces for which they speak representing nothing more than a triangle of ethnic futility. (1990, p. 12)

These broad societal factors may have led Abu Bakr to believe that his coup would at least lead to critical defections among the police and army, if not a popular uprising (Collihan and Danopolous, 1993, pp. 444–447). This was not an altogether fanciful expectation, there had been a serious military mutiny in the country in 1970 (Griffith, 1993, pp. 110–112).

Added to these factors was the dispute the Jamaat-al-Muslimeen had with the government over ownership of the property in Port of Spain on which the group had built its Mosque and related buildings. This dispute had been ongoing for more than twenty years (Bakr had been jailed briefly in connection with it in the mid-1980s). Two days before the coup, the High Court of Trinidad and Tobago had rejected an appeal by Jamaat-al-Muslimeen of an earlier judgment unfavorable to their claim of rightful ownership and declared them to be, in effect, "trespassers" (Deosaran, 1993, pp. 180–238). The coup, then, could be seen as a pre-emptive strike against the government-- taking control of it before it could act to remove the Jamaat-al-Muslimeen from the disputed property (Ryan, 1991, pp. 57–79). In this vein, Deosaran characterizes the attack on the government as "a Muslimeen quest for revenge" for their perceived mistreatment (Deosaran, 1993, p. 78). Bakr never mentioned the land dispute in his TV broadcasts to the citizens of Trinidad and Tobago.

External factors may have figured into the situation as well. A majority of the guns used by the Jamaat-al-Muslimeen in the coup had been purchased in Ft. Lauderdale, Florida, and after the coup had been put down, Prime Minister Robinson charged "that if we had the information which was possessed by the U.S. authorities in Miami, the coup would have been avoided" (Robinson as quoted in Ryan, 1991, p. 167). Ryan concludes that, while relations between the United States and the NAR government were strained over drug interdiction policy, the police in Trinidad and Tobago had contacted the wrong agencies in Miami (the FBI and the Miami Police), while the agency involved was the Bureau of Alcohol, Tobacco and Firearms. In response to the Prime Minister's charge, the U.S. Ambassador to Trinidad and Tobago indicated that in such situations, supposed "links" between the purchase of arms and a coup, tend to appear much clearer after the fact than before (Ryan, 1991, p.168). There does not seem to be any hard evidence that the United States knowingly and willfully withheld information that would have allowed the government to pre-empt the actual coup.

In terms of possible U.S. intervention in response to the coup, the evidence is mixed and somewhat contradictory. The Trinidad and Tobago *Mirror* "reported on August 3 that the USA did not want to intervene massively in Trinidad and Tobago since they did not know the terrain and any head on with Yasin Abu Bakr would have caused a lot of bloodshed" (Furlonge-Kelly, 1991, p. 125). It was acknowledged, however, that the aircraft carrier *Theodore Roosevelt* was "in the area," which would have made U.S. intervention possible, if it were seen to be necessary (Marajh and Robinson, 1990, p. 78; see also Terry, 1990, p. 30). In spite of Pentagon denials, Deosaran reports that "about 20 members of the antiterrorist Delta Force arrived from the USA and took over command against the Muslimeen." He also indicates that the U.S. Ambassador "was consulted twice a day by officials of the Trinidad Government" (Deosaran, 1993, p. 47). Both Ryan and Furlonge-Kelly confirm that a small number of the U.S. antiterrorist Delta Force were in Port of Spain, but claim that they acted only in an advisory role.

Far more significant as an international factor were Abu Bakr's links to Libya and its controversial leader Muammar Qadaffi. These connections were no secret, either in Trinidad or the United States. Earlier in 1990, the government of Trinidad and Tobago had refused to take delivery of $800,000 worth of pharmaceuticals that had been donated at Bakr's request by the Islamic Call Society, headquartered in Libya. In part at least, this was done on the grounds that Bakr was regarded "as a serious threat to National Security who had to be denied the legitimacy which accepting the offer of drugs would have afforded him" (Ryan, 1991, p. 54). It is also clear that at least thirty-five members of the Jamaat had received training in Libya. However, despite much smoke regarding the Libyan connection, Ryan concludes that there was no fire with respect to the actual coup attempt. He argues that Bakr and the Jamaat-al-Muslimeen "were part of Qaddaffi's proxy revolutionary army in the Third World and that Bakr had not only been seduced by Libyan largesse but had become a convert to much of what he had read in the *Green Book*. . . . Had the coup been successful, "Bakr . . . expected economic assistance and critical expertise from Libya . . ." (Ryan, 1991, p. 265), but "there is no documentary evidence to establish there was a Libyan connection [in the events of July 27] . . . . [Moreover]. . . when Libyan 'assets' in the Caribbean checked with Tripoli for instructions as to what response they should make to events in Trinidad, they were told to stay clear of it" (Ryan, 1991, p. 258).

Ryan points out that "opinion varied as to whether Bakr was a hero, a madman, a crook, a charlatan, a true social reformer or simply a misguided individual" (Ryan, 1991, p. 219). While it is clear that the vast majority of Trinidad and Tobago's population did not support his methods, it is also true that the issues that he raised—societal deterioration, economic want, and government inattention—resonated among a substantial portion of it, especially "dispossessed Blacks, who in [Bakr's] view continued to be economically powerless and dependent and discriminated against by the Christian based power structure" (Ryan, 1991, p. 11). In the final analysis, no popular uprising was triggered by the coup, save the fourteen hours during which "Port of Spain was mindlessly pillaged, ravaged and sacked" (Maynard, 1990, p. 42).

The Commander of the Trinidad and Tobago Regiment appeared briefly on television with two government ministers Friday evening after Bakr's announcement of the overthrow, assuring the citizenry that neither the Defense Forces nor the Protective Services (police) had or would collaborate with "the perpetrators of this crime." These critical security forces remained loyal to the government being run by ministers who were not held hostage. Later that evening, Trinidad and Tobago television signals were jammed, denying Bakr further direct communication with the population (Monfils, 1995).

By Saturday morning the Jamaat-al-Muslimeen were contained in two buildings (the Red House and T&T Television House) and a State of Emergency was in effect. The situation, in effect became a stalemated hostage crisis, although "never losing its potential for revolutionary upheaval" (Matthews, 1990, p. 12). A sense of urgency was added in that Prime Minister Robinson had been shot in the leg the night before when he had defied his captors' instructions to tell security forces to pull back and had instead ordered them to "attack in full force."

In the view of Deosaran, "there was in fact no 'take-over' of the government in place. . . The Government was not overthrown, it was hijacked. And political confusion reigned. . . Clearly Bakr was not in charge" (Deosaran, 1993, p. 26). As Judy Raymond expressed it, the Imam "seemed not to have read beyond Lesson One in the manual. . ." (as quoted in Best, 1990, p. D).

In these circumstances, Bakr issued a list of six demands to end the crisis peacefully:

1. Robinson to resign as prime minister
2. Other Ministers to support a new prime minister and interim government
3. The President to act on the advice of the interim prime minister
4. Elections to be held in 90 days
5. A Government of National Unity to include the heads of political parties and Abu Bakr
6. Amnesty for the coupmakers (*Daily Express,* 1990, pp. 68–69).

Negotiations to end the crisis began on Sunday, July 29 and, although the government was later to claim that it acted under duress, an agreement including amnesty for the perpetrators was reached that saw the release of P.M. Robinson on Tuesday July 31, followed by the release of the remaining hostages and the surrender of Abu Bakr and 112 members of the Jamaat-al-Muslimeen at two locations on Wednesday August 1 (Marajh and Robinson, 1990).

The entire group was detained at a special facility in Chaguaramas; two weeks later Bakr "was charged with 20 offenses including treason, 8 counts of murder, arson in destruction of the Police Headquarters and unlawful imprisonment of Trinidad and Tobago Television staff" (Furlonge-Kelly, 1991, p. 201).

Before a trial could take place, the question of whether the amnesty clause in the agreement signed by the government to end the crisis was valid or whether it had been signed under duress had to be settled. A complex and somewhat confusing set of legal appeals, involving courts in Trinidad and Tobago and the Judicial Committee of the British Privy Council (which acts as the final legal arbiter for the nation), ensued. In June 1992, Justice Brooks "ruled that the presidential pardon, the amnesty [was] valid and was not procured by duress" (Deosaran, 1993, p. 198). This ruling was appealed by the Government of Trinidad and Tobago to the Privy Council, which finally held that although the amnesty was in fact invalid it would not be politic to prosecute the group inasmuch as they had already been released, albeit incorrectly (Deosaran, 1993, p. 192). In effect, the Jamaat-al-Muslimeen escaped prosecution even though the amnesty was found to be invalid.

FINDINGS

News stories on the attempted coup appeared on major U.S. television networks for five-days, beginning on Saturday, July 28 (the day after the initiation of the coup attempt) and ending on Wednesday, August 1st 1990, the day the final hostages were released and the Jamaat-al-Muslimeen surrendered. There were a total of fifteen stories, five on each network.[3] There were no news stories on Trinidad and Tobago leading up to the coup, nor were there any follow-up stories in its immediate aftermath. In Iyengar's terms, it was a quintessential "episodic" event.

An examination of story characteristics summarized in Table 2.1 indicates that the producers of U.S. television news were at best uncertain about the importance of the events in Trinidad and Tobago. While a respectable 47 percent of stories related to the coup led off newscasts, with 67 percent running in the top three positions, these stories tended to be rather short in length—27 percent ran thirty seconds or less, with no stories running longer than three minutes. One-third of the stories were handled by the anchor alone in the studio; of those using a reporter, none featured more than one reporter in the field. Overall, 47 percent of stories used a reporter in Trinidad. These figures no doubt reflect the difficulty networks had, given the state of emergency, the closure of the airport, and related curfews, in getting information and film out of Trinidad and getting their reporters into the country to cover the on-going crisis. For example, while some film appeared in 93 percent of stories on the coup, the first visuals of the burning and looting in Port of Spain appeared on Monday, July 30 on CBS and NBC, which is when the first reporters actually started filing stories from Trinidad. Two academic experts on Trinidad, Professors Ken Boodhoo and Anthony Maingot, both of Florida International University, were interviewed on the first day of coverage of the crisis in an attempt to give the story some perspective. The position of the U.S. government on the crisis may be stated as follows: support for the Trinidad and Tobago government and a call for the rebels to lay down their arms; overall, 60 percent of stories legitimized this policy position and none opposed it.

Table 2.1
Story Characteristics N = 15

Characteristics	Number		Percent
Lead Story	7		47
1ˢᵗ Three Stories	10		67
30 Seconds and Under	4		27
Over 3 Minutes	0		–
Just Anchor Format	5		33
Use of Experts	3		20
Reporter in Trinidad	7		47
Two or More New Segments	0		–
Film With Story	14		93
Film of President Bush	1		7
Film of Prime Minister Robinson	6		40
Film of Iman Abu Bakr	11		73
Visual Violence	7		47
Libyan Connection	8		53
Tilt Favorable to U.S. Position	9		60
Tilt Unfavorable to U.S. Position	0		–
U.S. Involvement Index		1.4	

Also coded as a part of the study, on a five-point scale (1=low involvement to 5=high involvement) was the extent of U.S. involvement in the crisis. On this dimension,73 percent of stories received a score of 1, with only 13 percent getting as high as 3—the midpoint of the scale. Overall, the index score was 1.4, indicating a very low level of U.S. involvement. This lack of U.S. involvement no doubt played a role in reducing the importance of the event for media decision makers.

Data in Table 2.2 show the number of times leading sources (Barkin's news story "characters") actually appeared on camera or were quoted in the coverage of the coup. The use of sources by reporters is the first element in the journalistic gatekeeping chain, and is an important factor in how events are presented to audiences (Mermin, 1997). As pointed out by Steven Livingston, "most of the raw data used to construct news comes not from direct journalist exposure to an event but from sources, usually government authorities. Most of the power to define reality, in this view of the news process, resides at the point of reporter-source contact" (Livingston, 1996, p. 70).

Table 2.2
Number of Times Leading Sources Used (All Sources Used in Newscast)

News Source	Number
Jamaat-al-Muslimeen	5
Yasin Abu Bakr	4
Trinidad and Tobago Government Spokespersons	4
Trinidad and Tobago Military Spokespersons	3
Journalists (interviewed)	3
Trinidadians on the street	3
U.S. State Department Spokespersons	3
U.S. Experts	3

The list of sources used in coverage of the Trinidad coup list is significant for two reasons. First, there was a dearth of U.S. government sources. In most international crises, the president and the administration figure prominently in the list of sources. If there is political conflict regarding the appropriate U.S. response, opposition members of Congress usually lead the charge against the president's policy (Paletz and Entman, 1981). The relative absence of all U.S. sources in this case indicates the clear reluctance of the U.S. government to get involved in the crisis. The second point of interest is the extent to which the Jamaat-al-Muslimeen and Abu Bakr were able to command news attention; they were the story, with film of the Imam (mostly file footage) appearing in 73 percent of stories aired. The advantage held by the Trinidad and Tobago government in controlling communication after the first few hours of the coup did not seem to be exploited to the extent that it could have been. Indeed, during the first two or three days of coverage, more information regarding what was going on the country came from telephone interviews with a Trinidadian journalist than from Trinidadian government sources.

Data in Table 2.3 deal with the frames used by television news in making sense of the Jamaat-al-Muslimeen coup for American audiences. As mentioned, the coverage was primarily episodic. Basically the situation was portrayed as a "hostage crisis"—not as a political crisis—although some background information on Trinidad's economic and social problems was presented. The major focus of stories was on how, given the potential for significant loss of life, the situation would end. Within this hostage frame, violence figured prominently: the violence involved in staging the coup (the burning of the police headquarters building), the supposed wiring of hostages (including the prime minister) to explosives,[4] the shooting of the prime minister, and the burning and looting in Port of Spain. The negotiations to end the crisis were not reported in the context of dealing with social, economic, and political problems in Trinidad and Tobago, but rather in terms of what was necessary to secure the safe release of the hostages.

Table 2.3
Percentage of Stories in Which Media Frames Are Used

Frame	Primary	Secondary	Tertiary	Total
Hostage Crisis				
Number of Stories	12	2	1	15
Percentage	80	13	7	100
Violence				
Number of Stories	1	5	2	8
Percentage	7	33	13	53
International Terrorism				
Number of Stories	0	4	3	7
Percentage	–	27	20	47

One frame can be said to be thematic: that of international terrorism. Abu Bakr and the Jamaat-al-Muslimeen were clearly placed in the company of Libya's Muammar Qadaffi and portrayed in the tradition of the radical Black Power movement in the United States. While no hard evidence linking the coup to Qadaffi and Libya was actually presented, the prominence accorded the Libyan leader (the connection was mentioned in nearly half of the stories) makes it clear that U.S. audiences were being primed to see the coup as a part of an international terrorist conspiracy.[5]

Table 2.4
Text Evaluation of Major Participants

	George Bush (5 stories)	A.N.R. Robinson (15 stories)	Yasin Abu Bakr (15 stories)
Favorable			
Number of stories	3	7	0
Percentage	60	47	–
Neutral/Ambiguous			
Number of stories	2	6	7
Percentage	40	40	47
Unfavorable			
Number of stories	0	2	8
Percentage	–	13	53

Beginning with data in Table 2.4, we shall examine in detail how the major actors in the crisis were evaluated in television coverage of the coup attempt. In terms of text evaluation, first of all President Bush did not figure prominently in coverage; only five stories made reference to him, three in a positive context and two in a neutral context. He appeared on film (on vacation in Maine) in only one story. In contrast, all fifteen stories contained evaluations of both Prime Minister Robinson and Imam Abu Bakr. The balance of evaluation was favorable to Mr. Robinson (seven stories were positive, six were neutral or ambiguous, while only two were negative); for the Imam, none was seen as positive, seven were neutral or ambiguous, while eight were negative.

These figures are corroborated by the positive and negative codings of the words and phrases used to describe President Bush and the U.S. government, Prime Minister Robinson and the Trinidad and Tobago government, and Imam Abu Bakr and the Jamaat-al-Muslimeen as shown in Table 2.5. Again, the lack of valenced words and phrases attached to President Bush and the U.S. government (only six used overall), indicates the peripheral nature of U.S. involvement in the event.[6] In Trinidad, the prime minister and his government are generally portrayed favorably (two-thirds of descriptors positive, opposed to one-third negative), while the Imam and his group were portrayed in a virtual mirror image: negatively in 68 percent of descriptors and positively in only 32 percent.

Table 2.5
Percentage of Descriptors Reflecting Positively and Negatively on Major Participants

	Number of Descriptors	Percentage
Bush/U.S. Government		
Positive	6	100
Negative	0	–
Total	6	100
Robinson/Trinidad and Tobago Government		
Positive	23	66
Negative	12	34
Total	35	100
Abu Bakr/Jamaat-al-Muslimeen		
Positive	28	32
Negative	60	68
Total	88	100

CONCLUSION

In their coverage of what we consider to be the first post–Cold War crisis in the Caribbean basin, except for the limited treatment of terrorism discussed below, U.S. television news programs did not provide any clear thematic frame for the interpretation of the event. Trinidad and Tobago had never been the site of major confrontations during the Cold War and, compared with Cuba and Haiti, for example, was not seen as problematic from the point of view of U.S. decision makers. Thus a coup occurring there seemed to occasion the same degree of surprise within the U.S. government and U.S. media as it did for both the people and government of Trinidad and Tobago. While the country did suffer from both economic and social problems, it would be difficult to argue that these were any more severe than those that affected the region more generally. In short, Trinidad and Tobago was not seen as a likely place to attempt a coup d'etat.

The difficulty in getting information out of the country and reporters into the country, the watchful waiting stance adopted by the U.S. government, and the relatively violent character but brief duration of the coup all contributed to a style of coverage characterized by early placement in newscasts combined with minimal substance. The event tended to be treated in terms of an ongoing hostage crisis involving both societal and personal violence. Most stories dealt with the violence of the coup and fears for the lives of the hostages if negotiations to release them failed or the buildings in which they were being held were attacked by government forces. In effect, the news stories provided an ongoing narrative of what was happening, day-by-day, to resolve the crisis. The possibility that the coup might actually succeed in overthrowing the government of Trinidad and Tobago was never seriously considered.

While some discussion of economic and social problems facing the country was occasioned by the statements released by Abu Bakr, if there was a thematic frame, it was the international connection to the terrorist state Libya and its leader, Muammar Qadaffi. If the U.S. government had legitimized this perceived threat by the use of authoritative spokespersons and if it had become involved overtly in putting down the coup, without doubt the Libyan connection would have provided the justification for such involvement. Because the Jamaat-al-Muslimeen was a radical Muslim organization, and given the language used by U.S. media to describe Abu Bakr and the group, one can see the possibility of combining Samuel Huntington's clash of civilizations thesis, positing fundamentalist Islam as providing the next global challenge to the United Sates (Huntington, 1993), with Qadaffi's well-established reputation as a sponsor of anti-American terrorism.

An important theme not dealt with at all in TV news coverage is the vulnerability of small states to the kind of political violence characteristic of the Jamaat-al-Muslimeen coup (Best 1990, p. A; Ryan, 1991, p. ix). For example, there was nothing in news coverage placing the coup in the context of earlier successful ones in Grenada in 1979 (led by Maurice Bishop) and Suriname in 1980 (led by Desi Bouterse), and the consequences these coups had for their respective societies. Outside of North America and Western Europe, elections are not uncontested as the means of changing governments (Soderlund, 1970); and following the coup, A.N.R. Robinson claimed that "like it or not, the coup d'etat has emerged as the standard mechanism of political change in Third World Countries" (as quoted in Furlonge-Kelly, 1991, p. 156). It is not entirely fanciful to claim that "the Caribbean is full of causes looking for a leader and opportunity" (Canute James as quoted in Furlonge-Kelly, 1991, p. 190).

The reality is that coups definitely pose a threat to democratic governance in the Caribbean, where many small states lack the military capacity and discipline to respond in the manner seen in Trinidad and Tobago, which in the Caribbean context is considered both a large and economically developed country (Griffith, 1993). If Abu Bakr had more men at his disposal or a more well-thought-out plan, or if substantial elements of the nation's security forces had defected to the coup makers, the outcome of events in Trinidad and Tobago in July 1990 might have been quite different. Needless to say, a different outcome would have led to serious consequences, not only for Trinidad and Tobago, but for the entire Caribbean region.

APPENDIX 2.1

PRESIDENT BUSH/U.S. GOVERNMENT

Descriptors Coded Positive
- Voiced support for the elected government/voiced strong support for the government held hostage
- Called on Muslim rebels to lay down their arms
- Condemned the attempted coup
- American specialists are providing advice to the government on how to deal with a hostage crisis in America's back yard

Descriptors Coded Neutral or Ambiguous
- Closely monitored developments/following developments closely
- State Department is saying very little
- U.S. intervention is highly unlikely/there has been no thought of a U.S. military intervention
- United States has ten ships said to be on routine exercises in the Caribbean

PRIME MINISTER ROBINSON/TRINIDAD AND TOBAGO GOVERNMENT

Descriptors Coded Positive
- Being held captive/taken hostage/held hostage by a Black Muslim group that tried to seize power/one of the government leaders held hostage for four days
- Army is on the side of the government
- [PM] wired to explosives/reportedly shot in the leg/shot in both legs, tied to a chair, and wired to explosives/shot in both legs and badly beaten/wounded
- Anything he does is due to extreme coercion
- Released [from captivity]/released at twenty past one
- "The Prime Minister of our beloved country is now safe"*
- Is in good spirits
- Government denies a deal to get Robinson released/refused amnesty to rebels/denies an agreement with rebels and claims surrender was unconditional/insisted surrender was unconditional
- Talking in optimistic terms about an economic recovery program

Descriptors Coded Negative
- Unemployment and political dissent increasing/admits rising discontent due to a faltering economy/ general discontent in the population/blamed for the spread of poverty
- Police were slow to respond to looting
- Conceded that looting continued in Port of Spain

Descriptors Coded Neutral or Ambiguous
- Prime Minister
- Appears ready to strike a deal
- Has reached an agreement with Muslim rebels
- Will agree to resign, turn over power to a new government and hold elections in ninety days/agreed to resign and elections are to be held in ninety days/would step down and call elections/to resign/said to have resigned ad will call new elections
- Amnesty is not confirmed by the government
- "A small faction of the government made a coup"
- Will the government honor the agreement the Muslims say they have with the government?

ABU BAKR/JAMAAT-AL-MUSLIMEEN

Descriptors Coded Positive
- Well-known Trinidadian political figure
- Promised free elections
- "This is not democracy—Let us see a peaceful transition and in ninety days we will have another election free from fear and free and fair"
- "We have a signed agreement for the immediate release of everyone"
- Took over the government to help the poor
- "We did it to remove corruption and repression in society"
- Emerged with a triumphant gesture

Descriptors Coded Negative
- Muslim rebels/Muslim radicals/Muslim gunmen/Muslim extremists radical Muslims/ radical Black Muslims/radical Muslim gunmen/Black Muslims
- Muslim fundamentalists
- Took hostages/held hostages/took control of parliament, the TV station and one radio station/took Prime Minister hostage/"we are in charge of the Parliament building and the Prime Minister"/ holding hostages/holding top government officials/continue to hold 40 hostages/ still holding hostages/holding top government officials
- Threatened to kill hostages/wired the Prime Minister and others with explosives and threatened to kill them without an agreement/threatened to blow up themselves and their hostages if a rescue attempt is made
- Shot the Prime Minister in the leg/shot the Prime Minister in both legs
- Beat the Prime Minister badly
- Rebels/rebel gunmen/rebellion leader/rebel leader
- Has ties to Libya/frequent guest in Tripoli, Libya/has visited Libya and Vietnam/ Libya is suspected as a source of support/frequent guest in

> Libya of another radical Muslim, Muammar Qadaffi/has strong ties to Libya/has received money and supplies from Libya/allegedly linked to Libya/claims to have close ties to Muammar Qadaffi/he and his followers armed and trained by Qadaffi/got help from the Middle East, including Libya

- Had a lot of run-ins with police/has been in trouble with the law before
- Becoming almost desperate
- Police afraid of them
- Released the prime Minister because they didn't want him to die
- Was the first to surrender/surrendered to the military
- Nothing to suggest that they are ready to give up
- Does not appear to have wide-spread support/no indication of wide-spread support/no indication of widespread support for the coup/does not appear to be getting much popular support/ failed to win wide-spread support/rebellion not widely supported
- As long as they [the rebels] are free, Trinidad will not return to normal
- Radical convert to Islam, with connections to Libya's Muammar Qadaffi

Descriptors Coded Neutral or Ambiguous

- Former policeman/former Trinidad and Tobago policeman
- Muslim leader
- Called for public support
- Have a lot of money
- Follows the laws of Allah, not the laws of men
- Want their own safety assured/demanding amnesty
- If this agreement is implemented, it would be a victory for rebel leader Abu-Bakr
- Agreed to release the Prime Minister and other hostages in return for safe passage to their compound
- Denies that he will seek asylum in Libya
- wants to release hostages and go free
- Charged that the government is corrupt, undemocratic and ruined the economy
- Freed Prime Minister Robinson/freed wounded Prime Minister/released the hostages
- Would get amnesty/to be given amnesty
- Established his [religious] sect in 1980
- Roots [of the movement] grew out of the Black Power movement that blossomed in the United States
- Watched his men turn over their rifles to security forces
- Say they surrendered after winning a promise of amnesty
- Felt they did nothing wrong
- Surrendered without conditions

- "We did this for Almighty God, that they may get to their senses and change"
- Called for concessions from the government

* Descriptors in quotation marks indicate statements made by sources.

NOTES

1.   Where information in this section is not footnoted, it is derived from a private videotape of TV broadcasts aired in Trinidad and Tobago during the coup. This tape included, among other material, the initial and follow-up announcement of the coup made by Abu Bakr, the reassurances of Colonel Brown and two cabinet ministers, along with a post-coup interview with Prime Minister Robinson. I am indebted to Phillip Fortuné for making this valuable tape available to me.

2.   In term of ethnic origin, Trinidad and Tobago's population is roughly equally divided between Africans (40.8 percent) and East Indians (40.6 percent), with 16.3 percent reported as mixed. With respect to religion, 33 percent are Roman Catholic, about 30 percent Protestant, 25 percent Hindu and 6 percent Muslim, with 6 percent not stating religious preference (Deosaran, 1993, Table 1, p. 53).

3.   Also of comparison, the 1991 coup in Haiti that resulted in the removal of Jean-Bertrand Aristide from the presidency, generated twenty stories on the same three U.S. networks (see Chapter 3).

4.   Although the Jamaat-al-Muslimeen claimed to have wired hostages to explosives to be detonated in the event of a rescue attempt, once negotiations began on Sunday, this was known to be false. However, from post-coup interviews, there is no doubt that the hostages were targeted for death, had either the T&T Television House or the Red House been stormed.

5.   As an example, Professor Boodhoo was asked by a reporter not *if* Qadaffi was involved in the coup, but *what he had to gain* by sponsoring it.

6.   The term "valenced" is used to designate a descriptor that carries with it either a positive or negative value.

3

The Military Coup in Haiti, 1991

Ralph C. Nelson and Walter C. Soderlund

While the latest episode in the involvement of the United States in the affairs of Haiti can be dated fairly precisely from February 1986, with the "assist" given in the removal of Jean-Claude Duvalier, the history of U.S. involvement in the country goes back to the time of Haitian independence early in the nineteenth century. At one point during the independence struggles, U.S. warships were dispatched to aid Haitian general Toussaint L'Ouverture, who was involved in a dispute with another Haitian general. This, however, proved to be the extent of U.S. aid. Fear of a possible slave rebellion in the Southern United States, coupled with a rapprochement with France, resulted in a U.S. trade embargo in 1806 that "began a century of commercial ostracism," leading to Haiti's isolation from the world economic system (Abbott, 1988; see also Stinchcombe, 1994).

Although the twentieth century would bring a quantum increase in U.S. involvement in Haitian affairs, most would argue that the overall result was not beneficial to the island nation. As the Western world moved into a new round of imperialism and colonial expansion, the United States came of age as a world power. And it was, as geography largely determined, the Caribbean Basin—the U.S.'s so-called "backyard"—that caught the attention of U.S. strategic thinkers. Within the Caribbean, Haiti's strategic position and its domestic instability, combined with perceived foreign (particularly German) interest in acquiring a coaling station on the island, led in 1915 to a U.S. military occupation of the country that lasted formally until 1934. Full financial autonomy was not restored until 1952 (Abbott, 1988, p. 46).

While it is impossible to deal fully with this important formative period in U.S.–Haitian relations, a summary judgment is that any gains that were made in areas of creating an economic infrastructure and improving health were at least offset by the importation of U.S.-style racism and a refusal on the part of the United States to give any real substantive meaning to the concept of democracy. Another legacy of dubious value left by the Americans was the Haitian Army, organized as the *Garde d'Haïti* by the United States Marine Corps, which quickly took up an unintended political role upon the American departure

(Bellegard-Smith, 1990). Of course, the social divisions between a mulatto economic, social, and political elite and the mass of black Haitians persisted (Nicholls, 1996). It is unfair to blame the United States for the Duvalier dictatorship (father and son), which began in 1957; but the United States certainly set the stage for it and supported the dictatorship at various times in the context of the Cold War (Danner, 1993b; Fauriol, 1988).

The thirty years of Duvalier family rule, which combined extraordinary economic greed with brutal political repression carried out by the feared Tonton Macoutes, proved catastrophic for Haiti (Fauriol, 1988). Even the Army was not immune to Duvalier's wrath; according to Abbott, "Macoutes had the right of life and death over any member of society, and could with impunity punish or kill even the men in olive green, the soldiers Duvalier feared so pathologically" (Abbott, 1988, p. 87). The dictatorship led to some of the most talented members of Haitian society (the mulatto elite) being forced into exile; as well, vast wealth was siphoned off by what Maingot has referred to as a "kleptocratic state" (Maingot, 1986–87, p. 83). The result was that in 1986, when Haiti was finally rid of the dictatorship, the country was gripped by poverty, illness, and misery, with a huge gap existing between a few very rich and vast majority who were very poor (Hector, 1988, pp. 6–7).

In the aftermath of the Duvalier dictatorship, the United States pursued a policy of "restoration of democracy," although it could be argued that democracy had really never existed on the island and talk of restoring it was misplaced. The widespread hope that things would be different in Haiti did not last very long. While a new constitution was enacted, the first democratic elections held under its provision in November 1987 were marred by military-condoned violence, which led to their annulment (Abbott, 1988, pp. 1–7) The military staged another election in 1988 (boycotted by most democratic candidates) but the "winner" himself succumbed to a military coup within months of taking office. Yet another coup followed before free and democratic elections were held in December 1990 (Nelson and Soderlund, 1992). In the 1990 election a parish priest, an exponent of liberation theology and a champion of Haiti's poor, Jean-Bertrand Aristide, swept to victory with slightly more than two-thirds of the popular vote. He was genuinely viewed by Haiti's masses as a political savior.

This democratic decision, however, was not allowed to stand. Seven months after taking office as the duly-elected President, Aristide was overthrown on September 30; 1991 by a coup d'état carried out by the Army led by Lt. General Raoul Cédras, appointed by Aristide in part at least because of his commitment to democracy.[1]

The coup was an inside job, triggered by a rebellion of army enlisted men. While these soldiers might have been frustrated with violence carried out against them by Aristide supporters, it appears that they were led by Lt. Col. Michel François, commander of the Port-au-Prince police (Farmer, 1994, p. 183). Early in the coup attempt, there was a possibility that Aristide might be killed, and, in an interview with a British journalist, General Cédras indicated that he did in fact intervene to save the president's life:

There were a great mass of them here in my office, rankers [enlisted men], the lot...They were enraged, ready to tear the president limb from limb...so I jumped in front to him to shield his body, and I told them not to touch a hair on his head. That's not the way we do things here any more. (Cédras as quoted in Evans-Pritchard, 1993, p. 24)

Aristide's version of the same event differs considerably. In the days before the coup, rumors of an army mutiny had been circulating in Port-au-Prince; when queried by Aristide, Cédras dismissed these rumors. However, when Aristide's house "was surrounded and bullets were spattering against its walls," the president traveled to the National Palace "to get to the bottom of things..."

It is a trick! The building is surrounded!...We leave the palace as prisoners, headed for the army general headquarters. Cédras is there; he hid his cards very well...He tells me plainly, with a glowing countenance; "From now on, I am the president."...I myself have my hands tied. They try to humiliate me. The military discuss my fate in loud tones. "We ought to kill him." They almost get into an argument about who will have the pleasure of doing it...They hesitate...The pressure applied by the democratic countries wins the day: I will leave. (Aristide as quoted in Perusse, 1995, p. 18)

Not only was Aristide's life spared, he was allowed to leave the country; first landing in Venezuela, then moving on to Washington where he remained for the majority of coup coverage.

While the president survived, many of his supporters were killed during the coup. According to Aristide, "the corpses were counted in the tens and hundreds" (as quoted in Perusse, 1995, p. 17). Pamela Constable, puts the number of Aristide supporters killed during the coup at "several hundred" (Constable, 1993–93, p, 179); Paul Farmer (citing Bishop Willy Romulus) claims more than 1,500 were killed in the first few days after the coup (Farmer, 1994, p. 183). Whatever the exact number killed, the coup merely began a period of systematic terror and killing directed against the organizations that supported Aristide. According to George Packer, "Since the coup, the military regime has set out to destroy the unions, the media, the more politically active schools and universities, the peasant groups, and the neighborhood organizations that make up the fragile shoots of a civil society in post-Duvalier Haiti" (Packer, 1993, p. 298).

In evaluating the coverage of Aristide's overthrow on U.S. television news, it is important to examine some aspects of his rise to political power and his brief tenure of office to understand not only why he was deposed, but why critics, who were far from justifying or in any way endorsing his overthrow, came to have misgivings about him. In this undertaking it is necessary to examine both the structural and the personal problems that beset the Aristide presidency from its inception.

First and foremost, it is important to understand that Haiti's 1987 democratic constitution was motivated by the fear of a new Duvalier-type dictatorship and had been designed to promote a weak presidency (Haiti, 1987).

The mass of the people, to be sure, apparently wanting a strong benevolent leader, had no idea of the constraints built into the constitution. Further, at the time, Aristide was the leader of a movement, not a political party and there was tension between the Lavalas Movement and the one political party allied to Aristide (Packer, 1993, pp. 303–304). In short, the people looked for strong presidential power, while the constitution was designed to prevent that outcome. As explained by Mark Danner:

> [I]t fell to Aristide to govern under a constitution that had as its presiding idea not the facilitating of the programs of an extremely popular leader but the prevention of the rise of another dictator...and it is only one of the many ironies of history that when he took office in February, 1991, with the great ambition of launching a 'social revolution', it was the constitution that stood squarely in his way. (Danner, 1993c, p. 50; see also Danner, 1993a and 1993b)

According to observers, Aristide envisioned a system of direct democracy (Danner, 1993c, p. 50; Packer, 1993, p. 303). It might be more accurate to call it a conception of plebiscitary democracy, in which the leader appeals directly to the people and uses their support to override or control the legislature. With respect to Aristide and revolution in Haiti, Danner argues that "...he seems utterly unaware of the contradiction in trying to attain such a revolution—which would include 'a redistribution of wealth freely discussed'—by the strictly limited means which the election and the constitution had placed in his hands....Aristide misses the contradiction, of course, because for him it doesn't exist" (Danner, 1993c, p. 50). Moreover, according to Danner, the resort to mob intimidation in governance convinced many among the political class ..." that President Aristide, when it comes down to it, had no more respect for the constitution than any other Haitian ruler" (1993c, p. 50).

Second, when faced with the power of the legislature and its opposition to the manner in which the Prime Minister was appointed, there seemed to be two obvious courses open to Aristide. On the one hand, he could have recognized the limitations of his office and attempted some kind of concertation with the legislature, a course clearly indicated by the constitutional division of power. On the other hand, if he failed to win support for his policies from the legislature and the controlling parties, he could then turn to the masses "that had always been his strength." An appeal to the masses, however, would have meant an effort to use them to intimidate other elected officials and would have raised the anxiety level of those "who relied on the institutions of established power: the officers and the elite" (Danner, 1993c, p. 50).

Because, based on its past performance, Aristide realized that the army could not be relied upon, he "had begun to create his own civilian security force, a contingent of well-armed bodyguards that would be trained by French and Swiss experts and would be loyal only to him. The prospect of another armed force, even a small one, deeply disturbed many within the military" (Danner, 1993c, p. 50). Needless to say, such a move would have replicated one of the most salient and hated features of the Duvalier regime.

Nor did Aristide come to the presidency without any baggage; before his election his relations with the church hierarchy were not good. In the late 1980s he was pressured to leave the religious order to which he belonged, the Salesians (Danner, 1993b). He was distrusted because he was seen as promoting Christian base communities (*Ti Legliz* in Creole, *la petite église* in French) in opposition to the ecclesiastical hierarchy (Aristide, 1990). From 1971 to 1986, "a new concept of mission involving a prophetic outreach toward rural Haitians and away from the urban, mulatto elite, was reinforced by liberation theology and the growth of basic Christian communities" (Hogan, 1994, p. 22). After the papal visit in 1983, the Haitian bishops issued *Une Charte de l'Eglise pour la promotion Humaine, (A Church Charter for Human Advancement)* late in the same year. On this basis, there seemed good reasons for seeing an agreement on the part of the hierarchy with the growth of the base communities. However, Aristide was perceived as supporting the latter against the former. Thus, when John P. Hogan, director of Catholic Relief Services in Haiti, wonders why the church hierarchy was opposed to Aristide, whom he describes as "one of her own" (Hogan, 1994, p. 24), he seems to ignore the extent to which most members of the hierarchy saw in Aristide an enemy of the institutional church. This negative perception explains why the Vatican was alone in recognizing the regime of General Cédras, which took power in 1991 after Aristide had been overthrown.[2]

Aristide's strong preference for the poor should be seen as a pastoral policy of the church and must be distinguished from a political program aimed at social revolution based on a popular electoral victory. The traditional distinction between the mission of the church and politics tended to be blurred by certain practitioners of liberation theology. There was also the issue of recklessness—exhibited earlier by Aristide before he became a candidate—and the predictably cautious stance of the church.

The Catholic Church was one of the first to suffer Aristide's wrath when he assumed power. Over a two-day period in January 1991, his *lavalas* mob (which critics call his answer to the Tonton Macoutes) destroyed the old cathedral and gutted the home of the archbishop. According to the Puebla Institute, a Catholic human-rights organization, they then burned the Vatican embassy, broke both legs of the priest serving as First Secretary, and threw him into a ravine. The Nuncio himself narrowly escaped lynching. (Evans-Pritchard, 1993, p. 24)[3]

Perhaps the most notorious incident in the brief first period of his presidency was the speech Aristide gave on September 27, two days before the coup d'état. The speech has been used to discredit him, to support a charge of mental instability, and to indicate his advocacy of mob rule. In any case, it is difficult to attenuate the bad effects it created both domestically and abroad. Hugeux states it this way in *L'Express:* "Finally, the 27 of September, 1991, when Titid at bay praised, amid rumors of a coup d'état, the dissuasive virtues of 'Père Lebrun,' the Caribbean version of South African necklacing" (Hugeux,

1994, p. 35). Following is a version of the same incident from a clearly unsympathetic source:

> Aristide's preferred instrument of terror was Père Lebrun—necklacing with a burning tire. It was mostly used for dispatching Tonton Macoutes. "If you catch one, do not fail to give him what he deserves," Aristide said on Radio Nationale, during a bout of mob justice. "What a beautiful tool! It's lovely, it's cute, it's pretty, it has a good smell; wherever you go you want to inhale it." (Evans-Pritchard, 1993, p. 26)

Regardless of the "spin" placed on these remarks, they hardly could be interpreted as responsible statements by a leader who was charged with establishing the rule of law in a country that had known little of that tradition.

With respect to the U.S. position on Aristide, it was generally acknowledged that in the 1990 presidential election, the U.S. government supported Marc Bazin, a politician who was experienced in political matters, competent, and, comparatively speaking, conservative, or, at least predictable. Aristide, on the contrary, whose previous activities were as a local priest, was politically inexperienced, an advocate of liberation theology, a critic of the U.S. role in third world societies, and a promoter of social revolution. Washington's choice was understandable. In fact, there were few reasons for the United States to support Aristide.[4]

However, once Aristide had been elected overwhelmingly in what was reported as the fairest election in Haitian history, the United States became committed to support the new democracy and later to restore the rightful president after his overthrow. The question confronting the United States in responding to the coup was not whether Aristide should be restored to power, but rather concerned the means to achieve that end. It was quite clear early on that although the Bush administration condemned the coup, froze Haitian assets in the United States, and called for the restoration of Aristide to the presidency, it was reluctant to use force, especially U.S. force, to effect that restoration. Once it became clear that (1) there was no outside influence involved in the coup; (2) Americans in Haiti were not in any immediate danger; and (3) the army would not voluntarily surrender power and allow Aristide to return, the policy adopted by the United States was to persuade the junta to step down through freezing Haitian financial assets in the United States, and implementing a commercial embargo through the OAS.[5]

FINDINGS

News stories dealing with the 1991 Haitian coup overthrowing President Jean-Bertrand Aristide appeared on the main evening newscasts of the three major U.S. television networks—ABC, CBS, and NBC—for a nine-day period, beginning on September 30 (the day the coup took place) and continuing until October 8, when it became clear that the Haitian military under General Raoul Cédras was not about to give up power and allow the early return of the president. This meant that there would be no reversal of the coup without at least the application of economic sanctions by the United States.

There were a total of 20 stories on the coup' distributed unevenly among the networks: CBS accounted for nearly half (nine), as well as all of the stories filed by reporters in Haiti, NBC for six and ABC for five. Some historical context to events in Haiti had appeared on U.S. television news within the preceding year: Aristide's election victory in December 1990 was covered in seven stories, and an attempted coup against him in January 1991 (before he took office), occasioned one further story. Of course, after the September 1991 coup, Haiti became a serious, ongoing problem for the United States under both Presidents Bush and Clinton. Attempts on the part of the United States to restore Aristide to power in 1993 and 1994 will be investigated in Chapters 4 and 5. Actual language used by U.S. media to describe President Bush and the U.S. government, President Aristide, and their chief opponents after the coup, General Cédras and the Haitian army, by anchors, reporters, and news sources as recorded, collated, and coded, may be found in the Appendix to Chapter 3.

The twenty stories that ran from September 30 to October 8 constitute five more stories than were seen in the reporting of the Trinidad and Tobago coup of little more than a year earlier. Given the degree of U.S. involvement in Haiti over the years—for example, Kaplan refers to Haiti as having "at least partial client state status" (Kaplan, 1983, p. 59)—the relatively sparse coverage does not indicate any overwhelming media interest in the event.

When we look at the story characteristics shown in Table 3.1, we see further evidence that media interest in the coup was at best marginal. For example, only one coup story garnered lead status (5 percent) and just 25 percent of stories were shown in the first three positions in the newscast. Anchors alone in the studio reported 50 percent of stories; and 35 percent of stories ran just 30 seconds or under, with none exceeding three minutes in length. No story featured more than one reporter, with only 25 percent of stories using a reporter actually in Haiti (all on the CBS network). Although stories tended to be brief, 80 percent were accompanied by film. Violence featured quite prominently in coverage, mentioned in 85 percent of story texts and shown visually in 40 percent of stories. Somewhat surprisingly, President Bush appeared on film in only 20 percent of stories, while President Aristide appeared in 55 percent. General Cédras was not given much visibility, appearing on film in only three stories (15 percent of the total). Overall, 55 percent of stories were coded as expressing opinions favorable toward the American position in the crisis, which might be stated as follows: strong condemnation of the coup and a call for the restoration of Aristide to the presidency; the latter to be done, however, without American military intervention. Only 10 percent of stories were coded as opposed to the U.S. position, with the remainder seen as either neutral or ambiguous. Significantly, on the U.S. Involvement index (1=low involvement and 5=high involvement) the mean score for coverage of the Haitian coup was 2.1, well below 3, the midpoint of the scale.

Table 3.1
Story Characteristics N = 20

Characteristics	Number		Percentage
Lead Story	1		5
1st Three Stories	5		25
30 Seconds and Under	7		35
Over 3 Minutes	0		–
Just Anchor Format	10		50
Use of Experts	1		5
Reporter in Haiti (All on CBS)	5		25
Two or More News Segments	0		–
Film with Story	16		80
Film of President Bush	4		20
Film of President Aristide	11		55
Film of General Cédras	3		15
Visual Violence	8		40
Tilt Favorable to U.S. Position	11		55
Tilt Unfavorable to U.S. Position	2		10
U.S. Involvement Index		2.1	

Data in Table 3.2 show the leading news sources used in news stories on Haiti, either on camera or quoted. The list is quite interesting, with Aristide himself the most important news source (used eleven times), followed by spokespersons for the OAS (used ten times). George Bush and spokespersons for the U.S. State Department were also used ten times. All of these sources were heavily involved in attempts to restore the exiled Aristide to power. General Cédras, on the other hand, was not given much opportunity to state his case to the U.S. people, as he was used as a source only three times. Interestingly, foreigners living in Haiti appeared as news sources far more often than did ordinary Haitians in the street (seven to three). U.S. Congressional sources, who generally provide the main opposition to presidential policy, were totally absent (Paletz and Entman, 1981).

Table 3.2
Number of Times Leading Sources Used (All Sources Used In Newscast)

News Source	Number
Jean-Bertrand Aristide	11
Organization of American States	10
Foreigners in Haiti	7
George Bush	6
State Department Spokespersons	4
Haitian Government Spokespersons	4
Raoul Cédras	3
Haitians on the street	3

Table 3.3 shows how the Haitian coup was framed in television news stories. The major frame was thematic—the restoration of democracy—a policy in tune with the 1989 declaration of President Bush that dictatorship was no longer acceptable as a form of government. Aristide's fate was determined early on, so there was little suspense regarding the coup's outcome. Aristide's visits to Congress, the White House, the OAS, and the UN, accompanied by appropriate supportive video footage, dominated the restoration-of-democracy frame. Most stories pointed to Aristide's democratic credentials based on his overwhelming electoral victory in 1990. Only one story presented any sustained criticism of his record in office. Violence, primarily textual, focused on killings by the army and police (in staging the coup, in attempting to consolidate power in its aftermath, or simply acting out of control) and also featured prominently in coverage. Increasingly, as it became clear than no early reversal of the coup was likely, the social instability frame came into play, as stories highlighted the difficulties that any political faction would have in controlling events in Haiti. Thus, while the need to restore democracy, which involved the return of President Aristide to his rightful office, was the paramount frame, it was nearly always combined with either the violence and/or the societal instability frames, indicating that (1) the restoration was not likely to go smoothly, and (2) even if it were accomplished, a restored Aristide would have no easy task in governing the country.

Table 3.3
Percentage of Stories in Which Media Frames Are Used

Frame	Primary	Secondary	Tertiary	Total
Restoration of Democracy				
Number of Stories	9	6	1	16
Percentage	45	30	5	80
Violence				
Number of Stories	5	4	0	9
Percentage	25	20	–	45
U.S. Foreign Policy Decision Making				
Number of Stories	6	1	0	7
Percentage	30	5	–	35
Societal Instability				
Number of Stories	0	4	2	6
Percentage	–	20	10	30
Protection of Americans				
Number of Stories	0	2	2	4
Percentage	–	10	10	20

Two frames involved U.S. foreign policy decision-making with respect to the coup. The first centered on the degree to which the United States would become involved militarily in attempting to restore Aristide to power. The answer to this question came early on and decisively, as President Bush made it clear that while the United States condemned the coup and called for the restoration of Aristide, such a restoration would have to be accomplished without U.S. military involvement. Indeed, while Bush flirted with the possible deployment of a multinational force under the auspices of the OAS, clearly he hoped the coup could be reversed without any use of force. Once this hope was dashed, the only other factor that might have prompted a U.S. military response was the possible need to evacuate American citizens if violence got out of hand. While troops were moved to the Caribbean to facilitate such an evacuation, the U.S. State Department made an effort to downplay the likelihood that such action would be necessary. After October 4, when Presidents Bush and Aristide appeared together, no U.S. government spokespersons were used as news sources. Thus, roughly midway in the coup coverage, President Bush handed the ball off to the OAS and focus shifted away from the role of the United States to the OAS's attempts to negotiate the return of Aristide to power. Contrary to Jorge Castañeda's predictions regarding post cold-war framing, not a single story was framed in terms of the implications of the coup on the flow of Haitian refugees to the United States (Castañeda, 1993, p. 298).

While the frames used tended to be thematic, the coverage of the coup itself lacked depth. For the most part, Aristide was given legitimacy solely on the basis of his democratic electoral victory. Literally nothing was said about his pre-1990 radical and anti-American positions, and only one news story (a CBS report from Haiti), dealt with Aristide's actual record in office in a critical way.

Nor were the events leading to the actual overthrow of Aristide on the first day of the coup examined in detail. While early reports referred to a "military uprising," as coverage continued, the role of General Cédras as the "leader" of an organized military coup was more or less taken for granted. According to Evans-Pritchard, the situation surrounding the coup was in fact far more chaotic; it began with a revolt by enlisted personnel, and Cédras' role in its initiation was unclear (see footnote #1). In light of the media prominence given to the coupmakers in Trinidad and Tobago in coverage of a crisis occurring a little more than a year earlier (see Chapter 2), the infrequent use of Cédras as a news source may be seen as somewhat puzzling. He appeared on film on three occasions and was also used as a source three times. However, only once, where he was quoted as having taken over the country "to rescue it from the horrors of uncertainty," did his version of events find its way into news stories. We must be mindful of the possibility that Cédras was seen as the problem and thus deliberately marginalized (Herman, 1985). No alternative explanation of the coup gained media exposure.

No such lack of exposure was accorded President Aristide, as he was seen arriving in exile in Venezuela and later in the United States, where he appeared at various centers of power and influence. In general, his portrayal was positive, and some sentiments that the United States should perhaps do more to restore him to power were mooted. The coup, then, was framed as a setback for democracy in the hemisphere and needed to be reversed. This would have to be done, however, not with U.S. military force, but through diplomatic and economic pressure coordinated by the OAS. If there was a sour note to this consensus, it was the ongoing violence and societal instability in Haiti, which featured prominently in coup coverage and made any solution to the country's situation appear problematic.

Data in Table 3.4 compare the way in which President Bush and the U.S. government, President Aristide, and General Cédras and the Haitian Army were evaluated in textual presentations on U.S. network television news. President Bush and/or the U.S. government were evaluated in fifteen of the twenty stories; 47 percent of text evaluations were positive and only 13 percent were negative. President Aristide also came off quite well; half the stories reflected positively on him, and only on CBS did one story reflect negatively overall on the Haitian president. With the exception of the one CBS story, negative information on Aristide did not appear prominently in U.S. television news coverage of the Haitian coup.

Table 3.4
Text Evaluation of Major Participants

	Bush/U.S. Government (15 stories)	Aristide (20 stories)	Cédras/Haitian Army (19 stories)
Favorable			
Number of Stories	7	10	1
Percentage	47	50	5
Neutral/Ambigous			
Number of Stories	6	9	4
Percentage	40	45	21
Unfavorable			
Number of Stories	2	1	14
Percentage	13	5	74

This was not the case for Aristide's chief political opponents after the coup, General Cédras and the Haitian Army, who in nineteen of twenty stories were evaluated quite negatively. Only one story (on NBC) presented what was judged as a sustained positive verbal portrayal of the leader of the military government, stressing his flexibility in negotiations with the OAS over the return of Aristide. On the negative side, 74 percent of stories conveyed unfavorable verbal information on Aristide's primary adversaries.

Table 3.5 shows the evaluations of President Bush and the U.S. government, Aristide, and Cédras and the Haitian Army on television news based on the actual balance of positive and negative descriptors used with respect to the various actors. In light of the apparent consensus in Washington regarding the wisdom of President Bush's response to the coup, it is not surprising that 94 percent of Bush/U.S. government descriptors were positive. With respect to the Haitian participants, however, we see the only evidence of more than the most cursory and stereotyped presentations of the two sides. Negative features of Aristide's character and performance were indeed mentioned, accounting for just over one-quarter of total valenced descriptors. These negative references were largely contained in one story that detailed Aristide's abuses of power while he served as president; this story aired on the final day of coup coverage. Even with the negative references in this story, fully

74 percent of Aristide's evaluative descriptors were positive. Regardless of how one chooses to evaluate the impact of this one negative story, at this micro level his image is somewhat less pristine than is conveyed by overall story evaluations.

Table 3.5
Percentage of Descriptors Reflecting Positively or Negatively
on Major Actors

	Number of Descriptors	Percentage
Bush/U.S. Government		
Positive	15	94
Negative	1	6
Total	16	100
Aristide		
Positive	26	74
Negative	9	26
Total	35	100
Cédras/Haitian Army		
Positive	5	19
Negative	22	81
Total	29	100

In contrast to Aristide, General Cédras comes across a good deal less villainous than the Haitian Army that he led when the actual language used to describe them is examined; all positive references in the Cédras/army category 5 are to him as an individual (Appendix 3.1). While Cédras certainly does not escape condemnation, it is mainly the activities of the Haitian Army that contribute to the 81 percent of negative words or phrases.

CONCLUSION

The establishment of democratic governance in Haiti had been a priority policy for the U.S. government at least since 1986, when the Reagan administration played a key role in getting Jean-Claude Duvalier to leave the island. While some progress toward this end clearly had been made by 1991, given the various misadventures along the way (aborted elections, rigged elections, successful and unsuccessful coups, and societal violence), by the time of the September coup, it was obviously too early to proclaim that the goal was even close to being achieved.

Yet this seemed to be the premise underlying television news coverage of the coup that overthrew President Aristide. When the coup occurred, U.S. television news interpreted it primarily as a setback on Haiti's road to democracy, with almost no questioning of how far along that road Haiti had traveled, much less whether it was even on the right road. There was virtually no discussion of either the necessity or wisdom of returning Aristide to power. Congressional opponents, who emerged rather prominently in the later Haitian crises of 1993 and 1994, were silent on this issue—at least silent on network television news. While the U.S. public was given some preparation with respect to the almost certain difficulties that lay ahead in governing the island nation, this tended to take the form of cautious pessimism. The immediate issue was getting rid of the Haitian Army, and here the predominant sentiment conveyed was that the Haitian generals were extremely vulnerable to economic sanctions—in the words of the one expert interviewed, "once the [oil] tankers stop, the lights go out." Reality, of course, would prove to be far different.

Looking broadly at television news reporting of the Haitian coup, we have to conclude that overall coverage was thin and neglected any in-depth treatment of Haitian society and the roots of problems besetting it. Moreover, it was inordinately focused on personalities (Aristide in particular) and on violence. Further, with respect to Aristide, with the exception of CBS, coverage was unidimensional, presenting a far more simplistic and positive image of him than his record both before and after his election to the presidency would seem to have warranted. Network television news presented to the U.S. public a largely simplified and sanitized image of the Haitian president, highlighting his credentials based solely on winning a democratic election and omitting his less-than-reassuring prior record, and mentioning his actual performance in office in only one story. There was no hint of the change in U.S. policy towards Aristide that was reported to have taken place on the week end of October 5–6 (see footnote #5). Thus to the degree that television is important in attitude formation, the American public was primed to accept the need to restore democracy in Haiti without examining the difficulties, both structural and personal, that this entailed. Haiti's problems were presented as personal rather than systemic, and their solution centered on removing an illegal military government and restoring the democratically elected President Aristide to power. Moreover, in light of sanguine predictions on the effectiveness of economic sanctions, this restoration was presented as likely to occur rather quickly as soon as the impact of the OAS-imposed sanctions was felt.

In reality, of course, Haitian problems are so pervasive, deep, and multifaceted, that any nation wishing to help resolve them has to be prepared to be involved in the country for the long haul (Mintz, 1995). The framing employed in U.S. television news reportage on the Haitian coup did not give the American people this message in any strong sense. Instead, it combined the presentation of serious problems with relatively simple answers to them. In this respect the coverage is quite congruous with the ambiguity in American policy toward Haiti followed by both the Bush and Clinton administrations in the years leading up to Aristide's eventual restoration in the fall of 1994 (Morley and McGillion, 1997).

APPENDIX 3.1

PRESIDENT BUSH/U.S. GOVERNMENT

Descriptors Coded Positive
- strongly condemned the coup
- called for the restoration of a democratically elected leader/wants the restoration of Aristide
- cut off all aid to Haiti/suspended $8 million in aid/cut off military aid
- refuses to recognize the junta that seized power
- "the coup will not succeed"
- "the junta will be treated as a pariah"
- assured Aristide of U.S. support
- Secretary of State Baker backs Aristide
- freezing Haitian assets in the United States
- "He's helping us to have democracy back"

Descriptors Coded Negative
- should have done more

Descriptors Coded Neutral or Ambiguous
- ordered U.S. troops to the Caribbean
- playing down talk of intervention/seems reluctant to intervene militarily/disinclined to use American force/reluctant to use force/hopes coup can be reversed without U.S. military support/no promise of U.S. military help
- raised the possibility of a multinational force going into Haiti
- give sanctions a chance/believe sanctions have a very good chance of working/counting on economic and diplomatic pressure to reverse the coup
- does not want to use force unless U.S. lives are at stake/will not use force to remove the military dictatorship unless U.S. lives are threatened
- wants the OAS mission to succeed without the use of force/hopeful that matters can be resolved without multilateral OAS intervention

PRESIDENT JEAN-BERTRAND ARISTIDE

Descriptors Coded Positive
- popular/enjoys strong support/enjoys support of poor
- champion of the poor
- first democratically elected President/first freely elected President/took office in February as Haiti's first freely elected President
- legitimate President/elected President
- promised to return to power
- got help from OAS

- willing to give his life for democracy
- rallying point for fighting back
- powerful lobbyist for his own cause
- walking, talking accusation against the military who overthrew him
- assured of America support/got warm words from Bush
- considered a hero
- pleased with U.S. policy
- "If he does not come back we will all be dead"
- would welcome intervention by the OAS

Descriptors Coded Negative
- man elected as a democrat becoming a demagogue
- distributed hatred
- promoted social warfare
- employed thugs to murder opponents
- covered up atrocities
- incited mob justice against opponents
- delivered a chilling speech condoning summary executions by placing a burning tire around the victim's neck

Descriptors Coded Neutral or Ambiguous
- priest/former priest
- President
- deposed President/ousted President/exiled President/President, still in exile
- thirty-eight years old
- arrested/reportedly arrested
- served just seven months in office
- fled to Venezuela/flew into exile in Venezuela/exiled in Venezuela/ forced into exile
- warned of possible new bloodbath at the hands of the coup leaders
- delivered a call to arms
- reported to have signed a letter of resignation
- took his appeal for help to the White House
- pleading his case at the UN

GENERAL RAOUL CÉDRAS/HAITIAN MILITARY

Descriptors Coded Positive
- took over the country to rescue it from the "horrors of uncertainty"
- indicated Aristide's return might be negotiable/trying to work out a compromise/seen as flexible
- an intelligent man

Descriptors Coded Negative

- criminal
- pariah
- working as marauders
- rebels/rebellious soldiers/rebellious army troops
- in disarray
- not clear who is in control/will be some time before military government can consolidate power
- isolated politically, diplomatically and economically/needs to be isolated
- "he wants to shoot us down"
- will never accept the restoration of Aristide
- no popular support for the junta
- shows no signs of wanting to give up power
- could not guarantee Aristide's safety
- coup leader
- forcing the hand of the legislature with the power of the gun
- unable to control troops at the airport
- opened fire on the national palace/spraying the capitol with random gunfire
- opposition to the junta is growing

Descriptors Coded Neutral or Ambiguous

- General/Lt. General
- Army Chief/Army Commander
- still in control
- aware of the seriousness of what he has done
- may have made their first mistake—allowing Aristide to leave the country

NOTES

1.   According to Perusse, the coup was initiated by a group of enlisted men under the leadership of Major [later Lt. Col.] Michel François of the Haitian police who sent a group of armed men to the home of General Cédras. "Cédras was taken at gunpoint to military command headquarters, where François was waiting for him. François told Cédras to assume his role as general, or he would be killed or sent away. Cédras complied" (Perusse, 1995, p. 19).

2.   Not only did the Vatican give diplomatic recognition to the military regime, but the Nuncio, the Vatican ambassador, had very friendly relations with Madame Cédras.

3.   While these attacks did take place, they were justified as retaliation for alleged Church support for the January 1991 attempted coup (Danner, 1993c, p. 49).

4.   Indeed, in light of Aristide's record. U.S. acceptance of his electoral victory seven years after the invasion of Grenada can be taken as a clear indicator that the Cold War was over.

5.   There is evidence that Bush was backing away from support of Aristide within a week of the coup. Ives indicates that over the weekend of October 5-6 U.S. policy shifted 180 degrees and the "slow strangulation of Haiti's first democratically elected president and his nationalist program had began" (Ives, 1995b, p. 66; see also Morley and McGillion, 1997, p. 365).

4

The Attempted Restoration of Jean-Bertrand Aristide to the Presidency of Haiti, 1993

Walter C. Soderlund and Ralph C. Nelson

BACKGROUND

The United States, while supporting the restoration of Aristide to the presidency from which he had been removed in 1991, decided not to intervene militarily to accomplish that end. After it became clear that the Haitian army would not voluntarily surrender power, the policy adopted by the United States was to persuade the junta to give up power through the implementation of a commercial embargo conducted in the name of the OAS and the UN.

It has been reported that President Bush changed his opinion regarding Aristide's return and that the "slow strangulation of Haiti's first democratically elected president and his nationalist program had begun" within a week of the coup (Ives, 1995b, p. 66; Morley and McGillion, 1997, p. 365). Whatever U.S. operational policy might have been, the rhetorical policy of returning Aristide remained in place. It did not, however, achieve early success. By early November 1991, the Bush administration had to contend with growing numbers of Haitians taking to the sea to get to the United States. For about six months, refugees were taken to the U.S. naval base at Guantanamo Bay, Cuba for processing. In May 1992, however, Bush "ordered the Coast Guard to forcibly repatriate [to Haiti] all refugees interdicted at sea without an asylum interview" (Constable, 1992–93, pp. 185–186).

By early 1992 it was clear that the Bush administration had developed an ambivalence toward Aristide's restoration, and this ambivalence continued through Bush's final year in office. According to Doyle, the administration "sent a signal to the de facto regime that the United States (and by inference, the rest of the international community) was less than fully committed to isolating it and pressing for Aristide's return" (Doyle, 1994, p. 51). Further, she argues, "by the time of the U.S. presidential elections [November 1992] the Bush administration's mistrust of Aristide was an open secret" (p. 52). While an estimated 3,000 murders had taken place in Haiti since the coup and U.S. intelligence agencies estimated that up to 100,000 Haitians were ready to take to the seas (Perusse, 1995, p. 29), support for the restoration of Aristide to be achieved through the economic embargo remained the official U.S. Haitian policy inherited by the Clinton administration when it came to power in early 1993.

During the presidential campaign, Clinton had supported the restoration of Aristide on the ground of restoration of democracy and had criticized Bush's policy of forced repatriation. However, when he assumed the presidency, he found himself faced with the reality of dealing with the other dimension of the Haitian crisis—the pending flood of refugees to the United States. According to Morely and McGillion,

> Within days of his inauguration, ...Clinton backtracked on his position [dealing with Haitian refugees] following warnings that the United States might soon be confronted by a new wave of at least 200,000 Haitians fleeing the brutality of military rule. Sensitive to the electoral damage suffered by the Carter administration in the wake of the 1980 Mariel boatlift of over 125,000 Cuban refugees to Florida, Clinton tumbled from the high moral ground of the election campaign and announced that the existing policy would remain in place. (1997, p. 367)

In viewing his options, Clinton decided to put the policy of support for the restoration of Aristide on the front burner, "...thereby resolving the political crisis that had created the refugee flows in the first place" (Doyle, 1994, p. 52).

In pursuing this goal, the Clinton administration had to contend not only with getting the military to give up power in Haiti, but with a serious division within its own ranks (not to mention a partisan divide in Congress) over the wisdom of restoring Aristide. What resulted was a policy conflict that would make a textbook case of governmental politics (Allison and Zelikow, 1999), and did much to undermine the president's policy of restoring Aristide to power. Specifically, the U.S. State Department favored Clinton's policy, while the CIA and the Pentagon had severe reservations about Aristide and U.S. military involvement in Haiti. Moreover, the CIA seemed to work actively to undermine the president's policy by organizing a violent, anti-Aristide paramilitary organization, the Front for the Advancement and Progress of Haiti (FRAPH) (Morley and McGillion, 1997, p. 365). Nairn reports that FRAPH, under the leadership of Emanuel "Toto" Constant (at the time on the CIA payroll), orchestrated the dockside violence leading to the retreat of the USS *Harlan County*, the decisive event in the failure to return Aristide to the Haitian presidency in the fall of 1993 (Nairn, 1994a; Nairn, 1994b).

Progress toward the restoration of Aristide was first seen in March 1993 with the appointment of Lawrence Pezzullo as U.S. special envoy to Haiti. In the following months, working in conjunction with the UN mission in the country, pressure was applied to both the Haitian military and President Aristide to come to an agreement that would see him return to the presidency. Two factors were seen as crucial to a solution of the problem: "to get the military to the bargaining table, and to create guarantees for Aristide's safety" (Doyle, 1994, p. 53).

To get the attention of the Haitian generals, economic sanctions against the country were intensified in June (Danner, 1993a, p. 26). As well, Aristide's arm was twisted on the issue of granting amnesty to those who had perpetrated the coup against him and who had terrified and killed his supporters in the interim (Perusse, 1995; Morely and McGillion, 1997). These pressures worked; in July of 1993, President Aristide and General Cédras were brought to New York, where a compromise known as the Governor's Island Agreement was worked out, whereby the Haitian generals would leave power voluntarily, thus allowing the return of Aristide. Although Aristide signed the agreement, he did so reluctantly, as he (and others) saw the duplicity of the military regime.

The Governor's Island Agreement "had been hailed as a unique triumph: for the first time, a successful restoration to power, by peaceful means, of a democratically elected president ousted by a military coup d'état" (Martin, 1995, p. 73).

> The agreement provided for the nomination of a prime minister by the president; a political dialogue necessary for the prime minister's parliamentary ratification and passage of essential legislation; suspension of sanctions; international assistance for development and administrative and judicial reform, and the "modernization of Haitian armed forces and creation of a new police with the presence of U.N. personnel"; an amnesty; passage of a law creating a new police force and nomination of a new chief of police; "early retirement" of Cédras as commander-in-chief, followed by Aristide's designation of Cédras's successor, who would appoint a new high command; and a return of the president to Haiti on October 30 [1993] (1995, p. 80)

Unfortunately, the Governor's Island Agreement turned out to be "a profoundly flawed and inconclusive document.... [Specifically] it contained no mechanisms for enforcement, no penalties for non-compliance, and dangerous concessions to the Haitian military leaders" (Doyle, 1994, p. 53).

In accordance with the agreement, Robert Malval became Aristide's prime minister at the end of August in preparation for Aristide's return at the end of October. Following this, the sanctions imposed on the military regime in June were lifted. The hope of a peaceful restoration was of course dashed by the failure of the military regime to carry out its commitments. The Haitian military, largely through the actions of the *attachés* (described as a group engaged in "franchise terrorism" (Packer, 1993, p. 298), began a new wave of violence. According to Danner, in Port-au-Prince alone, at least fifty people were assassinated in a period of about a month (Danner, 1993a, p. 26). The CIA-financed FRAPH played a major role in perpetrating this violence. Both the United States and the UN soft-pedaled these abuses in vain hopes that the whole agreement would not unravel.

However, on October 11, the USS *Harlan County,* bringing military trainers and engineers to Port-au-Prince, was confronted by a hostile *attaché* demonstration, organized by the CIA's asset, Emanuel Constant, and was not allowed to dock.[1] On the following day, in an all-too-visible act of retreat, the Pentagon ordered the ship to withdraw from Haiti.[2] Although negotiations for the return of Aristide continued, it was clear to all but the most oblivious that the Haitian generals had carried the day; it was "tail-tucking" time for the United States, and Aristide would not be returning to Haiti as president at the end of the month.

FINDINGS

News stories on this crisis appeared on U.S. television networks for about a month, beginning on October 8 and continuing until November 9, when it became obvious that the Haitian military under General Raoul Cédras was not going to honor the terms of the Governors' Island Agreement and permit the restoration of President Aristide. The failure to return Aristide to power set in motion the reimposition of economic sanctions, even though it was clear that crippling the already fragile Haitian economy would not be sufficient to remove the Haitian military from power.

During this period U.S. television networks ran a total of sixty-two stories, containing eighty-two news segments[3] dealing with the attempted restoration. These stories were more or less evenly divided among the networks: ABC ran nineteen stories, CBS ran twenty-one, and NBC ran twenty-two. By fall 1993, a good deal of coverage of events in Haiti had appeared on U.S. television news in the preceding two years: Aristide's election victory in December of 1990 and related events were covered in eight stories, the 1991 coup that removed him from power was covered in twenty stories (Chapter 3), and the Governors' Island Agreement in summer 1993 was reported in eleven stories. The failure of the 1993 attempt to restore Aristide to Haiti's presidency was a severe embarrassment to the Clinton administration and meant that the Haitian problem, in all its dimensions, continued for the United States. An attempt led by the United States a year later, which finally succeeded in restoring Aristide to power, constitutes another case in the series of post-Cold War crises to be investigated (see Chapter 5).

The actual language to describe President Clinton and the U.S. government, President Aristide, and the chief opponents standing in the way of Aristide's return to power, General Cédras and the Haitian military, used by anchors, reporters, and news sources, as recorded, collated, and coded may be found in Appendix 4.1.

The story characteristics shown in Table 4.1 reveal that in addition to generating sixty-two stories (more than three times the number that had reported the 1991 coup), U.S. media attached considerable importance to this foreign policy crisis.

Table 4.1
Story Characteristics N = 63

Characteristics	Number		Percentage
Lead Story	22		35
1st Three Stories	41		66
30 Seconds and under	14		23
Over 3 Minutes	19		31
Just Anchor Format	17		27
Use of Experts	5		8
Reporter in Haiti	39		63
Two or More News Segments	19		31
Film with Story	53		85
Film of President Bush	18		29
Film of President Aristide	21		34
Film of General Cédras	16		26
Visual Violence	26		42
Link to Somalia	8		13
Tilt Favorable to U.S. Position	6		10
Tilt Unfavorable to U.S. Position	28		45
U.S. Involvement Index		3.5	

For example just over one-third (35 percent) of stories led off newscasts, while two-thirds were run in the first three positions. Anchors alone in the studio reported just over a quarter (27 percent) of stories; only 23 percent of stories ran thirty seconds or less; and 31 percent exceeded three minutes in length, which corresponds exactly with the percentage of stories that featured more than one news segment. Another indicator of importance is the number of stories using a reporter in the field—63 percent of stories featured a reporter actually in Haiti. Film was shown in 85 percent of stories; and violence was featured quite prominently, mentioned in 58 percent of story texts and shown visually in 42 percent of stories. Coverage tended to focus on the personalities involved: President Clinton appeared on film in 29 percent of stories, President Aristide in 34 percent, while General Cédras, who had been largely ignored in coverage of the 1991 coup, appeared on film in 26 percent of stories, raising him to the rank of a more-or-less equal participant.

In fall 1993, while the attempt to restore Aristide was under way, the United States was engaged in a UN peacekeeping operation in Somalia, where a military operation had resulted in the deaths of U.S. servicemen. Parallels between possible developments in Haiti and those in Somalia were made in 13 percent of stories. Overall, in terms of degree of support for U.S. policy in this crisis, which may be stated as General Cédras should step down as agreed to at Governor's Island, to permit the peaceful restoration of President Aristide, only 10 percent of stories tilted favorably toward this position, and 45 percent of stories took an unfavorable slant. On the U.S. Involvement index (1=low and 5=high), the score for the attempted restoration was 3.5, slightly above the midpoint of the scale.

Table 4.2
Number of Times Leading Sources Used (All Sources Used in Newscast)

News Source	Segment 1	Segment 2	Segment 3	Total Number of Times Used
Bill Clinton	18	9	0	27
Haitians on the street	22	3	0	25
Jean-Bertrand Aristide	18	3	1	22
Haitian Government Spokespersons	15	4	0	19
U.S. State Department	11	7	0	18
Congressional Democrats	9	6	2	17
Congressional Republicans	7	10	0	17
U.N. Spokespersons	13	2	0	15
Prominent Haitians	10	2	0	12
U.S. administration	4	6	0	10
Raoul Cédras	9	1	0	10
Foreigners in Haiti	9	1	0	10

Data in Table 4.2 show the leading news sources used in news stories on the attempted restoration. The list shows an almost equal distribution of U.S. and Haitian sources, with UN spokespersons and foreigners living in Haiti also contributing to the total. On the U.S. side, President Clinton occupies pride of place in arguing the wisdom of his policy (twenty-seven appearances), followed by U.S. State Department spokespersons (eighteen) and administration spokespersons (ten). That there was conflict over the direction of U.S. foreign policy in this crisis and that this conflict got air time is evident in the number of Congressional spokespersons interviewed—seventeen Democrats and seventeen Republicans. If there is opposition to a foreign policy position, it is usually Congress that voices such criticism (Paletz and Entman, 1981); this case demonstrates the truth of this observation.

Haitians on the street, Aristide, Haitian government spokespersons (often Prime Minister Robert Malval), prominent Haitians, and General Cédras account for the majority of Haitian sources used, and were even more deeply divided with the respect to the return of Aristide than were the U.S. sources. Foreigners living in Haiti again appeared as news sources, but were featured far less prominently than they were in coverage of the 1991 coup.

Table 4.3 deals with the frames used in television news reporting on the attempted restoration. As with the 1991 Haitian coup, the major frame was thematic—the restoration of democracy (would Cédras step down as promised to permit the restoration of Aristide), appearing in 94 percent of stories. Again, as with the 1991 coup, the violence frame, associated chiefly with misdeeds of the Haitian military and attachés and focused heavily on the turning away of the

Table 4.3
Percentage of Stories in Which Media Frames Are Used

Frame	Primary	Secondary	Tertiary	Total
Restoration of Democracy				
Number of Stories	51	6	1	58
Percentage	82	10	2	94
Violence				
Number of Stories	2	16	5	23
Percentage	3	25	8	36
U.S. Foreign Policy Decision Making				
Number of Stories	8	6	6	20
Percentage	11	10	10	31
Refugees				
Number of Stories	0	7	4	11
Percentage	/	11	7	18

USS *Harlan County* and its military trainers and engineers followed in frequency.

Two frames seen in coverage of the attempted restoration involved United States foreign policy decision making. The first centered on the degree to which the United States should become involved militarily in attempting to bring peace and order to the world, not only in Haiti, but in Africa and Eastern Europe as well. The juxtaposition of the Haitian and Somalian crises served to highlight this dilemma, and in the discussion, President Clinton's foreign policy record was not portrayed as particularly reassuring. In addition to these broad concerns regarding a possible overextension of U.S. capabilities, there was strong dissent on the question of whether Aristide deserved U.S. support. On this issue, Republican Senators Dole and Helms led a chorus of attackers against the Haitian president. The second frame that appeared in crisis coverage involving the United States dealt directly with the implications that the failure to return Aristide to Haiti might have on a renewed "flood of Haitian boat people" attempting to gain illegal entrance into the United States. The return of Aristide had been promoted at least partially as a means of keeping Haitians in Haiti and, by extension out of the United States. While present in television news coverage, the question of uncontrolled migration (both Haitian and Cuban)[4] to the United States was an extremely sensitive topic, and as a frame it did not compete strongly with the need to restore democracy in Haiti as a justification for the restoration of Aristide.

Data in Table 4.4 compare the way that President Clinton and the U.S. government, President Aristide, and General Cédras and the Haitian Army, were evaluated in textual presentations on U.S. network television news. President Clinton and/or the U.S. government were evaluated in sixty-one of the sixty-two stories; of these only 11 percent of text evaluations were positive, and 36 percent were negative. On text evaluation, President Aristide came off ambivalently: 17 percent of fifty-two stories reflected positively and 19 percent reflected

Table 4.4
Text Evaluation of Major Participants

	Clinton/U.S. Government (61 stories)	Aristide (52 stories)	Cedras/Haitian Army (57 stories)
Favorable			
Number of Stories	7	9	1
Percentage	11	17	2
Neutral/Ambiguous			
Number of Studies	32	33	8
Percentage	53	63	13
Unfavorable			
Number of Stories	22	10	48
Percentage	36	19	84

negatively on the Haitian president. There was no such ambiguity for Aristide's chief political antagonists, General Cédras and the Haitian Army, who in fifty-seven of sixty-two stories were evaluated extraordinarily negatively. Only one story presented what was judged as a sustained positive verbal portrayal of the leader of the Haitian military. On the negative side, 84 percent of stories contained unfavorable verbal information on Aristide's primary adversaries. These figures represent even lower positive and higher negative totals than seen in coverage of the 1991 coup.

Table 4.5
Percentage of Descriptors Reflecting Positively or Negatively on Major Actors

	Number of Descriptors	Percentage
Clinton/U.S. Government		
Positive	39	43
Negative	51	57
Total	90	100
Aristide		
Positive	45	47
Negative	51	53
Total	96	100
Cédras/Haitian Army		
Positive	3	2
Negative	118	98
Total	121	100

Table 4.5 shows the evaluations of Clinton and the U.S. government, Aristide, and Cédras and the Haitian Army on television news based on the actual balance of positive and negative descriptors used with respect to these actors. Given the controversy in Washington regarding the wisdom of President Clinton's Haiti policy and his foreign policy record more generally, it is not surprising that only 43 percent of evaluative Clinton/U.S government descriptors were positive and 57 percent were negative. With respect to the Haitian

participants, as was the case with textual evaluation more broadly, positive and negative features of Aristide's character, mental stability, and performance more or less balanced out—47 percent positive and 53 percent negative. This distribution contrasts sharply with the 74 percent of Aristide descriptors that were positive in coverage of the 1991 coup that removed him from power.

Again, showing congruence with their overall textual evaluation, General Cédras and the Haitian Army came across as the villains in the piece. Nary a kind word was said about them, while 98 percent of evaluative descriptive words and phrases were judged to be negative.[5]

CONCLUSION

The 1991 coup that removed Jean-Bertrand Aristide from power was a real setback to the establishment of democratic practices in Haiti. While the Haitian generals were seemingly able to weather the economic embargo imposed by the international community, during spring and summer 1993 the United States put new pressure on Aristide and Cédras to make some compromises that would result in the President's return by the end of October of that year—just over two years after his overthrow.

While the Governor's Island Agreement appeared to hold the key to a peaceful restoration, such optimism turned out to be premature. Flaws and ambiguities in the agreement, conflicting policies of the U.S. State Department and the CIA, the Pentagon's reluctance to press ahead with an armed invasion in light of set backs in Somalia, opposition in the U.S. Congress, and the intransigence of the Haitian military, were all factors contributing to the collapse of the Governor's Island Agreement. President Aristide remained in exile in Washington, and economic sanctions against the defacto military regime were reinstated.

In its reporting of the October 1993 crisis, the U.S. media focused heavily on thematic frames—first and foremost the need to restore democracy in Haiti, followed by the pessimism generated by the ongoing violence in the country. Present as a frame in just under 20 percent of stories, the implications of the failure to return Aristide to Haiti on the flow of illegal immigration to the United States was not especially prominent.

This was not the case with the frame that focused on the proper role for the United States in ensuring peace and order in an unruly and violent post–Cold War world. In pursuing its policy of restoring Aristide to power, the Clinton administration was faced with the predictable partisan attacks from Republican opponents, and with a fatal division within its own ranks. This led the CIA to pursue a policy that, as it turned out (combined with Pentagon doubts about committing U.S. forces to ensure the landing of the USS *Harlan County*), effectively undermined administration policy. That Clinton's policy was reported favorably in only 10 percent of stories and unfavorably in 45 percent, indicates that the media was very unimpressed with both the president's overall foreign policy performance and this particular application of it to Haiti. At the same time, there was evidence of overwhelming opposition to the continued rule of the Haitian military, combined with a sober re-examination of Aristide's qualifications and record while in office. In this re-examination the Haitian president emerged far more blemished than had been the case in the reporting of the coup that had earlier deposed him.

In summary, in the two years after the 1991 coup, no progress had been made in Haiti: the generals still ruled, Aristide remained in the United States in exile, the Republicans had found and exploited yet another weakness in the president's foreign policy, and the prospects of continued large-scale illegal immigration of Haitians fleeing the violence and poverty of their homeland continued. These problems were addressed and at least lip service was paid to the need to restore democracy, but no consensus emerged regarding how deeply the United States should become involved in restoring of Aristide to power. Another year would pass before the Clinton administration decided to bite the bullet and commit U.S. military forces to drive the generals from power.

APPENDIX 4.1

PRESIDENT CLINTON/U.S. GOVERNMENT

Descriptors Coded Positive
- dead serious [re: junta] "We are serious about the implementation of economic sanctions"
- has no intention of sending American troops in until Governor's Island Agreement is honored
- working overtime
- administration support for Haiti policy is unshakable
- demanded an explanation from the junta
- demanded peaceful entry for U.S. troops into Haiti
- not giving up on the mission
- justified actions on grounds of safety of Americans and restoration of democracy/acted to protect American lives
- his actions applauded/supported by the Black Caucus
- prudent and wise
- acting responsibly
- promised help to restore democracy
- revoked visas and froze assets of those supporting violence
- sending Haitian military a high-powered message/putting serious heat on them
- doing exactly the right thing
- U.S. warships have silenced the gunmen
- administration has a good record on the big issues
- squeezing Haiti's military leaders
- likely to come through confrontation with Congress with his foreign policy powers in tact
- policy is beginning to have a dramatic effect [in Haiti]
- embargo is hitting hard
- first positive sign in a week
- warned Haiti's military leaders that they have made a grave mistake by blocking a return to democracy
- looking for more ways to put more pressure on [the military]
- backed a UN proposal
- strong belief among those who voted for Aristide that the United States would make good on its promise and return Aristide to power

Descriptors Coded Negative
- has second thoughts
- his credibility is in jeopardy

- major setback for U.S. policy/Round 1 goes to the Haitian military/has to deal with a major setback/ his Haiti policy has unraveled/events are a setback to restoration of democracy
- denies a reversal of policy/denies a 180° turn in policy
- somewhat anxious
- sending confusing signals
- why did the administration allow a U.S. ship to be turned away by a few thugs?
- is Clinton allowing United States to become involved in poorly conceived UN missions?
- will be challenged by critics in Congress/on a collision course with powerful members of Congress/ Congress is in open rebellion
- public support for humanitarian foreign policy is plummeting/public has lost enthusiasm for taking part in UN rescue squads
- his team is badly split/in the middle of another in-house fight: diplomats support Aristide, intelligence analysts don't
- administration has private misgivings about Aristide
- reacted angrily
- no one is planning exactly what is coming up ahead
- failed to consult Congress before acting
- he must understand that the American people are queasy
- this is gunboat diplomacy
- wavering and impotent
- pressure is building to limit Clinton's foreign policy initiatives/should get Congressional approval before taking new steps/Congress is trying to limit Clinton's ability to commit U.S. forces overseas
- people are not comfortable with the President's foreign policy behavior/steadily losing support on foreign policy
- admits that his policies are not as clear as they should have been made
- concedes that mistakes have been made
- can be badly hurt
- encouraged the gunmen terrorizing the country
- "The United States has deserted us"/led Aristide supporters out on a limb and left them there/ "the life and blood of Guy Malary is on the hands of the Clinton administration"
- on resolve and consistency the Clinton Administration has failed
- "'on the one hand...on the other hand'—can't run foreign policy that way"
- White House infuriated [with Congress]
- Administration lacks intellectual rigor
- foreign policy has been relegated to the back burner
- foreign policy characterized as on the job training
- foreign policy is adrift and the President must get a handle on it

- is having trouble because of the way in which U.S. military power has been used on his watch
- needs to be given a red light on putting U.S. forces under the UN
- in foreign policy, the first months not as strong as we would have liked
- 69 percent of Americans oppose sending U.S. troops to Haiti to restore Aristide
- 52 percent of American people disapprove of the way that Clinton is handling foreign policy
- 55 percent of American people trust Congress, 23 percent trust Clinton to deal with the rest of the world
- Senate fired a warning shot regarding Clinton's foreign policy and the use of U.S. troops
- conceded that hopes of reinstating Haiti's former President are slim
- forced to defend Haiti's exiled President against allegations of mental instability contained in a CIA report
- United States has done little about Haitian drug trafficking/not serious about drug trafficking in Haiti
- President Clinton has lost
- demonstrations in Haiti called for the resignation of the U.S.-backed Prime Minister
- CIA informants were members of the Haitian military

Descriptors Coded Neutral or Ambiguous

- President
- to press for reinstatement of economic sanctions
- learning hard lessons in Somalia
- believed the United States has new freedom to intervene against bloodshed and suffering everywhere in the world
- must solve another difficult foreign policy problem
- has no real choice [on Haiti]/really has no choice
- risks being blamed for Aristide's actions
- U.S. policy is pegged to the return of Aristide
- not laying the groundwork for an intervention, but not ruling it out either
- has not ruled out an armed intervention
- didn't rule out an evacuation of Americans
- big gamble for Clinton
- flexing military muscle
- not a prelude to a military intervention in Haiti
- believes that pressure of military sanctions will bring order
- hope expressed that he will take it easy
- speculation that he will use force to restore Aristide
- working on two fronts

- attempts to limit presidential decision making can encourage the Haitian military
- apparently has little room to maneuver
- despite doubts about Aristide and presidential policy, Senate is likely to sign on with the President on this one
- administration denied trying to pressure Aristide into a coalition government with antidemocratic elements
- backing Aristide in the face of growing criticism in Washington
- pressuring Aristide supporters who fled to Washington to return to Haiti
- hopes the stalemate has been broken
- United States would see any attempt to form another government in Haiti as a coup d'etat
- Administration and UN decided to ignore the CIA analysis and stick with Aristide as the centerpiece to restore democracy to Haiti

PRESIDENT JEAN-BERTRAND ARISTIDE

Descriptors Coded Positive
- civilian president
- man the United States is backing
- elected President/democratically elected President/democratically elected by two-thirds of Haitians/first and only democratically elected President of Haiti/won election victory with a percentage of vote higher than any leader in the Western Hemisphere/elected in free balloting/elected ruler
- his return is awaited by a majority of Haitians/his support is unwavering
- elected but now exiled President/elected but exiled President/exiled President elect/deposed but
- freely elected President
- supports Clinton's stepped up pressure [against the military]
- "he is our only hope"
- opened the door to a more inclusive government
- "god— that's him for us"
- "Without Aristide, democracy will never come to Haiti"
- "Personal experiences of those in the administration working with Aristide are a more valid indicator of his mental health than allegations are"
- vowed not to make concessions to military leaders who ousted him
- will return as planned on October 30
- met with members of the Senate Foreign Relations Committee
- his supporters are in danger
- his supporters are willing to compromise

- "he is the only one who cares"
- the impression that Aristide has lost the support of the population is false
- the man who inspired his countrymen can't go home

Descriptors Coded Negative
- can he govern effectively?
- psychologically unstable/suffers from emotional problems/suffers from emotional problems requiring psychological treatment and medication/takes an assortment of therapeutic drugs/suffers from bouts of depression and other psychiatric disorders/displays signs of megalomania/loses touch with reality/ "this man is a psychopath"/once took lithium and halidol, drugs commonly used to treat manic depression/has an unstable and volatile personality
- uncertain about returning to Haiti
- U.S. fears he might not be strong enough to exercise power
- worried about what the military might do next
- virulently anti-American
- U.S. has major misgivings about him
- frightened by new troubles
- paid little mind to democratic principles
- called for necklacing of political opponents/supported violence/sometimes encouraged violence/ "give them what they deserve"/encouraged necklacing/described necklacing as a beautiful tool/exhorting mobs to kill political opponents by putting a tire filled with gasoline around their necks and lighting it
- unable to control popular justice through mob violence/difficult, erratic, and given to support mobs/prone to violence
- not sure that bringing Aristide back will improve unsettled conditions
- attacked on the Senate floor
- "United States. has no business risking American lives to put him back into office"
- will be in very serious trouble
- is he part of the problem?
- spent the week denying that he was mentally unstable/called charges that he is unfit to govern "garbage"/denounced charges that he is mentally unstable as nothing but psychological warfare/ labeled allegations of mental instability as part of a campaign of character assassination
- the opposition is skeptical about his motives
- why did he chose a drug dealer to be Commandant of the Army?
- unfit to govern
- rabble-rouser
- his resignation would be seen as a patriotic act

- there are plans to replace him with a new president
- "cannot come back to this country without going to jail"
- opponents threaten to impeach him
- "He should never return, should be history"
- "He has destroyed the country"
- "He has lost"

Descriptors Coded Neutral or Ambiguous
- President
- ousted Haitian President/deposed Haitian President/former Haitian President/overthrown president/ exiled president/President of Haiti in exile
- called for UN sanctions against Haiti/ called for a complete UN blockade of Haiti to force military rulers from power/called for harsher world measures/called upon the world to get tough with the military leaders who took his job away/called for a total commercial embargo
- his return delayed beyond the end of October/unable to go home/return is in question/his return looks less and less likely/will take a miracle for Aristide to return on schedule/his return has been delayed indefinitely/prospects for his return are even gloomier
- remains in Washington
- supposed to return to Haiti on October 30/supposed to return in ten days to resume power
- failed to return to Haiti and reclaim power/could not return
- he will die if he comes back
- his triumphant return from exile is delayed indefinitely
- his home was vandalized after the coup
- his only hope is more negotiations [with the military]
- living in the United States
- won't go home until the generals running the country step down
- counting on Clinton to return him to power
- he will die if he comes back
- his triumphant return from exile is delayed indefinitely
- his home was vandalized after the coup
- his only hope is more negotiations [with the military]
- "he will come after us" [attaches]
- predicted that if democracy is not brought to Haiti, a new wave of immigrants will come to the United States
- Catholic priest/Father Aristide
- requested security
- lasted in office seven months
- lobbied Senators not to undercut efforts to restore him to power
- favors political reconciliation but would not say if he would accept an expanded government including ministers loyal to the Haitian military

- returning to Haiti only his first challenge, he must neutralize thugs and hitmen
- priest turned politician/former priest
- warned Congress about drug trafficking/charged military leaders of making up to $5 million a year in drug kickbacks
- Mr.
- posters with his photograph defaced
- no one dares mention his name in the streets
- pointless to talk about his return when his country is paralyzed by fear

GENERAL RAOUL CÉDRAS/HAITIAN MILITARY

Descriptors Coded Positive
- offered conditions for stepping down
- elements of the army have reached out to the government and brokered a deal
- Cédras is very honest
- Army is sincere

Descriptors Coded Negative
- on rampage
- stepped up campaign of terror
- all happened under his [Cédras'] eyes
- thugs/group of thugs/armed thugs/small group of thugs/a few thugs/anti-Aristide thugs/ thugs who control the streets/thugs with the guns/thugs that have captured the country and are holding it hostage
- militants
- turned back a U.S. ship/blamed for hostility to landing/blocked landing of U.S. advisors/blocked the port
- attaches/military-backed attaches/a paramilitary force that acts as a hit squad
- for extreme elements/civilian gunmen/armed civilians
- renegade leaders/renegade gunmen
- killers/killed seven/responsible for most of the killing here/they will be doing a lot of killing/ routinely use murder as a political tool/turned the church of Sacre Cour into a killing ground/killed people and left bodies in the street/brutally murdering people in front of
- the world
- will not cooperate
- chief military strongman/military strongman
- they have all the guns and the willingness to use them
- generals still in power and making everyone nervous
- enforced a general strike
- shouted anti-American slogans

- wanted a new and wider amnesty/will resign if parliament grants amnesty to the military/insists on a broader amnesty/demanding a new amnesty bill
- feeling emboldened
- will never relinquish power/will not step aside/no indication that he will step down/unlikely that he will resign/digging in their heels/continuing to defy UN agreement to hand over power/remains in power/still has not resigned/refuses to give up power/showed no sign of stepping down/show no sign of capitulating/very recalcitrant in moving forward with Governors Island Accord/still defying their own agreement with the UN to step down/failed to show up for a meeting with UN envoy/did not attend a meeting with UN envoy/refusing to talk about Governors' Island Agreement/refusing to honor Governors' Island Agreement/ still holding out/shows no sign of leaving/failed to leave in accord with the Governors Island Agreement/ continued to defy the UN/defiant/not budging an inch
- will kill every Aristide man in the country before he gets here
- man whom many believe is responsible for the violence
- gunmen/small group of gunmen/groups of gunmen
- most Haitians have little faith that the military will keep its word
- prepared to tough out sanctions and to ignore the deadline to surrender
- refused to guarantee the safety of men from the U.S. ship
- will not provide security for UN troops
- allowed thugs to attack journalists
- threatened people
- feels vulnerable over assassinations
- condemned for not controlling violence
- principal obstacle to the restoration of democracy/doesn't want the country to be democratic/thwarting democracy
- wants to prevent change
- military dictators
- trying to block Aristide's return/blocking return to civilian rule/preventing Aristide's return
- "will not stop the democratic train from going ahead"
- supporters threaten to use voodoo
- called the Governors Island Accord a dead end/responsible for the failure of the Governors Island Accord
- "these few hundred thugs have no alternative but to get off our backs"
- involved in drug trafficking/may make up to $5 million a year in drug kickbacks
- military coup leaders/led coup against Aristide
- broadcast threats against foreigners
- intransigent
- continue to ignore Washington

- big-business-backed military leaders
- recalcitrant
- expected to hold out while the Haitian people bear the brunt of the embargo
- leading military strongman
- threatening civilian politicians
- the reason for the terror
- target of UN sanctions
- has stood up to the international community
- has grown more defiant
- supported by far right-wing political parties
- intent on hanging on to power and risk the consequences
- his resignation is called for by conservative opponents of Aristide/his resignation called for by right-wing groups
- hardliners are talking up a new scheme to take even tighter control of the government
- remains firmly in control/tightened their grip on the country
- threatens Aristide's government with a coup d'etat

Descriptors Coded Neutral or Ambiguous

- General/Army General/Lt. Gen/top General
- head of military junta/military chief/military leader/military ruler/
- military high command/army leaders/military leadership/Generals who run the country/military authorities/military leaders
- apologized for "confusion" at the port
- defends Haitian Army
- opposes sanctions
- "blinked"
- came to power in the 1991 coup
- scheduled to resign on Friday
- Mr.
- wants the UN to hear his side
- are at a dead end
- can stop the violence
- promised to resign
- they feel they won a major battle/claiming victory in spite of even tougher sanctions/ "We won—Aristide lost"/Aristide's opponents performed a victory dance/believe they have won
- in light of the turmoil, it would be irresponsible for him to leave his post
- said that U.S. show of force was counter productive
- were supposed to cooperate with Aristide's Prime Minister
- beginning to use their brain and realize that there is no way out
- "We will not back down—We will not surrender"

- de facto regime
- have ruled the country since the 1991 coup
- eventually they will feel the pinch [of the blockade]
- "They may have won the battle this time, but they didn't win the war"
- Haiti's main man
- will decide the fate of the UN plan to restore democracy
- military and attaches jubilant that their prayers had been answered

NOTES

1.   According to Nairn, Constant "had openly announced his dockside rally the day before and apparently did not get any U.S. warning to call it off" (Nairn, 1994b, p. 461).

2.   Doyle reports that the United States "warned no one" that a decision had been made to remove the USS Harlan County from Port-au-Prince and claims that "all those linked to plans for the returns of Aristide were suddenly vulnerable" as a result of the withdrawal (Doyle, 1994, pp. 55–56).

3.   A "news segment" is operationalized as a part of a total news story given focus by a single reporter. When the full news report is read by the anchor, one news segment is counted. When a story is introduced by the anchor and turned over to a reporter or reporters, the number of news segments equals the number of separate reporters used, as the anchor's introduction is not counted.

4.   The flow of refugees from Cuba, Fidel Castro's strategic use of this weapon in 1980, and the more lenient U.S. policy applied to Cuban refugees historically, further complicated the issues for the United States as it was argued that racism lay at the root of a more stringent Haitian refugee policy. Castro's opening of Cuban beaches to "rafters" in the summer of 1994, at the same time that the United States was contemplating military force to drive the Haitian generals from power, refocused attention on differences in U.S. refugee policy as it applied to Cuba and Haiti. (see Chapters 5 and 7).

5.   In the study of more than a dozen Caribbean Basin crises occurring since 1953, no other leader or group (including Rafael Trujillo), has been so thoroughly vilified.

5

The Restoration of Democracy to Haiti, 1994

Walter C. Soderlund and Ralph C. Nelson

BACKGROUND

After the aborted attempt to implement the Governor's Island Agreement in October 1993, the UN and the OAS reimposed sanctions on Haiti. Also, President Aristide called for the use of a UN force to restore him to power. Thus, 1993 ended with a good deal of rancor; expressed, on the one hand, by Aristide against Clinton's perceived lack of determination, and, on the other, by the U.S. administration against Aristide's perceived "intransigence." Indeed, there was speculation "that the United States might simply dump him [Aristide], lift the embargo and accept the status quo" (McFadyen and LaRamée, 1995, p. 5). The Governor's Island initiative had clearly failed, yet the old dilemma remained; tightening the noose on Haiti's military leaders would only encourage more people to leave the island for the United States.

All indications are that relations between the Clinton administration and President Aristide continued to be difficult (Greenhouse, 1994, A-11). As the second year of Clinton's presidency began, there were signs of increasing U.S. annoyance with Aristide, especially over his disagreements with Robert Malval, the prime minister he had selected (Stotzky, 1999, pp 35–36). Neither was Aristide seen to be sensitive to the massive refugee problem faced by the United States. With thousands ready to board boats, Aristide called the American policy of interdiction "racist and criminal" and refused to discourage people from leaving the island (Ives, 1995c, p. 109). At the same time there was increased pressure from Jesse Jackson and the Congressional Black caucus on behalf of Aristide's return (Berman and Goldman, 1996, pp. 309–310).

The basic dilemma underlying U.S. policy (under both Bush and Clinton) was, that imposing tighter economic sanctions on Haiti to persuade the generals to leave had the effect of sending larger numbers of Haitians streaming toward U.S. shores in unseaworthy vessels (von Hippel, 1995, p. 13). To counter the charge that the policy of repatriation was racist and, to attempt to stem the tide of refugees, the administration tried various expedients: replacing Lawrence Pezzullo with William Gray III as special envoy in Haiti; encouraging Caribbean countries to allow processing of refugees on their soil; requesting Panama to accept 10,000 refugees; and once more sending refugees to Guantanamo, Cuba (Gordon, 1994, p. A-1). If the refugee problem had not been so acute, the administration might simply have persisted with the policy of economic sanctions and "toughed it out." This was not the case, however, and "the refugee issue was now pushing the Clinton Administration to resolve the Haiti question once and for all" (Ives, 1995c, 110).

In January 1994, Admiral Paul David Miller produced a white paper on Haiti in which he outlined what were termed three "bad options": (1) increased sanctions, (2) a strategic retreat, and (3) military intervention (Shacochis, 1999, pp. 55–56). Faced with these choices, the last appeared to be the least of the evils, and, as Karin von Hippel has argued, "the invasions of Panama and Grenada supplied the United States with the ultimate resolution to the Haitian dilemma" (1995, p. 13).

What had worked in those countries now served as the only logical recourse for Haiti as well. Planning for a military operation continued during the spring and summer under the concept of "adaptive joint-force packaging" developed by Admiral Miller (Shacochis, 1999, pp. 53–54). According to Peter Jakobsen, "a decision on 8 May to stop the automatic return of the boat people to Haiti effectively put US policy on a one-way street towards intervention, because it led to a dramatic increase in the number of refugees which only an intervention could stop quickly" (Jakobsen, 1996, p. 211). Indeed by June 1994, the U.S. Coast Guard was "rescuing" 2,000 to 3,000 Haitians per day (Berman and Goldman, 1996, p. 310). In July 1994, the military option became a matter for open discussion when the UN Security Council, following a request from the United States, authorized the creation of "a U.S. led multinational force...empowered... 'to use all necessary means' to restore the democratically elected government of Haiti" (Niblack, 1995, p. 5).

The military option, however, proved to be unpopular among decision makers outside of the White House. Even within the Congressional Black caucus there was division, and influential lawmakers in both Republican and Democratic parties voiced skepticism or opposition to a U.S. military invasion.[1] The President's position was that he would surely welcome congressional support for an invasion, but its absence would not deter him from acting, as such authority fell within presidential powers. As the summer was coming to an end, U.S. military forces were readied for a "hard entry" into Haiti on ten day's notice (Shacochis, 1999, p. 60). At the eleventh hour, a last-ditch attempt to talk the generals out of Haiti was commissioned in the form of a mission led by former President Carter, Senator Sam Nunn, and retired General Colin Powell. The "Carter Mission," as it came to be known, reached an agreement with General Cédras regarding the peaceful removal of the military government on September 17, when U.S. troops were in the air on their way to begin the invasion (Shacochis, 1999, pp. 74–77).

The agreement, described as a "sweetheart deal" for Haiti's generals (McFadyen and LaRamée, 1995, p. 7), negotiated by Carter and the U.S. negotiating team with General Cédras was not without certain ambiguities, which, as Bob Shacochis reports, became painfully apparent once U.S. forces occupied Haiti. However, given the lack of both public and congressional support, the administration was extremely lucky to have avoided a full-scale invasion (Greenhouse, 1994, sec. 1, p. 12).[2] Especially problematic was that the rules of engagement for the U.S. military changed virtually overnight. The Haitian Army and Police, seen as the enemy on September 17, became collaborators on September 18. Another problem resulted from the policy that initially had prohibited U.S. forces from becoming involved in what was termed "Haitian-on-Haitian violence" (Farmer, 1995, p. 29).

After the occupation was accomplished, the next task was to send the members of the junta into exile once they had been granted amnesty. Aristide had continually objected to this, and it had been a long-term stumbling block to cooperation between the Clinton administration and the exiled President. Aristide's return to Haiti under the auspices of the U.S. occupying military force was in itself not without irony. Aristide was long seen as a spokesperson in Haiti for radical, anticapitalist, anti-American positions; Kim Ives describes him on his return in mid-October as "a small figure on a regal chair in a bullet-proof cage, exhibited for the crowds like an animal in a zoo" (Ives, 1995c, p. 107).

Once the restoration of Aristide had occurred, the majority of U.S. troops were quickly removed, while order was maintained by UN forces until a new Haitian police force was in place. On January 30 1995 the UN declared that "a secure and stable environment" existed in Haiti and on March 31, the United States transferred responsibility for policing Haiti to the UN. Importantly, on April 28, 1995 the Haitian army (FADH) was disbanded by President Aristide (Niblack, 1995, p. 6, Stotzky, 1997, p. 43).[3]

FINDINGS

News stories dealing with the threatened September 1994 U.S. military invasion of Haiti that aimed at restoring Jean-Bertrand Aristide to its presidency were studied on the main evening newscasts of the three major U.S. television networks for almost a month. The stories began on September 4, and continued through the end of the month, which happened to mark the third anniversary of the coup that had removed President Aristide from power. While it is apparent from the preceding two chapters that Haiti had been an ongoing story for U.S. media for a number of years, in this case we are examining stories that focused on (1) the military planning for the immanent invasion, (2) the negotiations that turned the invasion into an intervention, and (3) the ensuing problems faced by U.S. forces in the initial period of their occupation of Haiti. During this period U.S. television networks ran ninety-three stories containing one hundred and eighty-one news segments, making this the most heavily covered of all the crises examined in this study. Of the ninety-three stories, ABC ran thirty-two containing sixty-three reporter segments, CBS ran thirty-five containing sixty-

five news segments, and NBC ran twenty-six containing fifty-three news
segments. Language used to describe President Clinton and the U.S.
government; President Aristide; and Aristide's chief opponents, General Cédras
and the Haitian Military, used by anchors, reporters, and sources was recorded,
collated, and coded is shown in the appendices to Chapter 5.

Table 5.1
Story Characteristics N=93

	Number		Percentage
Lead Story	49		53
1st Three Stories	71		76
30 Seconds And Under	5		5
Over 3 Minutes	57		61
Just Anchor Format	9		10
Use Of "Experts"	5		5
Reporter In Haiti	62		67
Two Or More News Segments	53		57
Film With Story	85		91
Film Of President Clinton	41		44
Film Of President Aristide	27		29
Film Of General Cédras	34		37
Visual Violence	45		48
"Tilt" Favorable To U.S. Position	20		22
"Tilt" Unfavorable To U.S. Position	26		28
"U.S. Involvement" Index		4.5	

The 1994 intervention and occupation generated a huge amount of media
coverage. Over a period of time that was five days shorter in length than that
studied for the aborted restoration of President Aristide in 1993, there were
thirty-one more news stories featured in network coverage, (93 total) containing
ninety-seven more news segments (181). As indicated in Table 5.1, virtually
every indicator of story importance points to events in Haiti in 1994 as being
extraordinarily salient: 53 percent of stories ran as leads; 76 percent of stories
occupied one of the first three newscast positions; 61 percent ran longer than 3
minutes, with only 5 percent running 30 seconds or less; 91 percent contained
film/video; and 44 percent featured President Clinton. Interestingly, for the first
time in the three Haitian crises studied as part of this research project, General
Raoul Cédras appeared in film/video in more stories (35 percent) than did
President Aristide (29 percent).

By early September 1994, President Clinton had made it clear that with or
without Congressional support, the Haitian generals were facing an immanent
armed invasion to remove them from power and restore President Aristide.
When the invasion turned into an intervention/occupation (literally overnight),
the one constant in U.S. policy remained the return of Aristide. Thus, in terms
of evaluation of overall U.S. policy, which we describe as the willingness to use
U.S. military force to rid Haiti of the military regime and restore President

Aristide to the presidency, 22 percent of stories were coded as "favorable" and 28 percent were coded as "unfavorable." Further, on the U.S. involvement index (1=low and 5=high) the score for coverage of the "intervention/ occupation" was 4.5, highest for all crises studied, and up a full point from that recorded in 1993 Haiti coverage. Clearly, by September 1994, the crisis in Haiti had fully involved the United States; as a result, it was treated as a major media event.

Table 5.2
Number of Times Leading Sources Used (All Sources Used in Newscast)

News Source	Segment 1	Segment 2	Segment 3	Segment 4	Total Number of Times Used
Haitians-on-the-street	35	26	4	2	68
U.S. military in field	46	12	9	-	67
Bill Clinton	23	18	8	1	50
Administration	17	16	6	-	39
Pentagon	18	11	5	3	37
Congressional Republicans	11	7	2	5	25
Congressional Democrats	9	8	4	4	25
Jean-Bertrand Aristide	5	7	4	5	21
U.S. Embassy in Haiti	9	6	3	-	18
Aristide Supporters	10	5	1	-	17
State Department	8	8	1	-	17
Raoul Cédras	8	2	2	1	13
Haitian Military	9	4	-	-	13
Prominent Americans	10	3	-	-	13
Jimmy Carter	8	2	2	-	12

Table 5.2 shows the leading sources (on-camera and quoted) used in network television news stories dealing with the Haitian crisis. The table shows the preponderance of American sources, with ten of the fifteen leading sources being American. Whether this amounts to preferential sourcing of U.S. government spokespersons is open for debate. Catherine Orenstein accused U.S. media of adopting this practice in coverage of the 1991 Haitian coup, to the extent that she claimed the media became "the voice of the State Department" (Orenstein, 1995, pp. 103–104). In this connection it is important to note that not all U.S. sources were necessarily favorable to the U.S. position. The president, his administration, the Pentagon, the U.S. State Department, the U.S. Embassy in Haiti, and, for the most part, former president Carter and U.S. military forces in the field, all supported the U.S. position. On the other hand, Congress (Republicans and most Democrats) was critical (see Paletz and Entman, 1981), as were a number of prominent Americans, who by and large

did not see a justification for military action to defend U.S. national interests. As expected, General Cédras and the Haitian military condemned the policy that was aimed directly at their removal. Interestingly, President Aristide, the object of the restoration, seemed to support U.S. policy only when pressured to do so by the administration. Haitians on the street and Aristide supporters, with some exceptions, tended to support the U.S.-led intervention and occupation.

Table 5.3
Percentage of Stories in Which Media Frames Are Used

Frame	Primary	Secondary	Tertiary	Total
Restoration of democracy	24	18	19	61
Occupation Problems	17	14	10	41
Military planning	16	9	6	31
U.S. Foreign Policy Decision-Making	18	19	10	29
Societal Violence	14	9	5	29
Negotiations	11	1	-	12
Campaign implications	-	4	2	6
Refugees	-	4	1	5

Table 5.3 examines the crucial issue of how the 1994 Haitian crisis was framed by the media for U.S. audiences. Data here are revealing. Although at various times during the crisis, episodic frames such as military planning (would U.S. forces prevail and at what cost in terms of casualties); negotiations (would the Carter mission succeed); and problems related to the occupation (would the United States somehow get sucked into a Somalia-like situation) were evident, the thematic frames of restoration of democracy and the proper role for the United States in the post–Cold War world continued (as was the case in 1993) to serve as the major lenses through which the crisis was interpreted by U.S. television news. It is significant that the refugee crisis, which in the analysis of many scholars was a stronger driving force behind U.S. policy than was a commitment to democracy in Haiti, was never offered as a primary frame; as a secondary or tertiary frame, it appeared in only 5 percent of stories. The significant underplaying of the refugee frame (down 13 percent from 1993) adds weight to Cynthia Weber's contention that in the 1994 Haiti crisis, "the focus on the protection of Haitian human rights served as a false cover for an issue closer to home—immigration" (Weber, 1995, p. 272). Whatever the cause, neither the possible electoral impact of the crisis in the United States nor the refugee question were featured as frames to any significant extent in media coverage.

Data in Table 5.4 compare the way in which the major participants in the crisis (President Clinton and the U.S. Government, President Aristide, and General Cédras and the Haitian Army) were evaluated in textual presentations on U.S. network television news. Stories were coded into one of four categories: (1) Favourable, balance of coverage positive; (2) "Unfavorable", balance of coverage negative; (3) Neutral/Ambiguous, approximately equal amounts of positive and negative, or hard to gauge the likely impact of coverage; or (4) not applicable, stories not dealing with the participant.

Table 5.4
Text Evaluation of Major Participants (percentage)

	Clinton/U.S. Government (90 stories)	Aristide (69 stories)	Cédras/Haitian Army (8 stories)
Favorable			
Number of Stories	21	26	1
Percentage	23	38	2
Neutral			
Number of Stories	41	33	24
Percentage	46	48	27
Unfavorable			
Number of Stories	28	10	62
Percentage	31	14	71

For all three major participants, 1994 evaluations are somewhat less polarized than they were in 1993. Policies and actions of President Clinton and the U.S. government were evaluated in ninety of ninety-three stories, another indicator of the central role played by the United States in this crisis. Of these stories, 23 percent were coded as favorable, and 31 percent were coded as unfavorable; a balance actually more favorable and slightly less unfavorable than coverage for 1993, where 11 percent were coded as favorable and 36 percent were coded as unfavorable. This appears to indicate that in terms of media evaluation, it is better to be perceived as doing something (even if this is not seen as especially wise or popular), than to appear powerless or indecisive (Kagay, 1994). Policies and actions of President Aristide were mentioned in only sixty-nine stories; 38 percent of these were judged to be favorable, while only 14 percent were seen as unfavorable. The percentage of positive Aristide stories increased significantly (from 17 percent in 1993), while the percentage of negative stories decreased slightly from 19 percent. Policies and actions of General Cédras and the Haitian Army were the focus of nearly as many stories as the U.S. participants—eighty-seven of ninety-three. In only 2 percent of these stories was commentary judged to be primarily positive, while in 71 percent it was judged to be negative. The percentage of positive stories was identical to that recorded in 1993, while the percentage of negative stories dropped from 84 percent, due primarily to the cooperative stance adopted by Cédras and the Haitian Army toward the U.S. intervention and occupation after the Carter Agreement.

Table 5.5 shows the evaluations of President Clinton and the U.S. government, President Aristide, and General Cédras and the Haitian Army based on the actual number of positive and negative descriptors appearing in textual commentary focusing on these actors. On this measure we find that the U.S. president and his government were actually treated more harshly than they were in 1993, with the percentage of positive descriptors falling from 43 percent to 34 percent, and the percentage of negative descriptors rising from 57 percent to 66 percent. This finding, combined with those in Table 5.4, indicates that although

5 percent fewer stories were deemed overall to have evaluated the U.S. president and government negatively in 1994 as opposed to 1993, those that did were far more vehement in their condemnation.

President Aristide's evaluation remained virtually constant between the 1993 and 1994 crises, with both years seeing a more or less equal distribution

Table 5.5
Percentage of Descriptors Reflecting Positively or Negatively on Major Actors

	Number of Descriptors	Percentage
Clinton/U.S. Government		
Positive	119	34
Negative	232	66
Total	351	100
Aristide		
Positive	67	49
Negative	70	51
Total	137	100
Cédras/Haitian Army		
Positive	35	14
Negative	222	86
Total	257	100

between positive and negative characterizations—47 percent positive/53 percent negative in 1993; 49 percent positive/51 percent negative in 1994.

Evaluations of General Cédras and the Haitian Army based on descriptive language, point to a continued, but less skewed, condemnation than was seen in 1993, where only 2 percent of valenced descriptors were positive, and 98 percent negative. Nevertheless, the 1994 distribution of 14 percent positive and 86 percent negative is hardly reflective of numbers that would likely inspire confidence in the American people that the continuation of a defacto military government in Haiti was in any sense a viable alternative to the restoration of the elected head of state.

Numbers alone, however, do not tell the full story. An examination of the appendices which list the actual language used by the U.S. media to describe the various actors, adds a good deal of context and nuance to the analysis. In Appendix 5.1 positive language used to describe President Clinton and the U.S. government more broadly, accounting for about a one-third of evaluative comments, falls into three major clusters: (1) machismo, in finally standing up to the Haitian generals who had embarrassed the United States so badly for three years; (2) siding with the angels, in getting rid of the notorious Haitian military, who had inflicted horrible abuses on the Haitian people and on restoring democratic government; and (3) statements of pride and congratulations over the accomplishments of the U.S. military forces in Haiti. Negative commentary, accounting for about two-thirds of evaluated descriptors, can also be categorized in three major clusters, although in this case they are not as tightly grouped: (1) congressional challenges to presidential authority to mount the invasion, combined with efforts to thwart or constrain Clinton's policies; (2) a focus on the lack of support from the American people for an invasion; and (3) criticisms of the Carter agreement and subsequent problems related to the occupation stemming from it. Very little positive or critical commentary focused on the refugee problem; the battle tended to be fought on whether the invasion/ occupation served the security interests of the United States and American lives should be placed at risk. To the extent that language is important, it is evident that the President's detractors carried the day.

An examination of Aristide descriptors in Appendix 5.2, shows that most of the positive descriptors focus on three elements: (1) his victory in a fair and free election (thus conveying legitimacy); (2) his championing the cause of Haiti's poor, and (3) his promise to bring both democracy and reconciliation to Haiti. Negative descriptive language used, both in volume and tone, reflects the serious partisan debate regarding Aristide's commitment to democratic practice, the wisdom of the U.S. policy of seeking his return to Haiti, and his lukewarm support for U.S. military efforts mounted on his behalf. Although we did not code descriptive language in terms of strength of impact, we conclude that in the case of Aristide, even though the number of positive and negative descriptors was about equal, negative descriptors tended to carry greater weight. Whatever the case, from 1990 to 1994, as Aristide became better known to the American public through media coverage, there was certainly an increase in negative information about him. Nonetheless, his supporters (in the United States and in Haiti) were certainly not shut out of the debate. Nor of course (and this is important in terms of understanding the context in which decisions in Washington were being made), were Aristide's military opponents in Haiti ever presented as a reasonable alternative for continued rule over the island.

Appendix 5.3 shows that the negative language used with respect to General Cédras and the Haitian Army focused heavily on their record of notorious human rights abuses and intransigence regarding their removal from office; virtually all of the sparse positive language came from President Carter and others, and focused on the general's cooperative behavior after the successful negotiations to remove them from power. With the generals no longer a threat, apparently there was no need to continue to demonize them.   However, President Clinton, who had been front and center in the preinvasion media campaign aimed at discrediting the Haitian generals, offered few positive remarks about them.

CONCLUSION

Establishing of democratic governance in Haiti proved to be elusive. Haitian reality, as Irwin Stotzky points out, has a nasty habit of getting in the way of good intentions:

> Authoritarianism cannot be overcome simply because people favor democratic methods for resolving conflicts and developing a nation. Powerful forces block the passage from dictatorship to democracy. In Haiti these underlying forces are an organic conception of society that leads to a dualistic vision of the social

order; corporatism; anomie and lawlessness; and extreme concentrations of institutional, economic, and social power. These forces are directly related to massive human rights abuses (1997, p. 208)

No one maintains that democracy is near at hand in Haiti, but most would agree that some progress toward this end has been made, especially in the democratic election of 1990. The 1991 coup removing Aristide from power, however, proved to be a real setback to the process. While the Governor's Island Agreement appeared to hold the key to a peaceful restoration of Aristide, such optimism was seriously misplaced, as in October 1993 the Haitian generals outmanoeuvred U.S. strategists.

This chapter examines round two in the restoration of Aristide, which occurred almost a year later and produced a different outcome. When faced with the sure prospect of being removed from power in a massive U.S. military invasion, the Haitian military leaders finally "saw the light" and agreed to relinquish power, allowing the return of President Aristide in October 1994.

In their reporting of this crisis, as was the case a year earlier in 1993, the U.S. media focused heavily on thematic frames—first and foremost the need to restore democracy in Haiti, followed next by pessimism generated by the ongoing violence in the country. Interestingly, the implications of the failure to re-establish a democratic system in Haiti on the stream of illegal immigration to the United States (the primary domestic factor driving U.S. policy), was largely absent in media framing (see Orenstein, 1995; Weber, 1995). This was not the case, however, with the frame that placed events in Haiti in the context of the proper role for the United States in ensuring peace and order in an unruly and violent post—Cold War world (Morales, 1994).

In the early years of his presidency, Clinton's foreign policy approval ratings in general were poor, as was the evaluation of the Haitian component of that policy. Mass media coverage of the 1993 and 1994 crises reflected and probably reinforced these judgments. Although there is evidence of overwhelming opposition in media coverage to the continued rule of the Haitian military, beginning in the fall of 1993 and continuing through to 1994, the media also reflected a new focus on Aristide's character and his record while in office, fueled largely by factions within the United States opposed to his return.

With respect to democracy in Haiti, the five years between Aristide's election in 1990 and his restoration to power in 1994, saw a serious regression in democratic practice. The generals had ruled brutally for three years, during which time Aristide remained in exile in the United States and the Haitian people and economy suffered enormously. Given the lack of support for the military option among the general American population and in Congress, it is probably fortunate that the Carter mission was successful in negotiating U.S. occupation of the country without the necessity of a military invasion.

The intervention and subsequent occupation at best only restored Haiti to where it had been in late summer 1991—i.e., a country ruled by a democratically elected civilian president. However, the extent to which Aristide was forced to make compromises and embrace the Washington consensus to ensure his restoration weakened him domestically (Ives, 1995b, pp. 69–84; Fatton, 1997, pp. 146–148).[4] As well, his popular movement in Haiti had been literally decapitated during the period of de facto military rule (Farmer, 1995, p. 226). In 1993 and 1994, the partisan debates in the United States on Aristide's character and suitability to rule were reflected prominently in media coverage and weakened any firm commitment of the Clinton administration to the elected and now restored Haitian president. As events unfolded, Aristide was increasingly perceived in Washington as part of the problem, rather than a part of its solution (Pastor, 1997, pp. 131–132; Stotzky, 1997, pp. 48–49).

How these factors specifically affected developments in Haiti from the time of Aristide's restoration to the present are beyond the scope of this research, but it would be safe to say that their impact would not have been positive (see Manwaring, et al., 1997; Gibbons, 1999). Whatever the case, since the restoration of Aristide few have argued either that democracy in the country has put down firm roots or that any of the elected governments (Aristide's, during 1995; Preval's, from 1996 to 2000, which was beset by long-term paralysis; and Aristide's since 2001) have moved very far in solving the country's pressing social, economic and political problems (Schulz, 1997; Bohning, 1998; Donnelly, 1999, Gonzalez, 2002).

APPENDIX 5.1

PRESIDENT CLINTON/U.S. GOVERNMENT

Descriptors Coded Positive

- served notice [on the generals]—expect American troops in Haiti soon "if [the generals] resist, we're prepared to take further action to see that they leave involuntarily"/his resolve to end the standoff appeared firm/warning that one way or another, Haiti's military leaders will go and soon/gave a stiff warning to the Haitian military that time is running out/U.S. patience is wearing thin, the endgame is near/applying more U.S. pressure on Haiti/putting very visible pressure on the military regime/told the Haitian military leaders in no uncertain terms that their time was up/one way or another, U.S. troops will be in Haiti in a matter of days/put the military on notice/no change in Clinton's position: generals out, Aristide in/"I will not be delayed, I will not be deterred"/his policy is absolutely firm/if the generals don't leave, he will give the order/"We're not interested in negotiating with dictators, they have to go"/all but gave Haiti's generals an ultimatum; there's still time to leave, but if they don't, there's no choice but to invade/is determined that the present government [of Haiti] will not stand and that the elected President Aristide will be returned to power/get out of town now; nothing is negotiable, or face an overwhelming U.S. invasion/"they have no choice; they can go easy or they can go hard, but they're going to go soon"
- human rights abuses alone warrant U.S. action/a regime this brutal must be ousted/more determined than ever to launch a military assault/cannot stand by and let the human rights of the masses be trampled by a small group/there is logic for doing something—doing anything—to make this suffering [of the Haitian people] stop/will describe the grisly atrocities in Haiti he showed in pictures yesterday
- tan, rested, and ready to confront the challenges ahead
- discussed the possibility of Israeli help in restoring democracy
- strong resolve in the international community in seeking the restoration of democracy/announced that seventeen nations supported the U.S. invasion
- has continually tried to talk about what are U.S. interests in Haiti
- failure to restore Aristide could have a very unfortunate impact on other policy areas around the world
- suggested that there could be a new wave of Haitian refugees to the United States if no action is taken/if military rulers are not forced out, United States faces a massive threat of refugees
- people in Haiti secretly applaud the invasion

- is giving Haitian military leaders one last chance to leave without a fight/dispatched a high-level delegation to Haiti/decided on a dramatic and very high-powered move
- "this is a right cause"
- spoke with passion on the Haitian invasion
- "need to give democracy a chance"/"mission is to assist the legitimate government of Haiti restore democracy"/it is under the umbrella of the U.S. military that President Clinton hopes democracy will arrive, finally, in Haiti/intervention is working to give the Haitian people a chance at freedom/mission gave Haitians their chance at freedom/first important step in creating an environment where democratic institutions can work/democracy has finally come to Haiti/if it comes to an intervention, it is not an intervention against, but on behalf of the people of Haiti/the United States cannot walk away from a situation like this in our own backyard/wants to restore democracy
- democratic countries make better neighbors
- it is his responsibility to pursue every alternative
- the Pentagon has no doubt it's ready for Haiti/making sure that the United States has overwhelming military superiority
- can look awfully good if this works
- radio poll in Miami's little Haiti revealed strong support for what the United States in doing
- will not pay for a luxurious life in exile for General Cédras
- poor in Haiti believe their lives can only get better when the U.S. soldiers arrive/people in Haiti encouraged by the U.S. presence
- U.S. forces cheered and welcomed as long-lost friends/U.S. troops received heroes welcome/greeted as conquering heroes/ "We welcome the Americans"
- U.S. troops the only protection seen in Haiti since Aristide was overthrown
- there was satisfaction and congratulations in Washington that an invasion was avoided
- had not come to Haiti to make war
- his credibility on using military force is intact
- praised for achieving his principles without an invasion/thanked for giving diplomacy one last chance
- condemned Haitian police violence/[violence] must stop and it must stop quickly/violence cannot be tolerated/"we strongly condemn yesterday's police violence"
- feels very confident about the ability of our armed forces to complete the mission/ peacekeepers are ahead of schedule/"we are succeeding in our objective"/the situation has improved/mission is going very well indeed/going very well/"I'm proud and I believe the American people should be proud of the truly outstanding performance of American military personnel in Haiti"/satisfied with the U.S. military's

progress/making confident predictions about the intervention's ultimate outcome/the trend line is positive/[Clinton] put out the word that he's pleased with the mission so far/progress has been good and the President is pleased with that/is proud of the work that the U.S. military has done there
- stood up for a policy that was unpopular with the people and Congress
- resistance on the part of the Haitian military and police would be met decisively
- "more and more Americans are seeing what we are doing there is good and supporting democracy"

Descriptors Coded Negative
- invasion is on a fast-track in spite of little public support and no clear strategy for getting out
- will try to reassure a sceptical public by downplaying the invasion; it will be more of a police action than an invasion
- the Clinton administration, like the Bush administration before it, is a paper tiger/this administration's track record is not very strong in following through with its threats
- there is practically no optimism regarding Haiti
- criticized for waiting too long to return the exiled president
- thinking of invading Haiti to increase his standing in the polls/real reason for the invasion is to give the Clinton administration a boost before the midterm elections/accused of using the invasion to increase his approval ratings
- simply a diversionary tactic to get the spotlight off all his scandals
- "the president does not have the constitutional powers to invade Haiti"/"does not have the authority to go into Haiti in these circumstances"/preventing the Senate of the United States to speak on the risk to lives of young Americans/"We don't think there should be a monarch taking American sons and daughters into war without an expression of approval by members of the Senate and the House"/an immediate [Congressional] vote demanded the deployment of U.S. forces to Haiti/ "You must ask Congress before you invade"/"I think we would have faced a real constitutional crisis"/Congress put off by President's decision to send in troops without consultation/so worried about the political reaction that he moved up the timing of the invasion 24 hours to get it over before Congress could vote on it/in the Senate, the President's overall Haiti policy took a tremendous beating/ Republicans felt free to attack the President
- "I don't think the President can make his case"
- "not one American life if worthy of President Clinton using Haiti to demonstrate his political prowess"
- "credibility lost by political bungling should not be redeemed by American lives"

- the public opposes the invasion; 23% 'yes'; 73% 'no'/two-thirds of the American public oppose sending U.S. troops to Haiti to restore the democratically elected president/"You do not embark on a military exercise without the support of the American people"/the public is not behind the idea/is pressing ahead with invasion plans without much support from the public or the Congress/not so fast, back here opposition is growing/even Democrats are concerned that the president is willing to give the go-ahead with only thin support from the public and Congress/in Congress, there is formidable opposition to an invasion/on Capitol Hill, opposition to an invasion continued to grow/if a vote [in Congress] were taken today, the president would lose, big time/Congress would hand the president a crushing defeat/virtually no support for an invasion on Capitol Hill in both parties/if there is an invasion and it goes wrong, the president is going to be very much on his own/ There will be very few from Capitol Hill coming to his defense/"I don't think it has the support of the Congress"/clear that Congress would vote against an invasion/no shortage of opposition to the invasion/policy is receiving a firestorm of criticism/very little, if any, support for an invasion/ "talk show America' is up in arms against an invasion of Haiti/two-thirds of those questioned say "no" to an invasion/friends and foes took aim at the President/massive public opposition to an invasion/tremendous unhappiness here [in Washington]/his Haiti policy has come under fire from across the political spectrum/political criticism of the Clinton Haiti policy grows louder/if things go badly on the ground in Haiti, there will be no shortage of critics here [in Washington]/public is unimpressed with Clinton's Haiti policy/the American people have a right to know why we are about to make this mistake
- getting trapped by the same impulses that went into intervening before
- American troops may arrive as liberators, but the honeymoon is likely to be brief
- "risking American lives to restore Aristide to power is not an option; it is not a good option"/Haiti is not worth the lives of American armed forces/"Don't waste these troops, they're human lives, not Dixie Cups"/ "It is not worth the sacrifice of a single American life to return Mr. Aristide to power"/"How many brave men will we squander in ill-conceived foreign adventures that have nothing to do with American security?"/American lives should not be risked in an invasion/"Your Haitian policy is a mistake; you shouldn't risk American lives and we should get out of Haiti."
- "We have problems in our own country and we're not dealing with those; we're dealing with everyone else's all the time"
- "We cannot restore democracy at the point of a gun"
- Roman Catholic Bishops of the Western Hemisphere also sent a letter to the President saying they're not persuaded that the use of force is morally justified

- "We have not been given sufficient justification for an invasion"/not the national interest to invade Haiti/must do a better job than he has done so far explaining why he wants to risk American lives in Haiti/ "little old Haiti does not pose any threat to America"/"Why did the President waste so much time, money and prestige in a tiny island that posed no security threat to the United States"
- "it's never too late for Bill Clinton to get some combat experience; let him lead the invasion into Haiti"/"I wonder if [Clinton] would be willing to be the first stepping off the boats, leading the charge; not on your life"/as a young man he declined to risk his life in combat for this country
- will public opinion and support in the Congress still be there when the body bags and coffins come through Dover Delaware/"his policy has to pass the Dover, Delaware test—with support thin, can't afford to have many coffins brought home"
- "If the President thinks he can come in here and take the country over without bloodshed, he's a fool"/is underestimating the real dangers of an invasion
- losing the political battle over Haiti
- "Haiti has never had a democracy...you can't restore what was not there"
- U.S. action is triggering a last-minute campaign by Haiti's military to wipe out Aristide's supporters
- for those parts of the [U.S.] military not involved [in the invasion] there is less of everything. In the long run this could drastically reduce how well the U.S. military is able to do its job
- the Pentagon's gunboat diplomacy suffered an embarrassing gaff
- "I think the invasion is dead wrong"/he must go forward in terms of U.S. credibility; that's too bad because the policy is misguided/he's out there so far now he can't back off/how could the ultimate political animal go ahead with something so many people don't want/there are serious question with this policy/policy is mind-boggling/the underlying policy is flawed/Mr. Clinton's approach termed "Voodoo foreign policy"/doomed to failure
- [Clinton's] Haiti policy twists and turns
- Americans were chased away in 1993
- has put out feelers offering the generals a life of ease in exile
- "I disagree with the use of American force there"
- could be a quick in, but a dangerous stay
- warned that all Americans might have to be evacuated
- he blinked
- no-win situation for Clinton/immersed in his most serious foreign policy crisis, a crisis his critics say he helped manufacture/no way the invasion will be a political plus for the president/best that can happen [to Clinton] is that he breaks even

- if the President gives the order to invade, he will outrage Congress and sink any hope he has to pass key measures such as health reform
- the intervention would be like the Somalia situation, which will be very dangerous and not something members of Congress want to see U.S. troops participating in
- Congress will try to constrict the President's policy/Congress may try to put some time limits on U.S. presence in Haiti/Congress attempting to tie the President's hands on Haiti/setting a six-month limit on U.S. military operations in Haiti
- important that the President not be seen to "wimp out" at the last minute
- "Bill Clinton, Haiti is not Panama"
- unfortunate when a president has so squandered his credibility that he feels left with no option other than military action
- back-pedalling
- has a long way to go before he gets out of this one
- struggling to persuade the American people that he is up to the job
- embarrassed when the U.S.S. *Harlan County* was driven into retreat by an unruly mob
- his policy is as erratic as the flow of Haitian boat people
- getting painted into a corner by events
- "U.S. troops are here by the law of force, not legally"
- Bush administration charged with responsibility for the 1991 coup/Bush administration wanted Aristide out
- U.S. not on the side of democracy in 1915
- [occupation of] 1915–34; the Americans left a few roads and a few schools, but no democracy
- [Carter Agreement] a risky, last-minute deal/whole deal negotiated with "calculated ambiguity"/pressed to explain why he approved an honorable retirement for Haiti's military dictators/a deal made for Cédras/more caution than celebration [over the deal]/"We're inheriting Haiti's problems"/agreement is an insult/"U.S. policy was not what we expected"/sounds like a cozy relationship between the U.S. military and those responsible for so much of their misery/mission became awkward and dangerous/ mission neither simple nor safe/will have to run a very chaotic country/may have opened Pandora's box of troubles for the United States/growing number of second thoughts/Republicans are almost certain that occupying Haiti will be a political disaster/"We are headed in a dangerous direction"/"If you're opposed to the invasion, I don't see how you can support the occupation"/many believe that 'Operation Uphold Democracy could well turn violent/ "We're placing American troops basically and fundamentally in an untenable situation"/"American troops should begin withdrawing from Haiti immediately"/nobody has a clear sense here of what comes next and who is in charge/unclear as to who is pulling the strings and who is

doing the dancing/"What we are about to see is a classic example of what we call 'mission creep'"/not clear about what American troops are supposed to be doing down there/does not intend to go far enough to dismantle the Haitian military to make a difference/has reneged on a promise to disarm the Haitian military immediately/saddled with the task of supervising and even paying the salaries of soldiers and police earlier branded as thugs/U.S. troops doing nothing to protect people/ "How can Clinton say he is helping the people when the dictators are still here"/clearly worried about the potential for further civil disorder/could be in an awkward position of having to use force against those they came to liberate/[U.S. troops] are the "patron saints of anarchy"/naive to believe that the weapons buyback program will work/fear that Haiti is slipping into chaos, with looting and violence on the rise/U.S. troops could be caught in the middle/do not want [U.S. troops to be the only police force in the country/things took a turn for the worse/U.S. mission is looking more and more problematic/no one is using the term "quagmire" yet/[U.S. troops] are in the middle, their mission changed, they are the victim of what the military calls "mission creep"/quickly becoming saddled with the job it least wants; maintain order in a strife-torn nation/violence is likely to accompany the process of restoration of democracy/did not respond to violence/did not intervene when the trouble began/20,000 troops watched over another day of looting and shooting/ violence set off alarms in Congress/still very worried for the potential for violence/"I'm extremely concerned about 'mission creep'...It is imperative that we get our young men and women out of harm's way"/for many in Washington, the situation is bad enough/ "It's America's war"/"Where are the Americans? Why don't they disarm the police and the attackers"?

- furious with Jimmy Carter
- Carter ashamed of U.S. embargo/ashamed of U.S. policy in Haiti
- discouraged by press criticism of his handling of Haiti
- [Clinton] has problems of his own
- too often has allowed special interests to dictate foreign policy/caved into the Congressional Black caucus
- clearly playing for time
- never instructed Jimmy Carter to get General Cédras out of the country
- has yet to find the right White House staff or foreign-policy team
- State Department inflexible and vehemently opposed to Carter's recent mediation trips/Warren Christopher objected to Carter's role in Haiti
- struggling to assert leadership before the rest of the world

Descriptors Coded Neutral or Ambiguous
- a military invasion is virtually inevitable and most likely will take place early next month/accelerating planning for an invasion of Haiti

- tried to jack up pressure on the Haitian generals who will not leave/more hints from the highest levels in Washington; either get out or face a U.S. invasion/intensive training exercises underscore the possibility of U.S. invasion/another day, another warning to the generals in Haiti; our patience is wearing thin
- how much will this cost us? How long will [American troops] be there? And what kind of role will the United States play in the UN presence?
- White House operatives realize their credibility is on the line
- still has not decided to invade
- planning a war game dealing with getting out of Haiti
- considering a public relations campaign to sell the idea of an invasion to the public and Congress/stepped up its bid for public and political support/tried to ratchet up support for an invasion/trying to build momentum for his speech
- goes on TV tonight to tell a skeptical nation why he thinks it's necessary to invade Haiti
- will not issue a public deadline for Haiti's leaders to leave
- aides are trying to lower expectations [for the speech]
- it's not whether to invade, but when/D-Day in Haiti now appears to only weeks or even days away/all that remains is for Bill Clinton to pull the trigger
- surprising that the president has not made more of an effort to build support [for an invasion]
- hopes Haiti's rulers will finally believe that time is running out
- "We have exhausted every diplomatic alternative"/has exhausted every available option/has exhausted diplomacy
- will address the nation from the Oval Office
- will be police work, not war/U.S. forces will not become involved in nation-building [as in Somalia]/Haiti was not to become another Somalia
- administration's plan was to emphasize the urgency
- faces a tough audience Thursday night
- urged to seek Congressional approval
- there should be one last-ditch effort to get the generals out peacefully/likely to send on last diplomatic mission to tell Haiti's rulers that their time has run out/will likely send an emissary to Haiti after the speech
- U.S. Ambassador is not optimistic that an invasion can be avoided
- is aware that public opinion does not support an invasion/is aware that public opinion is strongly against the invasion/knows that neither Congress nor the American people support the invasion
- an action can be contemplated with the best intentions; even with the best of intentions, that's easier said than done/even with the best of intentions there's a lot of room for things to go wrong/pacifying Haiti will be a real challenge

- working overtime trying to keep Aristide on board
- knows that the United States could not nor should not be the world's policeman
- it may be the best-advertised military invasion in American history
- in spite of opposition...he no longer feels he has any choice/still extremely reluctant to order the invasion/still looking for some last minute way to get the Haitian generals to leave on their own/desperately hoping for a breakthrough/looking for a glimmer of hope/hopes that Cédras will get the message and leave voluntarily
- careful not to provoke anything
- this is a tough one for Bill Clinton
- a plan for war is an exercise of intimidation
- if Mr. Clinton can get the generals to leave, that will be good. But if he has to make concessions to get that to happen, that will damage U.S. credibility and that will hurt Mr. Clinton
- somber
- very dependent on Jimmy Carter
- worried about the personal security of the Carter mission
- Clinton's first major military decision
- represents a dramatic change in his foreign policy/his new approach is a daring and risky proposition
- shoring up support for his Haiti policy
- the United States has intervened and occupied a neighbor in the hemisphere, now it gets complicated/the job [in Haiti] is certainly more ambiguous/he may have secured an interim victory...but he has not solved the dilemma of the U.S. long-term role in Haiti/acknowledged that there were dangers ahead/complicated, ambiguous mission/road ahead will be long a full of pitfalls
- "Bill Clinton has survived another tough situation; he is a very fortunate man"
- Senate passed a resolution calling for the orderly withdrawal of American troops from Haiti/set a date certain for the withdrawal of U.S. troops/Congress approved the U.S. action but set a date certain for the withdrawal of American troops
- [Clinton] opposes any time limit to the mission
- can and should intervene in Haitian violence/will take a more active role in policing
- encouraged Haitian military and police not to beat up on their own people
- advised not to talk about Haitian violence
- regretted loss of [Haitian] lives
- defended U.S. policy in Haiti
- far from upset with killing [of Haitians]; it sent out an important signal

- U.S. forces quickly learning to be cops in a land ruled by the gun/have their hands full/keeping order not easy
- denies that "mission creep" has already occurred

PRESIDENT JEAN-BERTRAND ARISTIDE

Descriptors Coded Positive

- when a democratically elected president is overthrown by a military dictatorship, it gives a very bad signal as to what is tolerable in the Western Hemisphere
- elected president/exiled elected president/legitimate president/elected but exiled president/won a landslide victory in Haiti's only free election/legally elected president
- man the generals illegally replaced
- has pledged to step down when his term ends next year/will only serve out his current term and not run for re-election/pledged to step down from the presidency in a year
- wants to restore democracy/committed himself to democracy and economic reform
- "only hope of preventing violence is for Aristide to get here quickly and calm the people down"
- will take no retribution against his enemies/"no vengeance, no retaliation—let us embrace peace"/promised there would be no reprisal against the Haitian military/ "no to vengeance, no to retaliation"/pledged to forgive his enemies when he returns/"I don't believe that Aristide will go back with a sense of vengeance and retribution"/urged his followers to move to reconciliation/asking for reconciliation, not violence
- his supporters are reluctant to speak out for fear of reprisal
- base of his support is in the masses/most of the poor majority in Haiti voted for Aristide as president/most of the people are for Aristide/represented to poor as a priest and as a politician/support is wide indeed among the poor masses
- the elected president, Aristide, will return
- some of his supporters were murdered in the streets/at least 500 Aristide supporters have been killed/ friends and supporters murdered
- day of deliverance for Aristide supporters
- "we shall succeed"
- "stop the violence"
- survived three assassination attempts
- young priest in the poor neighborhoods
- "long live Aristide"/"Vive Aristide"/"We want Aristide"/"Aristide-Aristide"
- "Return Aristide—Thank you President Clinton"

- gave a very public display of support for the Clinton administration's efforts to put him back in office/publicly thanked the United States for leadership in removing the generals/"My many thanks for joining in these endeavors for peace"
- "In less than twenty-four hours, I will join you in Haiti"
- "I need Aristide to come back"/"We need Aristide"
- wants Haiti's military disarmed
- "We know that when Aristide comes back, everything will be alright"
- his support is increasing/his supporters took to the streets calling for his immediate return
- called for calm
- "When Aristide returns, I'll feel even better"
- appeared on Capitol Hill and struck a positive note
- "We shall succeed in restoring democracy to Haiti"
- has the trust of the people—therefore he should be allowed to return to his country"
- his return will bring the light of justice, the warmth of reconciliation

Descriptors Coded Negative

- "risking American lives to restore him is not a good option"/"We are not going to allow American lives to be expended in Haiti where we do not have a vital national interest"
- "he is doomed—is doomed forever"
- "will have to have American Marines watching over him until this term comes to an end"/Aristide supporters feel very uncomfortable having their former hero here brought in by U.S. Marines; they're not sure what kind of president he'll be sitting on top of an American occupation
- elected president whose stability has been questioned by some members of Congress
- restoring Aristide by force is a mistake/his return [to Haiti] is a mistake
- "there must be a solution that will keep Mr. Aristide out of here for another year and a half"
- after his election in 1991, some of his supporters tore his enemies apart limb-from-limb—Aristide did nothing to stop them/urged his followers to give the rich people what they deserved/once urged his followers to burn opponents alive
- "is as much of a thug as the ones who are down there"
- many have doubted his commitment to the democratic process that elected him/there are doubts about his commitment to democracy
- "I don't want Aristide in Haiti, he don't want Aristide in Haiti"
- "he was a real dictator—the real killer was Aristide"
- "Aristide no; democracy yes"/"democracy yes; Aristide no"

- "We want your skin Aristide; if you don't believe us, come see"/"If my Mother came here with Aristide, I'd kill my mother"/"I swear on my life, there is no way Aristide can put his feet on this ground"/"We hate Aristide so much that if they bring him back, we'll take him from them and kill him"
- "Down with Aristide"
- has been implicated by an informant in payoffs to Haitian officers by Colombian drug traffickers/took payoffs from Pablo Escobar's cocaine cartel/seen as taking a suitcase filled with several hundred thousand dollars in payoffs
- "President of the Black people—a racist"
- "will have to resign"
- worries some Republicans
- known as a moody, unpredictable leader
- "hasn't shown a great disposition…backs away and blames people"
- censured by his own order for preaching class warfare
- surrounded himself with advisors that critics felt were anti-American
- consensus-building is a message he failed to master in spite of speaking eight languages
- "biggest enemy that we have had"
- "how dare that insolent man take objection [to the Carter deal with the generals] the proper response is not second guessing or nitpicking—the proper response is two words—thank you"/"no one has the right to demand to ride into Haiti on the shoulders of the U.S. military"/after three day of stony silence, he finally said "thank you"
- "get real—don't screw it up"
- released a terse statement that did not endorse the agreement negotiated by Jimmy Carter/not happy with the agreement/plainly not happy with the deal President Carter struck/does not view the agreement as legal/his political entourage is telling the media that Aristide and they do not like the agreement/angry with President Clinton and former President Carter for making a deal that did not immediately remove the military leaders from Haiti/not happy with the terms of the deal/ defiantly refused to endorse the U.S. deal/his supporters are angry with the deal
- raises questions whether he would live up to his end of the deal
- stayed brooding in his apartment
- has little support in Congress

Descriptors Coded Neutral or Ambiguous

- president/exiled president/overthrown president/deposed president/ ousted president/ controversial president/controversial exiled president/ president-in-exile/Haitian president overthrown by the generals/ returning exiled president
- Father

- in Washington awaiting his restoration by the United States
- man in the middle
- if, when he comes back on the shoulders of U.S. Marines, he urges reconciliation, that will be a revolutionary concept in Haitian politics
- don't know how Haitians will receive Aristide
- supporters remain in hiding
- had hoped for more
- does not believe the generals should get amnesty/does not want to extend a full pardon to the generals/thinks the president gave up too much to the Haitian generals
- "not possible for Aristide to return quickly"/told Congress that it is still too dangerous for him to return
- had no comment on U.S. deal with the military leaders
- balked at UN and US plans to impose economic sanctions and possible force
- inspires strong feelings in his friends and in his enemies
- known as "Titid," or little Aristide
- received backing from the Washington power structure, but attracted little sympathy from the American public
- his return is no guarantee for the return of democracy/"the return of one man, even though elected overwhelmingly, is not democracy"
- disturbed that the dictators that overthrew him will retain power for up to a month/worried that the deal does not disarm the Haitian generals/would challenge any general amnesty
- the man being returned to power/the man President Clinton wants to return to power
- will encourage the Haitian Parliament to consider amnesty
- had expected to return to Haiti in the wake of a U.S. invasion
- expects the military junta to leave Haiti
- offered condolences to those killed [by U.S. forces]
- declined to be interviewed
- unless he is brilliant, his return in October may cause more turmoil

GENERAL RAOUL CÉDRAS/HAITIAN MILITARY

Descriptors Coded Positive
- accepted the offer of the Carter mission/agreed to meet with Carter/welcomed meeting with Carter
- "Sons of the land"
- (generals) especially respect General Powell
- have realized it's time for them to go
- crowds cheered when Cédras stepped onto the balcony
- praised for keeping order in Haiti's first-ever free election
- hopes to prevent bloodshed by entering into a dialogue where, for the first time, the military's side of the story can be told

- cooperated with American troops/cooperative/welcomed American troops warmly/"is cooperating very well with our forces"/not resisting the occupation or the restoration of democracy/agreed to give up power and help the U.S. occupiers
- agreed to step down/agreed to leave/promised to step down/will leave office in a month/will leave/will give up power/intends to step down by October 15th
- "We will take peace instead of war"
- being treated with absolute respect [by American troops]
- on their best behavior
- Cédras] acknowledged that he had to get involved in this [violence] and make it stop
- a prideful man
- a proud man with the ability to be charming
- holds dear the institutions of the military, his country, and his family
- "He [Cédras] has never made a misleading statement to me"
- "[Cédras] never made a comment that was selfish on his part"

Descriptors Coded Negative

- overthrew the elected government/coup leader/initiated the coup against Aristide/toppled Aristide from power
- dictators/military dictators/military dictatorship
- illegal government/leader of the illegal government
- strongmen
- criminals
- decidedly anti-American
- their days are numbered/days are definitely numbered/one way or another, they're going to leave/the de-facto government will be leaving/if the generals running Haiti don't get the message, they're simply not listening/have not gotten the message/"He's going to leave, sooner rather than later"/they better get the message/considering an ultimatum; leave Haiti or be taken by force/the clock is moving; previously they saw the hour hand moving, now we're down to the minute hand, if not the second hand/the drums of war are beating and even the generals can hear them now/harder and harder for them to doubt our resolve/their best alternative is to leave and not try to resist/feeling the pressure/the Haitian generals must go/his time is up/they have to relinquish power and leave the country/"Cédras must go"/"General Cédras is not a democrat; General Cédras is a killer"/"he has to go"
- "Cédras will be in handcuffs"
- has ties to the old Duvalier regime
- human rights record of what is going on in Haiti is sick/they have not only murdered ordinary people, but a priest, and now they're shooting orphans for sport/people of Haiti have been subjected to assassinations,

executions, beatings, mutilations, raids, rapes, and other violent abuses and intimidations/has become among the worst violators of human rights in the world/the most brutal, the most violent regime anywhere in the hemisphere/300,000 Haitians are hiding in terror/officer cut off a victim's ear and forced him to eat it and carved his initials in the victim's flesh/sow great terror and fear in Haiti/ instrument of terror for the Haitian people/General Cédras and his armed thugs have conducted a reign of terror, executing children, raping women, killing priests/they are a cancer; they are killing our people/paramilitaries responsible for many of the atrocities committed over the past three years/killing, torturing, raping and arbitrarily arresting for three years/"all they [the Haitian Army] ever does is stage coups and shoot at people they should protect"/gunmen will terrorize the city tonight/the group that has been responsible for the violence and repression/killed and terrorized Haiti's poor/killed 3,000 people since taking power/"they split open heads"/right-wing death squads terrorizing the supporters of Aristide/has a brutal reputation/most violent people in the Caribbean/"I'll shoot them dead if they throw rocks at me; I'll break their ass"/accused of a reign of terror/beat crowd with sticks/nation's deadly police thugs/"they've been giving us hell"/attacked a group of Aristide supporters/"they beat you, they kill you; they come to your house at night"/police brutalizing people/cracked down hard on supporters of Aristide/has terrorized the country/responsible for a reign of terror/described as the leader of a reign of terror that included murder, rape, and terrorizing orphanages/the night still belongs to the henchmen of the regime/police and attachés terrorized civilians for years/have abused their authority/attackers are still at work murdering Aristide supporters/"We would kill Aristide without even thinking about it"/hired guns who ruled by terror/used automatic weapons to terrorize people/"They're criminals, killing people at night"/"If the people come after us, we'll kill them"/perpetrators of murders, rapes and massacres/"Only the Army is capable of something like this [a grenade attack]"/ruling country in a reign of terror/[FRAPH] fired on demonstrators and foreign journalists/

- the economy, miserable before, is now dead
- civil administration doesn't work
- defiant/show of defiance/reaction is of continued defiance/shouted slogans against the United States and the invasion/sent a message of defiance/show no signs of a change of heart/if you want us, you'll have to come and get us/putting up a brave front/there is no mood of giving up/remain absolutely defiant/no indication that the generals are going to leave/ standing their ground and refusing to budge/put on a public show of defiance/put on a defiant show/show no signs of stepping down/ show no signs of leaving/remains stubborn about when he will leave/"has no intention of leaving the country, ever"/still clinging to power/intends to stay in Haiti/

- voodoo forces will protect them if American forces come on land
- arming a civilian militia/might try to resist
- have taken the country hostage
- may target Americans
- busy trying to come up with tactics to confuse the situation
- controls paramilitary forces
- the military's way of waiting gives anxious citizens further cause to worry
- doubtful that "volunteers" will fight/practicing the maneuver that may serve them best; 'about face'/intelligence reports that they will cave in without a fight/once the invasion begins, Haiti's leaders will 'cut and run'/one general may be preparing to ride horseback into the Dominican Republic/will shed their uniforms and run at the first sight of an invasion/soldiers are taking off their uniforms so that they can blend into the civilian population
- gunmen/paramilitary thugs/Tontons Macoutes today are called attachés/civilian gunmen/gangsters, thieves, murderers, and thugs/ Tontons Macoutes/paramilitary gunmen
- had promised to step down but reneged when the deadline came
- military of 7,000 people, poorly trained, poorly equipped, who have never shown any instinct but to internally repress their own people/poorly trained and equipped/are no match for an American assault
- [drug] payoffs were going to Haiti's top three military leaders
- "No civilian has ever been as powerful as a man with a gun"/"We're carrying guns"
- "corrupt; may say they are going to leave, then not"
- his wife is deep into voodoo and tight with the Papal Nuncio
- "his decision to stay will hinder democratic reform"
- shaken
- enemies of the people/police seen as the real enemy
- the main opponents of democracy are still armed and very dangerous/can cause trouble if they wait around long enough/"They have lots of money, lots of guns, and they're still at large"
- "Arrest General Cédras"
- "as long as Cédras is around this kind of violence will continue/"He's responsible for the situation, as it is the failure of the police and army to protect the people"
- "Mr. Cédras and his cohorts should go as soon as possible"
- "Down with the dictatorship"
- they see no other way than to go out in a burst of aggression
- smuggled goods during the embargo

Descriptors Coded Neutral or Ambiguous

- Haiti's military leaders/military leaders/Haiti's ranking military officer/Haiti's top military man/top brass/top Haitian military command/high command
- military government/military regime/military commanders/military rulers/current military chief
- General/ Lt. General/generals/Haitian generals/military generals
- De-facto Haitian leadership/de-facto government
- junta/military junta/ruling military junta
- outgoing military leaders
- his native language is French
- 45 years old
- career soldier
- not a man who enjoys interviews
- have kept a low profile
- "When they step down from their positions, they'll fade into obscurity"
- "guaranteed, that with 15,000 U.S. troops in Haiti, [Cédras] will honor all the provisions of the agreement"
- Mrs. Cédras was sure her family was going to die
- have the right to stay in Haiti until Aristide comes back/have the right to stay in Haiti
- police have been tamed
- tormentors are being tormented
- is increasingly concerned and frustrated about mob action and looting/worried that Haiti was near to sinking into mob rule/concerned with the potential for violence
- believed that the Carter agreement was not being lived up to
- does not believe the full truth is known about the killing of ten Haitians by U.S. Marines
- have become accustomed to verbal threats from official Washington and if they have become anxious, there certainly has been no sign of it/they believe its all a bluff
- trouble in the ranks; some doubt the wisdom of opposing a U.S. invasion/reports of turmoil in the ruling regime/signs of friction within the junta/if General Cédras doesn't step down, a last-minute coup could remove him
- "Right is on our side; might is on the side of Mr. Clinton"
- "If it comes to war, we will be ready for this war"/not afraid to fight, even if it appears to be a losing battle
- has offered to give up power, but on terms unacceptable to the White House
- wanted new elections in which President Aristide could not run
- to be allowed to stay in Haiti
- "I cannot and will not be bought out"

- "as Commander-in-Chief of Haiti's armed forces, I have been ordered to defend my country"
- his mood changed/attitude is different
- hoping that the Carter delegation would bring something new
- followers are worried that their military leaders will abandon them/supporters believe he is history
- have responsibility for keeping law and order
- police is under military control
- "had no right to invite Americans into Haiti"
- informally surrendered the country
- has ties with the Haitian business community in the United States
- America's partners in bringing order in a country where stability is as rare as democracy
- wants amnesty before stepping down
- doesn't believe in the value of the amnesty law
- Macoute who ruled village by terror stoned to death

NOTES

1.   For different reasons, the military invasion was opposed by sections of the left as well as of the right in both Haiti and the United States.

Public opinion in the United States also remained cool toward the use of military force, even in the heat of the moment of its commitment. Surveys done on September 18 and 19, 1994 revealed the following with respect to U.S. policy:

	Before U.S. troops entered Haiti (%)	After U.S. troops entered Haiti (%)
Approve of the way Clinton "is handling the situation in Haiti"	33	55
Disapprove	55	39
Sending troops "is the right thing to do"	31	41
U.S. troops "should stay out of Haiti"	60	52
U.S. has the "responsibility to restore democracy in Haiti"	36	41

	Before U.S. troops entered Haiti (%)	After U.S. troops entered Haiti (%)
U.S. "does not have this responsibility"	56	53

Only 20% of those surveyed indicated that "what happens in Haiti is very important to the interests of the U.S." (Kagay 1994, p. A–16).

2.   This is certainly an arguable point. Bob Shacochis maintains very strongly that the ambiguity regarding who was friend and who was foe after the last- minute switch from a hard entry to a soft entry operation led to a "too close" relationship between U.S. forces on the one hand and the Haitian Army and the Front for the Advancement and Progress of Haiti (FRAPH) on the other. While this is no doubt the case, it is important to remember that the very hard entry by the U.S. military into Panama in December 1989 also resulted in a strong representation of ex-Panamanian Defense Force members in the new security organizations that replaced the Noriega-tainted PDF. In our opinion, a U.S. invasion would only have guaranteed more casualties—far more Haitian than U.S. While the end of FRAPH influence may have been facilitated by a hard entry, only a firm U.S. policy on treatment of suspect organizations after the occupation had begun would have guaranteed it.

3.   For an insider's critique of international effort aimed at reforming Haiti's problem-plagued justice systems, see Beer, 2001.

4.   Generally seen to include democratic government, IMF-type structural adjustment programs, and adherence to principles of the free market.

6

The Zapatista Rebellion in Chiapas, 1994

Walter C. Soderlund and E. Donald Briggs

BACKGROUND

Because Mexico and the United States share a border, relations between the two countries have a long and full history. Unfortunately, until World War II, these relations were far more conflictual than cooperative, with Mexico ending up on the losing side of most contested issues.

Following the birth of the American republic at the end of the Revolutionary War in 1789, the United States began adding to its territory, initially largely at the expense of Spain. After Mexican independence in 1821, the Monroe Doctrine was proclaimed in 1823 to protect the newly independent ex-Spanish colonies from reconquest. For Mexico, however, a possible Spanish *reconquista* was not the main concern. Problems stemming from the independence of Texas in 1836 led directly to the Mexican-American War of 1846–47, which resulted in the loss of approximately one-third of Mexico's territory to the United States (Rippy, 1926, 1–14). There also was a request from the government of Yucatan in the 1840s for military aid in putting down an Indian insurrection in return for U.S. "dominion and sovereignty" over the region. An armistice between the warring parties was achieved as legislation "enabling the President to 'take temporary occupation of Yucatan'" was being debated in the U.S. Senate (Rippy, 1926, 21–22). In his analysis of the period, Fred Rippy claims that emotions connected with "manifest destiny" ran strongly in U.S. attitudes toward its southern neighbor:

> The Yucatan episode...had revealed most of the forces which were to shape the Mexican policy of the United States for the next decade...eagerness to annex a part or the whole of Mexico,...sincere or alleged fear of European designs upon the region, and real or pretended sympathy for the Mexicans themselves—a strange mixture of greed, benevolence, and apprehension. (1926, p. 25)

After the end of its own Civil War in 1865, the United States supported the ultimately successful government of Benito Juarez against a French intervention in an ongoing Mexican civil war, and relations between the two countries remained on the whole reasonable during the long dictatorship of Porfirio Diaz that followed.

The epic Mexican Revolution, begun in 1910, plus the consolidation of power by a nationalist-minded, anticlerical revolutionary government in 1917, led to a period of strained relations between the two countries during the 1920s and 1930s. There had been U.S. interventions during the revolutionary fighting, but these were relatively short-lived. Anti-clerical policies pursued by the Mexican government during the 1920s, added an element of strain to the relationship.

To be fully appreciated, these factors need to be seen in the context of the negative stereotypes by which Mexico and Mexicans were characterized in the American press during the revolution. According to Mark Anderson, these include

> *backwardness,* encompassing retrograde thinking and material conditions, punctuated with childishness and violence; second, *racial limitations,* displaying the Mexican's presumed genetic inferiority, highlighted by obtuseness and physically engendered hedonism as well as a propensity toward barbarism; and third, *moral decrepitude,* highlighting Mexican dishonesty, a love of excessive (often gratuitous) violence, inherent cruelty and an inclination for theft. (1998, p. 26, italics in original)

The expropriation of oil interests of U.S. companies in 1937 marked the nadir of U.S.–Mexican relations in the twentieth century, and only the looming spectre of World War II led to a situation where cool heads prevailed to end a very conflictual situation. An agreement on compensation was reached in November 1941, less than a month before the Japanese attack on Pearl Harbor got the United States involved in the war (LaFeber, 1989, pp. 359–360).

The necessity of World War II cooperation extended into the postwar era, when under the umbrella of the UN, the OAS emerged as a regional organization to deal with hemispheric problems, succeeding the pre-existing Pan American Union. While generally the last fifty years have seen a marked increase in cooperation between Mexico and the United States, there have been continuing problems in the relationship; most notably, illegal immigration, narco-trafficking, and disputes over how to deal with revolutionary Cuba under Fidel Castro. On the last issue, Mexico (along with Canada) refuses to honor the U.S.-imposed economic embargo of the island. These problems notwithstanding, economic cooperation between the countries progressed to the point where, following the 1988 Free Trade Agreement (FTA) between the United States and Canada, the administration of Bush the Elder sought to widen the agreement to include Mexico (Ross, 1995, p. 46). Somewhat paradoxically, under governments in both Canada and the United States controlled by political parties that had been opposed to the FTA in 1988 (Liberals in Canada and Democrats in the United States), the North American Free Trade Agreement was signed in fall 1993, and went into effect January 1, 1994.

THE ZAPATISTA REVOLT

As the new year dawned in 1994, when NAFTA should have occupied pride of place on the media's agenda of issues in U.S.–Mexican relations, between four and seven towns (depending on the source) in the southern Mexican state of Chiapas were attacked and occupied by the Zapatista National Liberation Army (Ejército Zapatista de Liberacíon Nacíonal [EZLN]). Targeted towns were "occupied by an army of over 3,000 indigenous people demanding land, jobs, housing, food, health care, education, independence, freedom, democracy, justice and peace" (Harvey, 1998, p. 6; Conger, 1994, p. 115). As a part of their revolt, the Zapatistas declared war against the Mexican army, "the basic pillar of the dictatorship under which we suffer," and promised "to advance on the capital, defeating the Federal army as we march forward" (Ross, 1995, p. 10).

The rebellion seemed to take the Mexican government by surprise (Ross, 1995, pp. 7–14). According to Andrew Reding, the U.S. government was likewise unprepared for the uprising, seemingly believing its own press releases regarding the power of NAFTA to solve political and social problems; specifically that "by locking in market reforms, NAFTA would create conditions that would foster democracy and respect for human rights" (Reding, 1994, p. 11). John Ross is less charitable, arguing that the existence of the Zapatista guerrillas was known to the Mexican government as early as December 1992 and that an armed clash occurred between the army and the guerrillas in May 1993 (Ross, 1995, pp. 25–27; see also, Collier, 1994, p. 5). Moreover, he maintains that the U.S. government either should have known or did know about the existence of the EZLN for at least six months before the outbreak of the rebellion. Because no mention of an active guerrilla movement was made during the NAFTA debates in the United States, Ross concludes that the CIA either failed to tell the administration, or that upon hearing the news, the administration chose to withhold the information in light of a projected close Congressional vote on NAFTA in November 1993 (Ross, 1995, pp. 38–51). In any event, the New Year's Day insurrection presented a new set of problems for Presidents Salinas and Clinton and for the carefully crafted new North American economic relationship.

The Zapatistas were not destined to maintain control of the towns they had captured for any extended period. Mexican army units with between 12,000 and 15,000 soldiers (accounting for about one-fifth of the nation's total armed forces), swiftly retook the region, town-by-town. Within three or four days the Zapatistas had retreated from all captured towns into the surrounding mountains, where they came under attack from both land and air forces (Ross, 1995, pp. 83–111). The total number killed during the rebellion was at least 145, mostly Zapatistas (Harvey, 1998, p. 229), although other estimates of dead run as high as 400 (Ross, 1995, 150–151). Calls for surrender and for negotiation, were issued by the government early in the crisis, but both options were rebuffed by the Zapatistas. Finally, on January 12, President Salinas ordered a unilateral cease-fire (Ross, 1995, pp. 83–94). The Zapatistas in turn did not violate the cease-fire. Within weeks of the cease-fire declaration, negotiations began between the government and the Zapatistas, with Bishop Samuel Ruiz, Head of the Diocese of San Cristóbal de Las Casas, serving as a mediator. A tentative agreement regarding a package of economic reforms was announced on March 2, 1994 (Ross, 1995, pp. 227–249). The agreement (ultimately rejected by the Zapatistas) provided sufficient closure for the U.S. television networks to end coverage of the crisis.

As with many post–Cold War conflicts, agreements to end hostilities do not necessarily imply a return to conditions of peace, and this certainly has been the case in Chiapas. The Zapatista communities rejected the tentative peace agreement in summer 1994 (Stephen, 1995, pp. 88–89). Since then, the Mexican army has remained in the region, engaging in some limited military operations in February 1995. More seriously, however, pro-government peasants have organized as paramilitary units to oppose the Zapatistas at the grassroots level, resulting in continuous low-level societal violence. The most serious instance of this type of violence was the December 1997 massacre of 45 peasants by an anti-Zapatista paramilitary organization *Paz y Justicia* (Harvey, 1998, p. 5). June Nash also notes ongoing economic hardships suffered by Zapatista supporters in the region:

> The 60,000 inhabitants of the 'conflict zone' (where Zapatistas have a majority of supporters) are clearly identified with the movement and are encircled by the army which limits their movement beyond the military outposts. Their ability to sell their crops has also been hurt: they were forced to sell their cash crops...at a tenth of normal retail price. (1995, p. 27)

With the election of Vicente Fox to Mexico's presidency in summer 2000, a solution to the long-simmering Zapatista rebellion seemed possible. In spring 2001, with the new government's blessing, the Zapatistas marched to Mexico City and a spokeswoman addressed the Congress. While the Mexican military presence in Chiapas has been reduced, it remains unclear whether President Fox can command the political support necessary to meet the demands of the country's indigenous peoples; many other groups have joined the Zapatistas in calling for fundamental reforms.

Explanations of the Revolt

Explaining the origins of the Zapatista revolt is not a simple task. As anthropologist George Collier has observed,

> [Chiapas] the region behind the headlines is a complicated one. [It] is sometimes described as a picturesque backwater—a quaint stop on the tourist circuit where time has stood still and Maya Indians can be observed performing their age-old crafts and rituals. But beneath the surface seen by the casual visitor, Chiapas is filled with paradoxes that defy easy categorization. (1994, p. 7)

Indeed, some reasons for the revolt date back as far in history as the conquest; some stem from social, economic, and political changes that had occurred over the past thirty years; and some causes include recent amendments made in 1992 to Mexico's land-reform program, and NAFTA, which was signed in November 1993. In his attempt to explain the Zapatista revolt, Reding wisely claims that it "can only be understood as the result of a confluence of causes—economic, political, social and ecological—each of which reinforced all the others, driving a normally peaceful population to the breaking point" (Reding, 1994, p. 12).

In terms of its ultimate origins, without doubt the Chiapas insurrection can be traced to the Spanish conquest and to the set of colonial dominance relationships established in its wake, which placed the native Indian population at the bottom of the social and economic pecking order (Collier, 1994, pp. 17–22; Ross, 1995, pp. 63–66; Harvey, 1998, pp. 36–43). Mayan civilization, with its decentralized structure proved to be more resistant to military conquest than the more hierarchically organized Aztec civilization. Thus, final Spanish control over the Mayans was established only after nearly twenty years of guerrilla-type warfare (Gibson, 1966, p. 29). It is in this context of resistance to domination that Neil Harvey argues "the Zapatista rebellion can be seen as the latest in a long cycle of popular demands for dignity, voice, and autonomy" (Harvey, 1998, p. 37).

While acknowledging the impact of a long history of revolt against authority by native peoples in the region (uprisings in 1712 and 1867 being most prominent), Harvey argues that between 1960 and 1990 the combination of two factors, liberation theology and political organization based on Maoist principles (both operating in the context of the Cold War), led directly to the formation of the EZLN.

In the 1960s, liberation theology emerged as a serious movement within the Catholic Church and found official recognition at the 1968 Medellín Council of Latin American Bishops. Samuel Ruiz, then newly appointed Bishop of the Diocese of San Cristóbal de Las Casas (later to serve as a mediator in the 1994 crisis), attended this meeting, although Charlene Floyd points out that at this time the Bishop had not adopted the principles of liberation theology (Floyd, 1996, p. 151, no. 27). According to Harvey, at Medellín,

> The adoption of the preferential option for the poor occurred in the context of an emerging radical consensus that the causes of poverty in Latin America were structural in nature and were rooted in the expansion of U.S. imperialism. Marxist class analysis and dependency theory overlapped with the bishops' own concern for their largest and newest constituency— the rural and urban poor. If the church were truly concerned with renewal, then it had to confront the economic and political obstacles to liberation. (1998, pp. 72–73)

Between 1961 and 1993, more than 7,000 *catequistas* (lay preachers) were trained by the Diocese of San Cristóbal de Las Casas (Floyd, 1996, pp. 154–156) and at least 600 Christian base communities were active in the region. The effect of this organizational effort "was to create a network of community leaders who went beyond religious activity to inspire new forms of political and

economic organization that would eventually be absorbed by the EZLN"
(Harvey, 1998, p. 74).

On the political side, in 1974, in the context of renewed government interest
in promoting agrarian populism, an Indigenous Congress was held in Chiapas to
mark the 500th anniversary of the birth of Fray Bartolomé de Las Casas, an early
clerical champion of Indian rights. In preparation for this congress, Maoist
organizers came to Chiapas from the north of Mexico and stayed on as advisors
to the new *uniones de ejidos* (groups of indigenous landholding communities)
that were being created as a part of government policy. Significant for later
developments, government attempts to organize and co-opt the new
organizations largely failed. In 1983, Subcomandante Marcos, the military
strategist behind the 1994 revolt, as well as the symbol of and spokesman for the
Zapatistas during the rebellion, first came to Chiapas (Ross, 1995, p. 278). The
EZLN itself came into existence in November 1983 as an "armed self-defence
force" to combat peasant expulsions from claimed land (Harvey, 1998, p. 165).
Although in the following years there was considerable factional strife between
different Maoist groups operating in the region, they nevertheless worked
together to promote "horizontal links between the members of each community
rather than simply between the members and the delegates. Drawing on their
Maoist training, they promoted contacts and exchanges between different
communities at a grassroots level" (Harvey, 1998, p. 82).

Paradoxically, Mexican government policies enacted as part of a plan to
modernize and develop the region served as additional irritants to the already
marginalized population. As argued by Roger Burbach,

> For the past twenty-five years Chiapas has been convulsed by unprecedented
> economic transformations that have torn up the traditional agricultural
> economy and devastated the indigenous culture. The Mexican state, responding
> to the interests of the country's bourgeoisie and the demands of the
> international market place, has treated Chiapas as an internal colony, sucking
> out its wealth while leaving its people—particularly the overwhelming majority
> who live off the land—more impoverished. (1994, p. 115)

As a consequence, during the 1980s the mix of ingredients in Chiapas
became more volatile: conflict over ownership of land mounted; tensions
between Evangelical Protestants and Catholics increased (Collier, 1994, pp. 37–
66); guerrilla movements in neighboring Guatemala gave rise to Cold War
concerns in Mexico and the United States (Castañeda, 1993, pp. 90–96; Ross,
1995, pp. 157–158; Harvey, 1998, pp. 148–149), and government repression in
the region under Governor Castellanos Domínguez intensified (Ross, 1995, pp.
155–186). The amendment of Article 27 of the Mexican Constitution of 1917 by
the Salinas government in 1992, which was widely interpreted as a fatal blow to
land reform, added fuel to the fire (Nash, 1995, pp. 23–27; Ross, 1995, p. 241;
Floyd, 1996, p. 153). Finally, NAFTA, which for many implied the end of
subsistence farming in the region in favor of exports of timber, cattle, and oil,
proved to be the match that set off the explosion (Reding, 1994, pp. 14–15).
According to Floyd, "[NAFTA's] passage merely served to codify the

disillusionment and despair of Mexico's rural poor. Not all of the poor, however, accepted these changes." (Floyd, 1996, p. 153)

Although the rebellion can be traced to both old grievances and new problems, the years of community organizing (both religious and political) outside the scope of government control or co-option gave the rebellion its cohesion. As Harvey argues, "When the EZLN appeared on January 1, 1994, it was not a small band of guerrillas hoping to incite a popular uprising. Rather, it was a well-organized indigenous army with a mass base of support" (Harvey, 1998, p. 3).

FINDINGS

Stories dealing with the EZLN or Zapatista rebellion in Chiapas (named after Emiliano Zapata, a hero of the Mexican Revolution, 1910–1917) began appearing on U.S. television network news on January 2, 1994 (Womack, 1968). Coverage of this crisis continued for about two months, until March 2, when a tentative peace agreement between the Zapatista rebels and the Mexican government was announced. The revolt, timed to coincide with the inauguration NAFTA, highlighted both new and old grievances of indigenous peoples in what was, as measured by most indicators, the poorest region in Mexico (Burbach, 1994, p. 114–115; Collier, 1994, pp. 16–17; Ross, 1995, pp. 71–73). In that membership in NAFTA was widely promoted as a symbol of Mexico's transition into the developed world, the rebellion not only presented the Mexican government with immediate security concerns, but with long-term public relations problems as well (Ross, 1995, pp. 120–139).

Only sixteen news stories dealt with the Zapatista rebellion during the entire two-month period of study. Coverage was concentrated in the week immediately following the start of the rebellion on New Year's Day (thirteen of sixteen stories) and focused largely on the counterattack launched by the Mexican Army, which drove the Zapatistas back into the mountains from the towns they had captured. Coverage was evenly divided among the networks: ABC ran five stories, CBS ran five, and NBC ran six.

Actual language used to describe the U.S. government; President Salinas, his government, and the Mexican Army; and the Zapatista rebels by sources, reporters, and anchors as recorded, collated, and coded may be found in Appendix 6.1.

There seems to be little doubt that if the Zapatista rebellion had occurred some eight to ten years earlier, at the time President Reagan was invading Grenada, supporting the Duarte government in El Salvador, and attempting to oust the Sandinista government in Nicaragua by promoting the cause of the "contras", it would have been framed by U.S. television news as a classic Cold War communist insurgency. In fact, it probably would have been linked directly to the decades-long civil war in neighboring Guatemala, where many of the same social and economic issues were in play, and where anti-Communism prevailed as the dominant media frame (Schlesinger and Kinzer, 1983; Gleijeses, 1991 and Castañeda, 1993). By 1994, however, the Cold War was over, and an event that a decade earlier most surely would have occasioned massive interest on the part of both the U.S. government and U.S. media, in fact received very little attention from U.S. government spokespersons and, at least partly as a consequence, garnered relatively light coverage on U.S. network television news. In terms of its framing for American audiences, it was presented quite differently from the communist-inspired guerrilla insurgency that had dominated the interpretation of similar events in the region during the previous three decades.

Table 6.1
Story Characteristics N = 16

	Number		Percentage
Lead Story	1		6
1st Three Stories	3		19
30 Seconds And Under	6		38
Over 3 Minutes	0		-
Just Anchor Format	6		38
Use Of "Experts"	1		6
Reporter In Mexico	8		50
Two Or More News Segments	0		-
Film With Story	13		87
Film Of President Clinton	0		-
Film Of President Salinas	2		13
Film Of Subcomandante Marcos	1		6
Visual Violence	10		63
Link to NAFTA	4		25
Tilt Favorable to U.S. Position	1		6
Tilt Unfavorable To U.S. Position	2		13
U.S. Involvement Index		1.25	

First, in terms of media salience, that there were only sixteen stories on the major U.S. television networks for a two-month period indicates that the Zapatista revolt was not treated as a major event. In addition to meagre numbers, data in Table 6.1 indicate that only one of the sixteen stories on the rebellion led off a newscast, with only three appearing in the first three positions. Six stories (38 percent) ran for thirty seconds or less in the anchor-read format, while none exceeded three minutes in length. Half the stories featured a reporter in Mexico (mostly from Chiapas) and no story used more than a single contributing reporter; thus, the number of news segments equals the number of stories. Only one story made use of a U.S. expert for background information on the crisis. In short, nothing here points to strong media attention.

Video/film accompanied 87 percent of stories, most of which featured violence focused on military operations and captured or dead Zapatista rebels. Interestingly, there was little visual presentation of the high-profile personalities who potentially could have dominated coverage: President Salinas was shown twice, President Clinton not at all. The U.S. president was never quoted or mentioned, while President Salinas was mentioned or quoted five times. Perhaps the most interesting and certainly the most curious finding to emerge from this study is the media's treatment of the Zapatista leader, Subcomandante Marcos. He was not used as a source, was never referred to, and was shown only once (in the very last story broadcast on the insurrection on March 2); on this occasion he was neither identified by name, nor did he speak.

Another surprising element in network coverage of the Chiapas revolt, given the overall historical importance of Mexico to the United States, and particularly in light of the unique circumstances surrounding NAFTA, is that U.S. involvement in the crisis was given minimal play. Only one story (6 percent) supported the U.S. position (ill-defined though it was), that *NAFTA was not responsible for the revolt,* while two (13 percent) took the opposing position. On a 5-point scale (1=low and 5=high) U.S. involvement registered at 1.25. Significantly, this mean score was lower than scores for coverage of the 1990 attempted coup d'etat in Trinidad (1.4) and the 1991 successful coup in Haiti (2.1). The U.S. spokespersons never articulated a U.S. position on the rebellion on television news. However, the specific connection of the revolt to the inauguration of NAFTA was mentioned in only four stories (25 percent), with the pro-NAFTA, U.S. position supported in one story and opposed in two.

Table 6.2
Number of Times Leading Sources Used (All Sources Used in Newscast)

News Source	Total Number of Times Used
Mexican Government Spokespersons	8
Zapatista Spokespersons	6
Mexicans on the street	6
President Salinas	5
Mexican Military	4
State Department Spokespersons	2
Church Spokespersons	2
Foreigners in Mexico	2

Data in Table 6.2 show the number of times leading sources appeared on camera or were quoted in coverage of the rebellion. In that it represents a departure from the norm, what is very apparent is the extremely limited use of U.S. sources (a U.S. State Department spokesperson twice and a U.S. expert once) in coverage of the Zapatista rebellion. Completely absent in coverage is any comment from President Clinton, White House spokespersons, or members of the House and Senate, either Democrat or Republican (Paletz and Entman, 1981). Clearly U.S. politicians of any stripe had no desire to play a role in the crisis, in spite of its declared connection to NAFTA and the latter's importance to U.S. global economic policy.

With respect to Mexican sources, there were nearly three times as many government sources used as there were rebel sources: government spokespersons were used eight times, President Salinas five times, the Mexican Army four times, and Zapatista spokespersons were used six times. Mexicans on the street (expressing both pro- and anti- rebel sentiments) also appeared six times, while foreigners in Mexico and spokesmen representing the Catholic Church each appeared twice. Although Subcomandante Marcos did appear on film once, he was never used as a source and his name was never mentioned in network news coverage of the crisis by sources, reporters, or anchors. This seems strange in the extreme in the light of the cult of personality that emerged around him, given television's well-known preference for reducing complex events to personalities.

Table 6.3
Percentage of Stories in Which Media Frames Are Used

Frame	Primary	Secondary	Tertiary	Total
Violence	9	3	1	13
Aboriginal Grievances	2	3	3	8
Human Rights Abuses	1	4	1	6
NAFTA	0	3	1	4
Social Instability	1	0	1	2

Table 6.3 shows the frames employed by U.S. network television news in coverage of the Zapatista rebellion. Clearly, the main frame was episodic—that of violence—appearing in a total of 87 percent of stories and serving as the primary frame in more than half of them. As mentioned, television cameras did not record the initial Zapatista takeover of the Chiapas towns, which meant that virtually all violence reported dealt with efforts of the Mexican Army to dislodge and pursue the rebels. Pictures of captured, wounded, beaten and dead Zapatistas (often quite graphic) dominated television coverage of the rebellion.

In addition to violence, four thematic frames were closely linked in coverage: aboriginal grievances, human rights abuses, the impact of the NAFTA, and social instability. Fully half the stories dealt with the problems faced by the indigenous peoples of Chiapas; for the most part, this treatment was quite sympathetic on issues such as poverty, social discrimination, and repression. Human rights abuses focused on what were portrayed as atrocities carried out by the Mexican Army in retaking Chiapas: the beating and execution of surrendered rebels and perhaps the killing of innocent civilians. NAFTA was identified as the trigger setting off the rebellion, and also played a prominent role in its framing. Both pro- and anti-NAFTA positions regarding the ability of free trade to remedy social inequality in Mexico were aired, but commentary was on the whole more negative toward NAFTA than positive. There was not even speculation that outside of the rebellion's impact on NAFTA, the United States might have to deal with it as a foreign policy issue. The fourth thematic frame dealt with social instability and encompassed discussions both of difficulties in resolving the basic issues underlying the Chiapas revolt and the possible spread of the violence to other parts of Mexico.

What is significant in media framing of the Zapatista crisis is the almost total avoidance of any discussion that would serve to link the rebellion to the Cold War, especially to the conflict that had raged across the border in neighboring Guatemala for more than three decades (LaFeber, 1983). Although there was one mention of "outside guidance," one instance of speculation that "Guatemalan guerrillas" were providing training, and the term "capitalist" was used twice (once coupled with "oppression" and once with "idealism," (the latter perhaps a mistranslation), these were passing references that were not followed up.[1] There was no discussion of the Maoist underpinnings of the EZLN, nor were any connections made between the Zapatista rebellion and other guerrilla movements still active in Latin America. Also of interest, Fidel Castro was missing from the rebellion's cast of characters. Nor was the paradox that Mexico, the one country in the Western Hemisphere in which revolutionary Cuba had never supported guerrilla insurgencies, was challenged by an insurrection after the Cold War had ended, ever mentioned (Falk, 1986, p. 21; Castañeda, 1993, p. 88). For the most part, the rebellion was framed as the unfortunate, but legitimate lashing out of an oppressed indigenous peasantry that had come to the end of its rope in dealing with centuries-old, systematic injustice, complicated by the pressures of modernization. Although NAFTA was cited as contributing factor to the revolt, there was no hint of a U.S. role (military or other) in putting it down.

Table 6.4
Text Evaluation of Major Participants

	U.S. Government (4 stories)	Salinas/Mexican Government and Army (16 stories)	Zapatista Rebels (16 stories)
Favorable			
Number of Stories	1	2	4
Percentage	25	12.5	25
Neutral/Ambiguous			
Number of Stories	1	8	10
Percentage	25	50	62.5
Unfavorable			
Number of Stories	2	6	2
Percentage	50	37.5	12.5

Beginning with data in Table 6.4, we shall examine in detail how the major actors in the rebellion were evaluated on network television news. The first point that needs to be stressed is that President Clinton never appeared on film, was never used as a source in a story, and was never mentioned in any way. The U.S. president, of course, has unique access to television news. For example, President Reagan once commented that he could be on the news every night if he so desired (quoted in Kegley and Wittkopf, 1991, p. 279). While this might be seen as somewhat of an exaggeration, the failure of President Clinton to connect himself in any way to the Chiapas rebellion can hardly be seen as accidental. Not only the president kept a low profile. Michael McCurry (then a U.S. State Department spokesperson) appeared twice early in the coverage of the rebellion to present the U.S. case that NAFTA should not be held responsible. This was the only of U.S. government commentary on the crisis. In all, the U.S. position, limited to a discussion of NAFTA, was presented in only four stories—one favorable, one neutral or ambiguous, and two unfavorable. Seemingly keeping a low U.S. profile on the rebellion was a higher priority for the government than was defending the new free trade agreement against charges that it would negatively affect indigenous and poor populations in Mexico.

In contrast, all sixteen stories contained evaluations of the two sides directly involved in the rebellion—the Zapatistas and the Mexican government/Army. Interesting, but not surprising in light of the framing of the crisis, the Zapatistas came off with more positive evaluations than did the Mexican government/Army. The position of the Zapatistas was portrayed favorably in four stories (25 percent) and unfavorably in two (12.5 percent). In contrast, the position of the Mexican government/Army was portrayed favorably in only two stories (12.5 percent) and unfavourably in six (37.5 percent). With respect to both sides involved in hostilities, half or more of stories were categorized as neutral or ambiguous. Thus, while ambiguous and neutral commentary predominated in coverage of both sides, in stories that did take a side, the Zapatistas clearly had the sympathetic ear of television journalists to a greater extent than did the Mexican government or Army.

Table 6.5
Percentage of Descriptors Reflecting Positively or Negatively on Major Actors

	Number of Descriptors	Percentage
U.S. Government		
Positive	2	50
Negative	2	50
Total	4	100
Salinas/Mexican Gov't. and Army		
Positive	23	48
Negative	25	52
Total	48	100
Zapatista Rebels		
Positive	23	61
Negative	15	39
Total	38	100

Table 6.5 presents the results of the analysis of the actual language used to describe the U.S. government, President Salinas, the Mexican government and Army, and the Zapatista rebels. The fact that there were only four evaluative descriptors used with respect to the United States underscores the marginal role the neighbor to the North played in media coverage of the crisis. President Salinas, his government, and the Mexican Army received the bulk of evaluative descriptors (forty-eight), 48 percent of which were coded as positive and 52 percent as negative. The Zapatistas were the object of thirty-eight evaluative descriptors, 61 percent coded as positive and 39 percent as negative. These data

are broadly consistent with those presented in Table 6.4, and show that the Zapatistas received "more favorable" press coverage than did the Mexican authorities opposing them.

CONCLUSION

In a book written before the initiation of talks leading to NAFTA, Pope Atkins makes the following observation on the relationship between Mexico and the United States:

> [Mexico] a major state that borders a superpower,...stands apart in Latin America because of its special structure of bilateral relations with the United States...Consequently, the Mexican–U.S. relationship is largely divorced from the greater inter-American arena. Many of the issues are "North American" in content and closely associated with the domestic concerns in each country; the relationship has been determined primarily by territorial proximity and increasingly integrated economic and social structures. (1989, pp. 30–31)

Arguably no country in Latin America and the Caribbean is more important to the United States than Mexico, and NAFTA, beginning in 1994, "represented a historic point of reference in relations" between the two countries (Bosworth, Collins, and Lustig, 1997, p. 1).

Indeed, in a book emerging from a Brookings Institution-sponsored conference focused on the impact of NAFTA, the editors contended that much was expected from the agreement:

> [It] was expected to bring about a substantial expansion of trade among the three member countries and to give a strong boost to economic growth in Mexico. It also represented a recognition of efforts, extending over the prior decade, to modernize and open up the Mexican economy to the global trading system. (Bosworth, Collins and Lustig, 1997, p. 1)

Whatever the long-term effects of NAFTA may be for Mexico, there was no immediate sign that it had provided a cure for either its political or economic problems. During 1994 Mexico suffered through assorted financial and criminal scandals relating to the family of ex-President Carlos Salinas de Gortari, the assassination of Luis Donaldo Colosio (presidential candidate of the ruling party), and the collapse of the peso near the end of the year. Only the last of these might in some way be tied directly to NAFTA, but they all helped to create a climate of uncertainty and unease in which grandiose expectations were even less likely to be fulfilled than is normally the case. Writing three years after the agreement's inauguration, Bosworth and colleagues assess its effect on trade, narco-trafficking, and illegal immigration as at best mixed. However, in the scholarly analysis of those authors, Chiapas and the Zapatista rebellion do not merit even a passing mention.

Perspective here is hard to establish. Perhaps it truly is that the economic and political problems that occurred in Mexico during the year after the inauguration of NAFTA bore little or no relationship to the Chiapas revolt and would have occurred irrespective of the activities of the Zapatistas. However, on the basis of a content analysis study of major U.S. newspaper coverage of Mexico for the fourteen months following January 1994, Josep Rota and Eileen McLaughlin argue that their "data reflect a connection between the Chiapas uprising and U.S. investments in Mexico" (Rota and McLaughlin, 1999, p. 10). The direct impact of the Zapatista rebellion on the unravelling of Mexico's image as a stable democracy and the effect this had on subsequent economic and political problems may be hard to ascertain. At the very least, however, the rebellion did serve to focus the attention of the international media on a set of problems in the country that neither Mexico nor its northern neighbor were especially anxious to have exposed. As argued by Collier,

> The uprising had thrown Mexico into crisis, calling into question President Salinas de Gortari's program to restructure and modernize the Mexican economy…[as well it] provoked public debate over government fraud, corruption, and dereliction of duty to Mexico's peasant and indigenous poor. (1994, p. 5)

It is also obvious that in terms of the extent of this exposure, U.S. television network news did little to heighten the embarrassment of the governments involved in NAFTA.

In general, governments have three responses to demands from marginalized populations for a more equitable share of society's economic resources: repression, co-option, and redistribution of resources. Before to the Mexican Revolution, the operative policy of the Mexican government had been one of repression, carried out by private paramilitary forces working for the landed economic and social elite, augmented by police and military power when necessary. While this response was not totally abolished in the post-revolutionary period, especially in Chiapas (Ross, 1995, pp. 68–71), the major thrust of government responses shifted to redistribution (especially both the reality and promise of land reform under Article 27 of the Mexican Constitution of 1917) and incorporation of peasant organizations into the ruling party, the Institutional Revolutionary Party (PRI), resulting in the co-option of significant portions of the peasant leadership to the side of the government (Harvey, 1998, pp. 52–67).

For Mexico as a whole this formula led to uncharacteristic social peace and political stability (Tannenbaum, 1966), albeit at the price of an unhealthy concentration of power among elites and widespread corruption. Life under PRI rule may have left much to be desired, but for key groups in society (labor and peasants, in particular) it marked an absolute improvement over conditions that prevailed before the revolution. During the long rule of the PRI, there have no doubt been instances of electoral intimidation and fraud of a magnitude that determined the outcome of elections (1940 and 1988 are mentioned most prominently in this regard) However, the party did not have to rely routinely on repressive tactics or electoral fraud to remain in power.

In the case of Chiapas, however, for a host of idiosyncratic reasons dealing primarily with the failure of getting land redistributed to peasants, in the 1970s the PRI lost control of a significant portion of the peasantry to organizations whose leaders had been trained in a combination of liberation theology and Maoist principles of political organization. Paradoxically, policies aimed at the modernization of Mexican society as a whole worked to further marginalize and alienate the Chiapas peasantry to the point where armed insurrection appeared to many the only way to remedy the situation.

The timing of the Zapatista revolt is crucial; if it had occurred prior to the demise of Communism we can be close to certain that it would have been treated quite differently by the U.S. government and mass media alike. For instance, had it occurred but a decade earlier it no doubt would have been linked to the ongoing insurgencies in Guatemala and El Salvador, the Sandinistas in Nicaragua, and of course to Fidel Castro. In particular, one obvious interpretive frame would have been that the evil empire of the USSR was conspiring to disrupt the launching of NAFTA by proxy.

The Zapatista revolt of course had the good fortune of occurring in 1994 rather than in 1984, and as a consequence it has been referred to as the "first post-modern rebellion" (Burbach, 1994, p. 113). Coming as it did, when Communism no longer presented a threat to the United States, the rebellion could be assessed by the U.S. government and media for what it was—a domestic problem dealing with redistribution of societal resources—not as a potential focal point for yet another instance of international Communist subversion in the hemisphere. This change in the international environment explains the U.S. governments muted reaction to the rebellion and the interpretative frame placed on it by mass media as a legitimate expression of desperation on the part of a long-trodden-upon indigenous population.

It might also be argued that the end of the Cold War changed not only the U.S. governments response to the rebellion, but that of the Mexican government as well. That the Mexican government's response to the rebellion shifted from one of military engagement with the guerrillas to one of peace negotiations as early as January 12 is significant. Once it became clear that the Zapatistas posed no real military threat to the survival of the Mexican government, common sense dictated that in a post–Cold War era it was counterproductive to pursue 1960s–style tactics of counterinsurgency such as those that had devastated large portions of neighboring rural Guatemala. That the international media were on hand to record every gruesome death intensified the public relations nightmare-in-the-making faced by the Mexican government. In short, in the absence of the Cold War, a policy to watch, contain, negotiate, wear down, and ultimately wait out the Zapatistas became both possible and desirable.[2]

If the Chiapas region is filled with paradoxes, there are at least two paradoxes surrounding the rebellion occurring there and the media coverage of it. The first has to do with the micro-timing of the revolt. In light of the demonstrated military weakness of the EZLN, it is fairly obvious that the Zapatistas could survive militarily only on their home turf, in a campaign of guerrilla warfare in which the Mexican Army obligingly played the role of witless pursuer. "Defeating the Mexican army" and "advancing on the Capital" were examples of brave but empty rhetoric and the Zapatista leadership, clearly not lacking political skill and sophistication, must have known this. The revolt was no doubt intended to raise the issues of indigenous marginalization to national and international salience, and in doing this it was extraordinarily successful.

If, however, the real purpose of the revolt was to somehow derail NAFTA, then the Zapatistas clearly missed their best chance. Had the revolt occurred even six weeks earlier (November 15 rather than January 1), it might have decisively strengthened anti-NAFTA forces in the U.S. Congress, where its fate was anything but certain (Ross, 1995, pp. 44–49). As evidence for such a conclusion, Ross cites an interview with a U.S. political officer in Chiapas during the rebellion, in which the official stated that "...if Congress had known about the guerrillas on November 17, NAFTA would have been dead..." (Ross, 1995, p. 51). This may put the matter in more definitive terms than is warranted, but there is little doubt that the Zapatistas had far more leverage on the outcome of NAFTA before this key congressional vote than after it had been passed and signed into law. A military victory was no more likely in January than it had been in November, so the question of why the Zapatistas did not begin their revolt six weeks earlier remains an item of some mystery.[3]

The second paradox surrounding the revolt is the virtual absence of Subcomandante Marcos in the television coverage of it. It is well-known, that television is particularly fond of dealing with complex events in the context of the personalities involved in them (Gitlin, 1980). The enigmatic Marcos, with his ski-mask, green eyes, and pipe, presented an alluring Zorro-like figure, made to measure for television cameras. While Marcos did emerge from the Chiapas conflict with a worldwide reputation, he did so without exposure on U.S. network television news; during a two-month period, his name was never mentioned and he appeared unidentified, one time, in a short video clip.

A number of explanations for this anomaly can be offered: (1) American reporters did not do an especially good job of covering the rebellion and were simply unaware of Marcos; (2) Marcos deliberately and successfully avoided TV cameras;[4] (3) for a brief time, coincident with the Chiapas revolt, television networks abandoned their cult-of-personality strategy in covering news events; or (4) there was a spontaneous or induced agreement at some level not to give the Marcos factor play. Whatever the ultimate cause, although the American public did learn the basic details concerning the Chiapas revolt from reports that were reasonably sympathetic to the insurgents, they certainly did not learn about the charismatic, green-eyed Subcomandante from network television news.[5] Perhaps Marcos will go down in history as the first hero created by the internet (Halleck, 1994; Cleaver, 1998).

One final point of speculation cannot be resisted. Because Chiapas was a part of Guatemala during the entire Spanish colonial period (not joining Mexico until independence in the early nineteenth century), perhaps the most tantalizing feature of media coverage of the Zapatista rebellion is that it gives us a flavor of what might have been if the Cold War had not intruded on the Guatemalan revolution that had begun in 1944. Although in social science research it is impossible to use control variables to deal with real world problems, based on the Chiapas case it is certainly possible to speculate that in the absence of an international Communist threat, the U.S. government would have reacted quite differently to the land-reform program undertaken by the Arbenz government in the early 1950s. Also, given that media coverage tends to follow, in general terms at least, government policy (Bennett, 1990), we might have seen a media interpretation of that revolution that was largely sympathetic to the plight of indigenous peoples in Guatemala, rather than the predominant Cold War frame that was applied to conflict in that country.

APPENDIX 6.1

U.S. GOVERNMENT

Descriptors Coded Positive
- rejected the claim that NAFTA would hurt Mexico's indigenous people
- NAFTA designed to promote economic activity that might address the concerns of those who suffer economic deprivation

Descriptors Coded Negative
- NAFTA was the catalyst of the revolt
- NAFTA dredged up old problems of poverty and violence

Descriptors Coded Neutral or Ambiguous
- sent investigators to monitor the situation

PRESIDENT SALINAS, THE MEXICAN GOVERNMENT AND THE MEXICAN ARMY

Descriptors Coded Positive
- Salinas] called for calm and opening a dialogue with the rebels
- [Salinas] understands rebel grievances, but violence doesn't help
- have brought order back
- slowly gaining the upper hand
- insist they are treating captives well
- appears firmly in control again/appears to have gained the upper hand
- called for negotiations/appealed to negotiate/decided that the only way to end the peasant uprising is at the negotiating table/offered to talk peace
- will address the inequalities in the region but will continue to put down the rebellion
- promised a thorough investigation [of all alleged atrocities]
- announced a unilateral cease-fire
- [Salinas] "If rebels want social progress, violence is not the way to obtain it"

Descriptors Coded Negative
- were not successful in putting down the uprising
- revolt was a big embarrassment for the government
- still do not have the situation under control
- "there was no protection of any kind when rebels came to town"
- [people] "afraid of government retaliation"
- [Mexico] a country in which dissent of any kind is barely tolerated
- government was caught by surprise
- can't rest easy

- accused of genocidal policies
- officials tried to cut off TV transmission of pictures of the rebellion/kicked out all reporters and photographers from Ocosingo/strafed reporters from the air
- eyes of the world are focused on Mexico's human rights record
- big danger to travel is the army itself
- trying to defend itself against charges of brutality and atrocities against its own people
- Mexico's image is crumbling
- said to have gunned down a young girl/insurgents with hands tied behind their backs, lined up and apparently shot by government troops/solid evidence that combatants had been shot after they had surrendered/accused of killing innocent civilians
- has yet to deal with the underlying causes of the discontent
- accused of a litany of abuses: "injustice, oppression, persecution, racist discrimination, and torture—so many things, over so many years"
- neglected the region
- failed to bomb the rebel force into submission

Descriptors Coded Neutral or Ambiguous

- Mexico's President/President
- Mexican army/Mexican military/army troops/government troops/ Federal troops/government soldiers
- police officers were killed
- responded with force/fought to quash a bloody rebellion/a show of force
- retook San Cristobal/on the move/regained control of several towns/have taken control of several cities/in control now/tightened their grip/mountain villages seized by EZLN rebels recaptured
- security forces
- [Salinas] claims to be improving the economy
- told Indian rebels to lay down their arms and surrender
- called in air force
- used bombs
- One-fifth of the Mexican Army descended on Chiapas
- making sure that the New Year's Day rebellion doesn't flare up again
- [Salinas] spent considerable time and money promoting Mexico as a modern western nation
- [Salinas] spoke for the first time

ZAPATISTA NATIONAL LIBERATION ARMY

Descriptors Coded Positive
- armed peasants/small, poorly armed but determined group of peasants/ group of peasants/ peasant army/a militia of Indian peasants/soldiers of a peasant army
- want their fair share of the region's wealth/demand land, education, and money/demand free elections, land, and economic help
- fighting on behalf of Mexico's disenfranchised Indians
- armed mostly with shotguns and hunting rifles/poor-man's uprising/ some only carried sticks for weapons
- poor people/"poor peasants—I feel sorry for them"
- "were driven—very brave"
- people who feel they are being left behind
- at the very bottom of the ladder
- their condition will not get better
- captured, bound, and say they were beaten, too/badly beaten
- claimed economic reforms were literally killing them
- many were massacred/some rebels appear to have been executed/some apparently shot, execution style
- "their demands are pretty straight-forward—the things they are asking for are legitimate claims such as the basic foundations of a healthy society— education, food, housing, land"
- agreed to a package of economic reforms
- "have been driven to desperation and things will not get better for a long time"

Descriptors Coded Negative
- trained by Guatemalan guerrillas/had outside support
- insurgents/Indian insurgents
- continued to snipe at government forces
- blocked roads
- failed to inspire a popular insurgency
- heavily armed and until now unknown EZLN/armed force
- guerrillas
- looted stores and government buildings
- fired on journalists
- refused to talk peace

Descriptors Coded Neutral or Ambiguous
- Zapatista Liberation Army rebels/rebels/Indian rebels/rebel force
- hold four towns/still holding four small towns
- Zapatistas, after Emiliano Zapata, hero of the Mexican Revolution
- never heard of before

- Indians/Mayan Indians/Native Indians
- fighting against capitalist oppression/fighting to end capitalist idealism
- issued a declaration of war/declared war on the Mexican government
- economic development following NAFTA could threaten their way of life/opposed to the NAFTA/free trade will lock them in poverty under U.S. domination/find NAFTA oppressive
- polite to tourists but brutal to local officials and land-owners
- more of an embarrassment than a threat to the Mexican government
- have retreated to the surrounding mountains/faded back into hills/running back into their mountain jungles/chased back into the hills/retreating force of armed peasants
- not sure whether their uprising is fizzling or if they are simply taking time to regroup
- promised to fight on
- stormed out of the hills
- under attack by aircraft
- warning they'll be back/gone for now, but are they gone for good?
- refused to give up, saying they will take their struggle under-ground/warned their uprising will continue until they win social and economic reforms
- wearing black ski masks
- rebel negotiators
- fought army troops
- vowed to take their fight to the capital

NOTES

1.   Connections between Chiapas and Guatemala during the brutal Cold War insurgencies in the latter country were in fact multidimensional (involving both leaders and refugees), long-lasting, and deep (Castañeda, 1993 and Harvey, 1998).

2.   It is significant that during the 1999 Papal visit to Mexico, a satisfactory solution to the problems underlying the Chiapas revolt was high on John Paul II's agenda.

3.   Citing interviews of Marcos in the media, Collier concludes that NAFTA actually had little to do with the timing of the revolt. He claims that rather than being a "cause" of the revolt, it was no more than a "pretext" (Collier, 1994, pp. 86-87). For his part, Marcos, while not dismissing the importance of NAFTA, claims that the Zapatistas were not prepared for an earlier uprising. The Zapatistas needed a holiday to mask the movement of their army. An offensive had originally been planned for October 12 (Day of the Virgin of Guadeloupe), but the Mexican Army had discovered a stockpile of Zapatista arms, thwarting that plan. Christmas was seen as problematic, as was December 28 (Fool's Day) because "when journalists reported the attack...no one would believe them. So we decided to postpone the date again until the 31st" (Benjamin, 1995, pp. 66–67).

4.   Max Para hints at just such a strategy, pointing out that the Zapatistas "took the unprecedented precaution of refusing entry to reporters from *Televisa,* a television monopoly" to the press conference marking the start of negotiations with the government

(Para, 1995, p. 65). Another element in the Zapatistas' quest to define their own image cited by Para is the Zapatistas' "use of video to record their own interviews which have then been distributed to reporters, or fax to issue press statements." This technology allowed the Zapatistas to "resist the attempts to make them fit into existing stereotypes."

5.   Nor was Marcos the recipient of a large amount of coverage in U.S. newspapers. Rota and McLaughlin (1999, Table 2, p. 24) found only 22 references to him in a total of 4,911 stories dealing with Mexico during a fourteen-month period beginning in January 1994.

7

The Cuban Balsero Crisis, 1994

Walter C. Soderlund

BACKGROUND

This chapter analyzes U.S. television network news coverage of the mass exodus of Cubans who attempted to cross the Florida Straits on home-made rafts in 1994. This emigration, which was encouraged by the government of Fidel Castro, reached crisis proportions in late summer, when the United States already had its hands full with the events in Haiti (see Chapter 5).

As with Haiti, U.S. involvement with Cuba extends back to the nineteenth century. From the time of the Spanish-American War, which led to Cuban independence in 1902, to the Cuban Revolution, and the saga of Elian Gonzales, there has been a continuous series of contentious issues on the Cuban-U.S. agenda. Evaluating this relationship, Gregory Treverton argued, "Depending on one's taste and definitions, ...the United States...has threatened Cuban sovereignty for much of the last century and a half" (Treverton, 1989, p. 63).

As Louis Pérez has observed, "the sources of the [Spanish–American] war reached deeply into the nineteenth century. The Americans began to contemplate Cuba very early on in that century, mostly in the form of musings on possession" (Pérez, 1998, p. 3). Acquisition of the island was complicated both by the issue of slavery (not settled in the United States until the U.S. Civil War, and even later in Cuba), and that Cuba, the "ever faithful isle," remained a colony of Spain after the Wars of Independence that had liberated most of Latin America from Spanish rule between 1810 and 1823 (Thomas, 1971, pp. 85–105).

The Ten Years' War (Cuba's First War of Independence, 1868–1878) ended indecisively; as has happened in more recent times, the outcome of that war led to an influx of Cuban refugees into the United States, the most notable being José Martí. This group of refugees pursued their goal of liberating the island from U.S. shores. As Gerald Poyo makes abundantly clear, Cuba's Second War of Independence in 1895 (which became the Spanish–American War in 1898) was to a significant extent organized and driven by the Cuban exile community in the United States (Poyo, 1989, pp. 110–111), with Walter Millis claiming that "secret orders were dispatched [from the United States] setting the night of

February 24, 1895, as the date for the rising" (Millis, 1931, p. 25; see also Thomas, 1971, pp. 305–306). The United States, however, had its own agenda to pursue. In the latter half of the nineteenth century, when the U.S. frontier had reached the Pacific, the idea of manifest destiny acquired a connotation of overseas expansion, which led the United States to acquire a de facto colonial empire, including Cuba as a protectorate after 1902. (LaFeber, 1963; Morgan, 1965).

There is some dispute over whether the Cuban insurgents could have defeated the Spanish without U.S. assistance (Pérez, 1998, pp. 10–12; 126–133), but there is little doubt that U.S. intervention was decisive in achieving a quick victory in summer 1898. There is also no doubt that the way in which independent Cuba was turned into a protectorate of the United States (by the Platt Amendment to the Cuban Constitution), was instrumental in setting the two nations on a path of conflict that resulted ultimately in Fidel Castro and the Cuban Revolution of 1959.

This revolution led to fundamental changes in Cuban politics and society and also to a new set of Cuban–U.S. controversies involving the USSR and the Cold War. Included here was Cuba's role in the "export of revolution," to Latin America and Africa (Domínguez, 1989). As summarized by Howard Wiarda, "Since 1959, Cuba has been the dominant preoccupation of U.S. foreign policy in Latin America" (Wiarda, 1989, p. 155); the dominant thread of that policy has been to isolate Cuba, both politically and economically (Waters, 1992, pp. 9–11). Early in the post revolutionary period, after the Bay of Pigs invasion of 1961, Cuba aligned itself with the USSR. That relationship, in turn, led directly to the Cuban Missile Crisis of 1962, an event that most analysts agree marked the closest point that the two superpowers came to nuclear war during the entire Cold War period (Allison and Zelikow, 1999). From the 1959 revolution to the present, the relationship between the United States and Cuba has remained antagonistic, and many believe that "no other political leadership in the world is as hostile as Cuba's is to the United States" (Domínguez, 1989, p. 21; see also Domínguez and Hernandez, 1989).

In relating the history of Cuban–U.S. relations to the *balsero* crisis of summer 1994, three factors need to be considered. The first is the large number of Cubans (primarily from the middle class and elite), estimated at 800,000, who fled the island until 1980; at least 85 percent of these settled on the U.S. mainland (Portes and Bach, 1985, p. 84). Most of these refugees prospered and have been prominent in setting the direction and tone of U.S. foreign policy toward Cuba until today (Rieff, 1995). The second is the Cold War that continued until the early 1990s, and which made Castro's communist Cuba the object of special consideration in U.S. immigration law. Under provisions of the Cuban Refugee Adjustment Act passed in 1966, Cubans who reached U.S. shores were virtually guaranteed refugee status and asylum, a provision clearly not extended to migrants fleeing other dictatorial regimes, especially Haiti. The third factor is the collapse of Communism; first in Eastern Europe between 1988 and 1990, and then the disintegration of the USSR itself in 1991. Taken together, these developments left Cuba without a major political-military ally and with an economy in absolutely desperate conditions (Schulz, 1993, pp. 90–97; see also Smith 1992; Oppenheimer, 1992).

Rather than attempting to use this latter factor as a bargaining point for improving relations with Cuba (Soderlund, Wagenberg, and Surlin, 1999), the response of the United States was to further tighten the screws on the Cuban government in the form of the 1992 Cuban Democracy Act (the Torricelli Bill) (Nazario, 1996). As economic conditions on the island continued to worsen, there were uncharacteristic popular challenges to state authority, culminating in a major antigovernment riot in Havana on August 5, 1994. Economic and political dissidents clamored to leave the island (Gunn, 1990). As had happened after the messy occupation of the Peruvian Embassy in Havana in 1980 (resulting in the Mariel boatlift), President Castro again decided to play the immigration card.

Using immigration to the United States as an escape valve to get rid of dissidents was by no means an untested arrow in Castro's quiver. Holly Ackerman and Juan Clark report that in addition to the mass exodus prompted by the revolution itself, Castro opened the escape valve in a modest way in 1965 (5,000 refugees left from the port of Camarioca), and in a major way in 1980, when nearly 125,000 Cubans left for the United States from the port of Mariel, creating consternation and chaos in Florida, which had to provide social services for the newly arrived Cubans (Ackerman and Clark, 1995; Clark, et al., 1981). Of lasting consequence, the Mariel boatlift created a major problem for the Carter administration, which was already tainted with suspicions of weakness over its handling of the Iran hostage crisis (Larzelere, 1988). The Mariel crisis occurred at a time when Cuban influence in the world was widely perceived to be as its apex; Howard Wiarda claims that 1979 was the peak of Cuban international influence (Wiarda, 1989, p. 17).

On the August 12, 1994, President Castro again sought to export his problems to the United States by issuing orders to his police and military to turn a blind eye to those leaving Cuban beaches for the United States. Unlike those participating in previous migrations by sea, which were carried out using small boats and helped by Cubans already in the United States, the 1994 migrants were labelled *balseros.* They were left largely to their own devices; many took to the seas in unseaworthy, homemade rafts. Ackerman and Clark describe the situation as follows:

> ...in mid-August [1994] from fifteen miles off Cuban shores, the seas from Mariel to Havana's eastern beaches were often literally dotted with a line of flimsy rafts, typically carrying nine people or less and shoddily made from anything that would float. (1995, p, 24)

The number of refugees increased during 1994 (the U.S. Coast Guard rescued 248 in January; 1,010 in July; and 21,300 in August); and President Clinton changed U.S. immigration policy on August 19. Previously, Cubans arriving on U.S. soil were accorded virtually automatic entry into the country; henceforth, those intercepted at sea would be taken to the U.S. naval base at Guantanamo Bay, Cuba. Those who actually made it to U.S. shores would be detained, pending an immigration hearing. This change in policy averted an immigration crisis in Florida, for which authorities were not prepared (Falk, 1997, p. 156). Clinton also put an end to charter flights, family visits, and most important, cash remittances from Cubans in the United States to their families in Cuba. By cutting off a major source of hard currency for the beleaguered Cuban economy, he sought to create some problems for Fidel Castro (Ackerman and Clark, 1995, p. 39, see also, Ackerman, 1996).

With both governments now having a stake in ending the balsero crisis, talks to resolve it began on August 26, and an immigration agreement was reached on September 9. When the new policy was implemented by the Cuban frontier guard on September 13 the crisis ended (Ackerman and Clark, 1995, pp. 39–40). The terms of the agreement called for the United States to provide a minimum of 20,000 visas to Cubans per year; in exchange, the Cuban government would reinstate border controls on the island's beaches and discourage would-be migrants by persuasive measures. Ultimately, the vast majority of those intercepted by the U.S. Coast Guard at the height of the crisis and interned at Guantanamo Bay (some 22,000) were, contrary to statements made by Administration spokespersons during the crisis, permitted entry into the United States (Rieff, 1995, p. 88).

FINDINGS

Television news stories studied for this crisis appeared from August 12 until September 13, when the immigration agreement between the U.S. and Cuban governments came into effect and effectively ended the flow of rafters.

A total of eighty news stories, containing one hundred and thirty nine news segments, dealt with the *balsero* crisis during this period. In terms of distribution, ABC ran twenty-five stories, containing forty-one news segments; CBS ran twenty-eight containing forty-seven news segments; and NBC ran twenty-seven stories containing fifty-one news segments. Coverage was heaviest on all networks immediately after President Clinton's August 19 reversal of the longstanding U.S. immigration policy regarding Cuban refugees. As the crisis continued to unfold, key events gaining media attention were conditions at the U.S. detention facilities at Guantanamo Bay, the decision by the U.S. and Cuban governments to engage in talks to resolve the crisis, the talks themselves, and the eventual implementation of the outcomes of the negotiations—an enhanced immigration quota for Cubans wanting to immigrate to the United States and Castro's agreement to close his beaches to illegal migrants. Language used by sources, reporters, and anchors to describe President Clinton and the U.S. government; President Castro and the Cuban government; as well as the *balseros,* as recorded, collated, and coded may be found in the appendices to Chapter 7.

Television networks in the United States began to pick up on the Cuban refugee story in mid-August, airing a total of eleven stories between August 12 and August 19, when President Clinton announced the change in U.S. immigration policy. This policy change really marked the start of the *balsero* crisis as a major media event; for the next two weeks, networks ran sixty-one stories, comprising one hundred and seven distinct news segments dealing with the story. A total of eight stories wrapped up coverage of the crisis from the time of the announcement of the Cuban–U.S. agreement on September 9 to September 13, when the crisis became a part of history.

As data in Table 7.1 indicate, although the *balsero* crisis was a major media event, it was not as salient as the concurrent crisis in U.S.–Haitian relations involving a possible invasion to restore Jean Bertrand Aristide to the Haitian presidency. U.S. television networks ran eighty stories on Cuba and ninety-three on Haiti, with 39 percent and 53 percent occupying the lead position in newscasts, respectively.   Thirty-five percent of Cuban raft-crisis stories mentioned a direct link to the ongoing Haitian crisis, sometimes a mere mention, sometimes an in-depth analysis. In a comparative context, of the seven crises reported in this book, the rafter crisis ranked second in overall media interest, more than likely as a consequence of its ranking second as well on the U.S. involvement index—4.0 for the rafter crisis versus 4.5 for the 1994 restoration of Haitian President Jean-Bertrand Aristide.

Table 7.1
Story Characteristics N = 80

Percentage of Stories	Number		Percentage
Lead Story	28		35
First Three Stories	49		61
30 Seconds and Under	7		9
Over 3 Minutes	49		61
Just Anchor Format	7		9
Use of Experts	9		11
Reporter in Cuba (including Guantanamo Bay)	39		49
Two or More News Segments	46		57.5
Film With Story	80		100
Film of President Clinton	23		29
Film of President Castro	14		17.5
Film of Rafters at Sea	71		89
Film of Rafters in Detention	42		52.5
Film of Demonstrations in the United States	6		7.5
Link to Haitian Crisis	28		35
Tilt Favorable to U.S. Position	7		9
Tilt Unfavorable to U.S. Position	19		24
U.S. Involvement Index		4.0	

Although overshadowed to some extent by events connected to Haiti, 61 percent of stories ran in the first three positions in the newscasts and the same percentage ran longer than three minutes; 57 percent contained two or more news segments, and 49 percent featured a reporter in Cuba. All of this indicates a major commitment of network resources to covering the crisis. Video/film was shown in every story, with 89 percent containing footage of rafters at sea, 52.5 percent showing rafters in detention (either in Florida or Guantanamo), while 29 percent featured the U.S. president and 17.5 percent featured the Cuban president. These percentages are lower than seen for Bill Clinton, Jean-Bertrand Aristide, and Raoul Cédras in the concurrent Haitian crisis. On balance, stories did not reflect positively on the U.S. position in the crisis, which was *to* interdict

Cuban refugees at sea and take them to the Guantanamo Bay naval base where they were to be detained, and finally to negotiate a resolution with the Castro government—9 percent were judged favorable, and 24 percent were judged unfavorable to the U.S. position, with the remainder coded neutral or ambiguous.

Table 7.2
Number of Times Leading Sources Used (All Sources Used in Newscast)

News Source	Segment 1	Segment 2	Segment 3	Total Number of Times Used
Cuban Rafter	39	35	7	81
Cuban exiles in the United States (Elite and Non-elite)	21	19	4	44
Cuban Government (Including Ricardo Alarcon)	30	6	3	39
Cubans on the Street	11	14	8	33
U.S. State Department	24	1	2	27
Clinton Administration	17	5	0	22
U.S. Military in the Field (Including U.S. Coast Guard)	12	7	1	20
Bill Clinton	17	2	0	19
Americans on the Street	2	5	1	13
Fidel Castro	8	2	2	12
Congressional Democrats	8	3	0	11
American Experts	5	5	1	11
Congressional Republicans	8	1	0	9
U.S. Justice Department	6	3	0	9

Table 7.2 shows the sources (either on-camera or quoted) that were used by the networks in constructing stories on the *balsero* crisis. Because reporters rarely witness news firsthand, selection of sources is an important element in how news is interpreted by American audiences (Shiras, 1996; Mermin, 1997). It has been widely documented that official government sources tend to have privileged access to television news (Herman and Chomsky, 1988; Orenstein, 1995).

The case of the Cuban *balseros* appears to qualify that judgment. While there is certainly a significant representation of official U.S. governmental sources, one hundred and ten connected to the administration, and an additional twenty from Congress (where one would expect opposing views to be expressed) (Paletz and Entman, 1981), reporting of this crisis was dominated by nongovernmental, and by and large, non-elite sources–eighty-one Cuban rafters, forty-four Cuban exiles in the United States (elite and nonelite), thirty-three Cubans on the street, and fourteen Americans on the street—a total of one hundred and seventy two. Cuban government sources were used fifty-one times, somewhat less than half of the one hundred and ten that, in varying capacities, had the opportunity to reflect the views of the Clinton administration.

In Table 7.3 we examine how the *balsero* crisis was framed by network television news programs for their American audiences. Two frames predominate in this coverage: foreign policy decision making (on the part of Cuba and the United States) and human interest concerns related to the fate of the rafters, at sea as well as in detention. The foreign policy decision-making frame fits neatly into Iyengar's (1991) thematic category. The history of Cuban–U.S. relations, especially from the time of Castro's successful revolution in 1959, was confrontational, and the strategies and tactics employed by both governments in this crisis were placed in the context of past hostilities and policies (see Falk, 1986; Falcoff, 1994).

Table 7.3
Percentage of Stories in Which Media Frames Are Used

Frame	Primary	Secondary	Tertiary	Total
U.S. Foreign Policy Decision Making	46	14	2	64
Human interest	10	16	21	47
Cuban Foreign Policy Decision Making	10	14	10	34
Conditions at Guantanamo	14	1	9	24
U.S.–Cuban negotiations	9	10	5	24
Societal Hardships in Cuba	7.5	7.5	9	24
U.S. Economic Embargo	1	9	4	14
Restoration of Democracy	0	3	7	10

Spokespersons representing the U.S. position attempted to limit discussion of the crisis to the immediate problem of getting Castro to reimpose border controls (i.e., a problem of immigration), while the Cubans interviewed for stories sought to link the economic distress driving the out-migration to the hardships caused by the U.S. trade embargo, maintaining that the U.S. immigration crisis could not be solved without a resolution of more fundamental problems in the bilateral relationship: (easing or removing the embargo). It was largely in this context that the frames of societal hardship in Cuba, the U.S. embargo, and, to a very limited extent, restoration of democracy were discussed. It is very important to point out that the discussion of restoring democracy to Cuba appeared in only 10 percent of stories, mainly as a tertiary frame. This is quite different from the concurrent situation in Haiti where 61 percent of stories contained the restoration of democracy frame. For whatever reason, in the case of Cuba, relatively little media attention was directed at the need to rid the island of its long-ruling dictator. That Fidel Castro would continue in power after the resolution of the crisis was more or less a given—what was seen to be important was that he stop the exodus of refugees and that he do this sooner rather than later.

The human interest frame was extremely important to the way in which the *balsero* crisis was likely to be interpreted by American audiences. It appeared in 47 percent of stories, mainly as a secondary or tertiary frame. Although this is a significant percentage, it actually understates its importance due to the impact of the visual dimension. Nearly 90 percent stories dealing with the *balsero* crisis

featured video footage of rafters at sea, and just over 50 percent showed them in
U.S. detention after their rescue. In this way the elements of human suffering,
human risk, human frustration, and human tragedy, added a personal-
involvement dimension to the coverage that cannot be grasped by analyzing it as
focusing primarily on the strategies of the two rival governments involved
(Robinson, 2000). In short, in framing the *balsero* crisis, the pawns were as
important as the kings, queens, and rooks; the human touch provided the lens
through which U.S. and Cuban government actions (or inactions) were seen by
American viewers.

Table 7.4
Text Evaluation of Major Participants

	Clinton/ U.S. Government (76 stories)	Castro/Cuban Government (75 stories)	Rafters (72 stories)
Favorable			
Number of Stories	7	4	36
Percentage	10	5	50
Neutral/Ambiguous			
Number of Stories	46	35	33
Percentage	64	47	46
Unfavorable			
Number of Stories	19	36	3
Percentage	26	48	4

Data in Table 7.4 show the textual evaluation of the major actors involved
in the crisis (Bill Clinton and the U.S. government, Fidel Castro and the Cuban
government, and the rafters themselves). Neither government receives favorable
press coverage, and here we see clearly the consequences of the focus on the
human dimension. While the U.S. side comes off somewhat better (its position
and policies given a favorable spin in 10 percent of stories and a negative one in
26 percent), the Cuban government's positions and policies were seen
favourably in only 5 percent of stories and unfavorably in 48 percent. The net
impact of these figures is that neither the two governments involved, nor their
respective leaders, were able to convince the press that their positions in the
crisis were especially meritorious and worthy of support.   This is quite
understandable with respect to Mr. Castro and the Cuban government, but that
Mr. Clinton and the U.S. government were not more convincing in putting
forward their case deserves some explanation.

First, in 1994 President Clinton was still relatively new to office and it was
fairly clear that he had a lot to learn about foreign policy. Specifically, his
handling of the Bosnian, Somalian, and Haitian crises in 1993 did little to
inspire confidence in his abilities on the international scene (Mandelbaum,
1996). Also, and of equal significance, literally as the U.S. Coast Guard was
busy plucking Cuban rafters from the seas in the Straits of Florida, other
elements of the U.S. military were preparing for a major invasion of Haiti to rid
the island of the generals who had deposed President Jean-Bertrand Aristide in
1991 (see Chapters 3, 4, and 5).

To say that President Clinton did not have the support of Congress and the American people for an invasion of Haiti is an understatement. Thus, that Mr. Clinton's policies on Cuban rafter crisis—a change in immigration policies (interdiction at sea and detention, rather than acceptance into the United States), tightening the embargo to further damage the Cuban economy, and finally negotiating with the Cuban dictator to resolve the crisis—were not more warmly received is understandable.

While most of the criticism of U.S. policy focused on the suffering it inflicted on the rafters as well as the Cuban people who were dependent on remittances from family members living in the United States, Clinton's policy was also attacked by those who wanted him to do more to free Cuba from the Castro dictatorship. Specifically, because United States was in the process of mounting an invasion to force out the Haitian generals, it was argued that the same solution should be adopted with Cuba. The argument was given added force because Cuban refugees were now being treated the same as Haitian refugees (i.e., interdicted at sea and interned at Guantanamo Bay) (von Hippel, 1995). In summary, Mr. Clinton's policies aimed at stopping the Cuban immigration inflow to the United States failed to generate any widespread support among television journalists covering the crisis.

Table 7.5
Percentage of Descriptors Reflecting Positively or Negatively on Major Actors

	Number of Descriptors	Percentage
Clinton/U.S. Government		
Positive	48	25
Negative	146	75
Total	194	100
Castro/Cuban Government		
Positive	20	15
Negative	117	85
Total	137	100
Cuban Rafters		
Positive	56	79
Negative	15	21
Total	71	100

Data in Table 7.5 summarize the positive and negative language used to describe the major participants in the crisis—the U.S. and Cuban leaders, their respective governments, and the Cuban rafters. Not surprisingly, there is a correspondence between this measure of linguistic support and opposition to the various actors involved with the more general measure of support analyzed in Table 7.4. In the "semantic environment" surrounding the crisis (Horlacher, 1990), only 25 percent of evaluative language applied to President Clinton and the U.S. government was coded as positive, and 75 percent was negative. The percentages for the concurrent Haitian crisis were 34 percent positive and 66 percent negative, indicating that there was no major group in the United States that backed U.S. policy toward Cuba whole-heartedly, as was the case with President Aristide's supporters. With the exception of the support offered by the

Cuban-American National Foundation (CANF), whatever support U.S. policies received was provided by spokespersons representing the U.S. government in varying capacities.[1]

Interestingly, the percentages of positive and negative descriptors applied to Fidel Castro and the Cuban government are virtually identical to those applied to General Cédras and the Haitian generals—15 percent positive and 85 percent negative with respect to the Cuban leadership, and 14 percent positive and 86 percent negative in describing the Haitian leaders. These percentages of negative descriptors are similar to those found for press coverage of some of the most unsavory Latin American political leaders, such as Anastasio Somoza Debayle, Roberto D'Aubuisson, and Manuel Noriega (Soderlund, 2001).

Confirming the observation made on the visual impact of coverage of the rafters, while there was nowhere near the amount of evaluative language used to describe them as there was for the two governments (especially the U.S. government), what there was tended to be highly favorable—79 percent was judged to be positive (largely in terms of human suffering endured), and 21 percent was seen as negative. There were some negative descriptors of instances of unrest and stone-throwing at Guantanamo late in the crisis, but primarily in unfavorable characterizations made by Cubans in the street who were loyal to the revolution and heaped rebuke on those who chose to leave.

CONCLUSION

The Cuban *balsero* crisis emerged gradually in 1993 and 1994 as economic and social conditions on the island deteriorated after the break-up of the USSR, the end of the Cold War, and, most importantly for Cuba, the end of a range of Soviet economic subsidies (Mesa-Lago, 1993). Rather than attempting to use this new situation to leverage change in Cuba (admittedly at best a long-shot in dealing with Fidel Castro, who listens intently to his own drummer), the United States took the opposite tack, intensifying the thirty-year-old trade embargo with the passage in 1992 of the Cuban Democracy Act (Vanderbush and Haney, 1999). This caused additional economic hardship on the island at a time when conditions were already desperate.

By the summer of 1994 there was sufficient unrest in Cuba that people began demonstrating against the government. Similar conditions had twice before (in 1965 and 1980) led Fidel Castro to employ the strategy of exporting his problems to the United States in the form of refugees. The United States was not about to let Cubans living in South Florida sail to Cuba to pick up those wanting to leave, so in 1994, the journey was far more risky. While raft technology improved as the exodus continued,[2] the change in U.S. immigration policy that returned fleeing to the U.S. naval base on the island resulted in a course of action that was unsustainable for any length of time.

President Clinton's policy changes had little effect on the number of Cubans taking the water route to the United States, and the question quickly became: How many refugees could be detained at Guantanamo, for how long, and at what ultimate cost? Complicating the situation was whether of the U.S. military would be able to deal with two crises in the Caribbean simultaneously. In this equation, it became clear fairly quickly that of the two crises, the Haitian one, where 20,000 U.S. troops were preparing for an invasion to restore the democratically elected president to power, was the more important.

In addition to exporting dissidents, Fidel Castro wanted to use the immigration crisis as leverage to get the United States to drop its trade embargo, something that President Clinton, who was concerned about his apparent weakness in foreign affairs (not to mention electoral consequences in Florida), was not about to do. In the talks that resolved the crisis, although the Cuban side failed to get any concessions regarding the embargo, it did persuade the United States to modify its immigration policy, allowing approximately 20,000 Cubans to immigrate to the United States per year, a significant increase over prevailing numbers.

The rival foreign policy strategies of the two governments were highlighted in media framing of the crisis. Here the United States wanted to achieve the short-term goal of stopping the flow of refugees by getting the Cuban leader to reinstate border controls. Cuba sought to link the solution to the refugee crisis to easing the U.S. trade embargo. The human desperation that drove the refugees to take to sea on perilous voyages was the third major frame evident in coverage; in presenting the positions of the rival governments, the link between the embargo and the economic and social hardships in Cuba was referred to more often than the alternative link (offered by the United States) between domestic political repression and those hardships.

In that the root cause of the crisis, as Ricardo Alarcón (the chief Cuban negotiator at the talks) referred to the embargo, was not addressed in the resolution to the crisis, an opportunity to place Cuban–U.S. relations on a more normal footing was lost. Granted, the likelihood of such an outcome was remote at best; in any case, if Clinton had relaxed economic sanctions under the circumstances, he would have been seen as making concessions to the Cuban dictator under duress. At the same time, with the Cold War over and with Cuba posing no military or political threat to the United States, some form of normalization of relations with the island was clearly called for; this was pointed out by a number of the President's foreign policy critics, Democrats as well as Republicans. For better or worse, in U.S. television news coverage of the crisis there were more calls for the United States to change its policies toward Cuba than there were calls for the initiation of democratic changes by the Castro government in Cuba. Despite the observation of Juan Clark and his colleagues in their analysis of the 1980 Mariel boatlift that "as long as a totalitarian oppressive system prevails in Cuba, the resumption of the exodus [of refugees] will always remain a possibility" (Clark, Lasagar and Reguer, 1981, p. 7), the U.S. media's framing the 1994 *balsero* crisis paid scant attention to the other root cause of the crisis. Cuba's aging and repressive political system (Grenier, 2000) barely made it on the media agenda.

This omission is especially curious given the intense attention being paid simultaneously by the Administration to the non-democratic status of the generals ruling Haiti; their removal and the reinstatement of a democratically elected government was seen to be so essential that it necessitated a U.S. military invasion. Clearly there was a major disconnect between the way that the U.S. government wanted the American people to interpret these two crises. The Cuban crisis was characterized as a matter of dealing with a flood of refugees, while the Haitian one was portrayed as a matter of restoring democracy to a nation suffering dictatorial rule. In their coverage of these two events, U.S. television news can hardly be charged with supporting Administration positions. However, coverage was not framed to draw attention to the significant differences in the ways the U.S. government sought to deal with them.

APPENDIX 7.1

PRESIDENT CLINTON/U.S. GOVERNMENT

Descriptors Coded Positive
- insist everything's under control/insist they can handle the exodus/seem to be able to handle the surge of immigrants in an orderly fashion/insists it all was going well/"We can manage this for some time/"We can certainly do the job as long as the job needs to be done"/expects to be able to handle up to 100,000 refugees
- "We urge the people of Cuba to remain at home and not fall for this callous maneuver"
- issued a stiff warning to Fidel Castro not to encourage Cubans to storm Guantanamo
- blamed the whole problem on Fidel Castro for encouraging them to come
- took action to stop the flood of refugees into the United States
- people in the United States don't want to see another Mariel boat lift
- defended his decision to the end the easy immigration policy/"We stand by our new policy to Cuba"
- believe this policy will have broad support/"We hope the American people are proud of the way the United States has responded to this humanitarian situation"
- policy will probably work in the short-run
- many people in South Florida are cheering the new policy/relieved about change in U.S. policy that will give Cubans second thoughts about coming here
- keeping the pressure on Fidel/wants to keep pressure on Fidel/holding to the hard line/trying to make life tougher for Fidel Castro/got tough with Cuba's leader, Fidel Castro/ordered new steps to further isolate the Cuban dictator/turned to economic pressure/tightening the screws/talking tough on Cuba and threatening to raise the ante against Fidel Castro/came out sticking to his hard line
- "We are extremely happy and also in full support of the President"
- "no quick fix, but we continue to be on the right track"
- condemned human rights violations in Cuba
- Florida officials liked what they saw
- did the right thing, addressed the issue with vigor and compassion/issued clear warning to Cuban refugees that to try to reach the United States by sea is not only pointless, but dangerous/ doing all it can to let Cubans know that if they try to come, they won't get in
- "Castro is paramount—the long-term goal is the liberation of Cuba, we must forego the short-term goal of immigration policy"/detention policy serves a larger goal/need to forego the short-term goal for the big goal, the liberation of Cuba/"We have to sacrifice the short-term gain for the liberation of Cuba"

- won't consider lifting the embargo unless Castro restores democracy in Cuba/remains firm in its demand that to end the embargo, Cuba must adopt substantial democratic reforms/island's repressive government hasn't gone far enough [toward reform] and refuses to lift the thirty-one-year trade ban/"If there are significant steps toward democracy, free market economy and human rights in Cuba, the United States will respond with carefully calibrated measures of its own"
- blames the failure of Cuban socialism on the immigration crisis/Cuba's failed socialist system created the crisis
- "It is not the time to deal with Fidel Castro—to show weakness in the face of Fidel Castro"
- "We must not let any nation…control the immigration policy of the United States"
- "We seek peaceful change—a naval blockage is an act of war"
- wants to avoid political extremes
- encouraged that the flow of refugees has slowed
- encouraged by the first round of talks/more optimistic about solving the crisis with Cuba
- the best is being done for them [detainees], be patient/"We have safe, humanitarian conditions"
- reached an agreement which should have a positive effect in directing Cuban migration into the United States into safe, legal and orderly channels/"These measures will help deter people from undertaking dangerous journeys on unsafe boats"/"It is a fair, good agreement–good for the United States—I'm pleased with it"

Descriptors Coded Negative
- accused of encouraging Cubans to flee their country/as long as preferential treatment [for Cuban refugees] exists, Cuban immigration will continue unabated
- [U.S.] "is covering up murder"
- refused Florida's request for a state of emergency
- the last thing Clinton needs right now is a foreign policy crisis
- [crisis] produced consternation in the White House/the White House seemed in disarray/tremendous confusion with new U.S. policy/clearly unprepared/left in a quandary
- "Don't change the policy in Washington, change the policy in Cuba"
- "What we have is a policy that is being formed about every twenty minutes"/policy is still in the kitchen/made an abrupt policy change/repeatedly adjusted policy on the fly
- selected the lesser of two unattractive political options/there's no way the Administration can win on this one/the Administration has no good options
- "They [the Americans] abandoned my country again"
- "[Administration] reacts, rather than anticipates"
- Clinton's move will backfire

- deliberately vague about how the new wave of refugees would be treated in the long run/ waffled on repatriation of Cubans
- policy punishes the rafters, not Fidel/not doing anything to Fidel/punishing the rafters instead of Fidel
- last week [Administration] downplayed the chance of a new influx of Cuban refugees
- "I'm not pleased with it [policy] as a Democrat and I'm not going to be proud of it as an American"
- "Reopen the borders and let the boats come"/"Clinton should let us in, we're risking our lives at sea"
- "Clinton—Coward"/"Clinton—Coward you"
- called upon to take the same steps as he has with Haiti's leaders/"If Cubans are to treated as Haitians, then Fidel Castro has to be treated as Cédras"/"We want one thing, for Cuba to be free and for this to be accomplished, we need a naval blockade, just as in Haiti/called upon to take military action to topple Fidel Castro/impose a total blockade/"We want a total blockade"/"We should give Fidel Castro an ultimatum that if he doesn't stop exporting Cuba's discontented in one month or three weeks, then the U.S. will proceed with a naval blockade of the island"/"Something should be done to accelerate the fall of Fidel Castro"/"Let's have an international embargo"/"Fidel has to go"
- new measures have not deterred those intent on leaving Cuba when they can/no matter what President Clinton does, thousands defy him/hasn't been able to do anything to convince Cubans to stay home/policy has no credibility in Cuba/continuing but so far fruitless campaign to stop the flow of refugees/no signs new U.S. policy is having any effect
- "In no time at all you will have what will be called by the Cubans concentration camps"/ "I hate the thought of people being picked up in boats and taken to Guantanamo/Listen, these camps in Guantanamo are not going to be pretty/what happens next here [at Guantanamo] is anybody's guess/[U.S.] troops are scrambling to set up more tents
- How long can the United States detain thousands of Cubans?/ Eventually the U.S. in going to do something with these people they have at Guantanamo/[detention] is shaping up as a huge problem for the Clinton administration/faces a potentially serious political and humanitarian problem/likely to be faced with the long-term detention of hundreds, if not thousands of refugees/"We are about to devote a substantial amount of the defense budget into setting up Guantanamo as a concentration camp"/dealing with both the Haitian and the Cuban situations [at Guantanamo] has become a huge drain on resources/barbed wire stings Cuban pride/only a matter of time before the system is overwhelmed/every day [the detention of refugees] becomes a bigger problem for the United States/"They're concentration camps detaining 21,000 Cubans and those inside have no hope of getting to the United States
- accused of a policy of inexperience and immaturity

- [the embargo] caused and is now causing tremendous hardships among Cubans/can't tighten the embargo and expect that people are not going to leave/banning dollars from the States won't change the situation, it will only cause more suffering/"Tell President Clinton that if you take away the dollar, we don't have anything. If he has kids he should think about the children in Cuba who have nothing to eat"/"11 million people [in Cuba] are suffering from the cutting off of the dollars"/without American dollars, families in Cuba will become desperate/[the policy] will not make the Cuban government suffer, only the people/must address the fundamental problem, which is the embargo/"If the Americans were to impose embargos on all countries that do not have the same electoral system, my God, you would run out of oil in a couple of minutes"/ "They will not solve this problem unless they are willing to discuss the fundamental problem, which is the embargo"/AT&T, Marriott, Chrysler, and Coca Cola are ready to invest in Cuba but are shut out by the embargo/"So why not lift the embargo on Cuba, and when that happens, I think that will encourage Cuba's movement toward a more open political and economic system/if the thirty-two-year trade embargo is not lifted, conditions will only get worse, spurring others to leave/U.S. embargo a critical factor, it's strangling the island's economy/ economic sanctions are not going to bring down Castro and the use of force is certainly not a feasible option with respect to Cuba/no reason not to broaden talks with Cuba and end this impasse/"If you want a real solution to the problem you have to go to the source, and that is the embargo"/"If the problem to begin with is an immigration problem, and we know that the immigration problem stems from lack of food and medicine, how can you keep tightening up on the country and not expect more immigrants/"U.S. embargo must be discussed" "The more that you turn the screws on the Cuban economy, there will be more people who find reasons to find better situations in other parts of the world, particularly in the United States."
- an opportunist
- can turn Cubans away from American shores, but cannot escape the headaches of caring for them
- Coast Guard is hard pressed to hold the refugees back/U.S. military is scrambling/Coast Guard is stretched to the limit/ Of the search-and-rescue operations for Cubans continues for any time, it will have a detrimental effect on the Coast Guard's other missions/
- "Imperialism gone wrong again"
- policy relies on patience in South Florida; Clinton can count on precious little/patience of relatives [of rafters] in America is wearing thin
- did not acknowledge the question, "Is your Cuban policy in trouble?"/did not acknowledge a question about Cuban refugees/"Mr. President, Is your new Cuba policy in trouble?"/avoided the issue/wouldn't answer when asked if his new policy had backfired/not talking about Cuba today/has had nothing to say about the refugees

- "Clinton—No more death"
- is being inflexible
- has miscalculated the level of desperation driving people to get out of Cuba while they can
- "[policy] is backward, short-sighted and dangerous"/"the administration's policy is short-term focused, reactive, and it seems to be improvised/the administration has no long-range policy toward Cuba/with two crisis points in the Caribbean, Washington is only focused on it problems of the moment
- Congress is calling for negotiation
- bipartisan call for tougher measures/needs to toughen his new Cuba policy
- apparently unwilling to pursue any kind of political or diplomatic solution to this problem/refusing to talk to Castro is a mistake/"This is 1994—the Cold War is over, maybe some people don't know that yet"/U.S. should begin talking to Cuba so that Castro can find a new way out/"If we're opening the door to Vietnam and North Korea, what in the world are we doing not talking to this guy who's 90 miles away"/the Cold War is over, Cuba's no threat, why shouldn't policy change?/the administration should be reaching out to Fidel Castro, discussing more than immigration to nudge Cuba toward democracy/the lesson [in moving Communist countries toward democracy] is to broaden and intensify contacts/"Cuba has changed, the world has changed, and the United States has changed, and that probably suggests that there should be a change in policy toward Cuba"/"This would be the right moment to use aggressive diplomacy, of negotiating, of trade and media to create new expectations within Cuba and create irreversible change"/Cuba is no longer a security threat to the U.S./"Cuba is a Third World country with an army that's crumbling, an economy that's in shambles. Its not a threat to anybody anymore, its not a model either, and its time that U.S. policy adjusted to that"
- Clinton's Cuba policy is under heave pressure/policy is already in trouble/his policy sinks deeper/President's policy continued to draw criticism/his Cuba policy is still under fire/
- was misguided by electoral advisors; instead of following a coherent foreign policy approach, he is following an electoral approach
- "We by no means want any negotiations with this man; its about time Cuba became free"
- "To allow the crisis to continue makes no sense, its juvenile"
- "They're trying to spend money on the Haitian and the Cubans, but not on us [American military dependents]"
- 20,000 visas won't be enough/quota guaranteeing legal immigration to the U.S. won't help many of the rafters who are poor, unemployed, and have no immediate family to claim them
- critics say that Mr. Clinton is reversing long-standing U.S. policy, asking a nation to crack down on people leaving/"Human rights meant

that people could leave their country, we're asking Castro really to violate a treaty we've signed—that isn't going to work very long"
- no one believes that the potential for crisis is over
- went from one rough spot to another
- an angry President Clinton declared that Fidel Castro would not be allowed to dictate U.S. immigration policy, but that policy was exactly what was on the table today
- a real solution may require a change of thinking in Washington
- the solution to President Clinton's Cuba problem will not come in Panama
- deal leaves out nearly 30,000 refugees detained at Guantanamo

Descriptors Coded Neutral or Ambiguous
- sending signals that it wants at least to at least stop the violence and prevent U.S. residents from aggravating the situation/will prosecute anyone going into Cuban waters to bring refugees into the United States/hoping to head off a potential flood of refugees/fears a repeat of the 1980 Mariel boat lift
- believes a large commitment of aid [to Florida] may attract even more refugees/does not want to do anything that might encourage more Cubans to come
- considering reversing the thirty-year-old policy of accepting all Cuban refugees/Cuban refugees will no longer receive special treatment/reversed a twenty-eight-year policy of accepting any refugee from the Communist regime in Cuba/officially ended an almost thirty-year-old open-door policy/reversed a policy that stood for three decades/reversing its policy on Cuban immigrants/has changed the rules of the Cuban immigration game/slammed shut the open-door policy for Cubans
- strategy is to scare Cubans into staying home/decided that changing the policy was the only way of preventing another mass exodus of Cubans to the United States/hoping new policy will discourage Castro from permitting people to leave and convince Cubans that there would be nothing to gain by going to sea/"We discourage you from getting on these boats"/hope the Cuban people will believe the new line.
- too soon to know if President Clinton can stop the Cuban refugee tide/no way of telling at the beginning of this outflow how high it would reach
- "[The United States] should mobilize international pressure against the Cuban leader"/the first step should be the removal of Fidel Castro/the United States should not act alone, should ask the UN for condemnation of Cuba
- new policy has the begrudging support of many Miami Cubans
- "concentrating all our efforts to deal with the migrant flow"
- security [at Guantanamo] is a concern/"Security concerns are something we worry about every day"/most of the camps [at

Guantanamo] have been quiet, but the military is worried that tensions will rise
- publically insists the policy will work
- sitting down with Castro would be political dynamite, a step that Bill Clinton is not about to take/hardly in a position to waver on remaining firm against Castro/does not believe it would be useful to have a dialogue with Castro/dead set against talking with Castro/for those who want to compromise with Fidel Castro, the answer is still no/anything that even look like a concession to Castro could set off unrest in the Cuban-American community
- "The United States has done everything, with the exception of an invasion of U.S. Marines, to destroy the Cuban revolution"
- bedeviled by Cuba's Fidel Castro
- pressures for a blockade of Castro's Cuba could become irresistible/raised the possibility of increasing restrictions on Cuba even more without a naval blockade
- rejected a call from Cuba's UN Ambassador for wide-ranging talks between the two countries
- Guantanamo may require 8 to 10,000 U.S. military personnel/costs [at Guantanamo] to run to hundreds of millions of dollars/forced to expand the base at Guantanamo to house 40,000 people/by the end of September the cost of looking after Cubans already at Guantanamo will exceed $100 million
- despite the setbacks, the president is satisfied with his new policy, his critics are not
- accused [by Fidel Castro] of buckling to pressure from the fascist mafia in Cuba's wealthy exile community
- surest way of ensuring the problem remains Castro's problem is to forcibly return the refugees
- at best coping with the crisis/is coping with the refugee flows so far, but the commitment is open-ended
- applauded Castro for moving to stop Cubans from bringing children on the their dangerous voyage to freedom
- could use an immigration deal with Cuba in a hurry/counting on talks between the United States and Cuba to reach an agreement to stop the flow of refugees
- no major effort [on the part of the Cuban-American community] to turn around Clinton's policy
- "[flow of refugees] is a concern and there is no question we are trying to address it"
- a certain urgency on the part of the Administration to make these talks work
- a sense of relief that the Cubans seem serious about wanting to make a deal

FIDEL CASTRO/CUBAN GOVERNMENT

Descriptors Coded Positive
- not encouraging, not stimulating this illegal immigration
- farmers are going to be allowed to freely sell their produce
- "Fidel Castro and the revolution gave us more food, and homes and medical care"/still appears to retain the support of many Cubans/"I still support Fidel Castro because I think its one of the best governments Cuba has ever had"/his power is intact
- "We are doing our best to find a solution"
- "I have no animosity toward President Clinton"
- remained optimistic/expressed cautious optimism
- extended an olive branch to the White House-has already begun cooperating with American authorities
- "It's [the ban on children leaving by raft] a good order, it will keep children from dying"/did the right thing for banning teenagers and children from joining the refugees
- no longer a security threat to the United States
- vast majority [of Cubans] chose to remain
- agreed to stop its citizens from getting into rafts and trying to illegally get into the United States/will stop refugees from putting to sea/promised to stop people from going to sea/making good on its promise
- promised to take no reprisals on those who want to return home

Descriptors Coded Negative
- attacking U.S. open immigration policy for Cuban refugees
- threatened to unleash a torrent of refugees/making good on his threat to let any Cuban who wants to leave/will not put any obstacle to this illegal immigration to the United States/encouraged the exodus/just sitting back and letting his people take to the seas
- flooded the United States with refugees in the 1980 Mariel boat lift
- conditions in Fidel Castro's Cuba continue to deteriorate/conditions of sheer economic desperation; sheer social desperation/social and economic conditions are deteriorating/the pressure cooker will explode/desperately needs U.S. dollars/economy is crippled/there are long lines for food, gasoline, and busses/"We are suffering the worst situation in the last thirty-five years of revolution"/burdened by a 75 percent drop in imports/conditions in Cuba are driving rafters to sea/his economy is going down the tubes, yet he seems to be the one calling the shots/faces a dire economic crisis/the economic situation is bad; there's no food, no jobs/severe shortages are common everywhere/people are hungry and desperate/conditions are deteriorating/country is in crisis/there is desperation to get out/economy is a disaster/as long as there is a way to escape the hunger and poverty that they say is afflicting them, they will continue to go/if things don't get better economically, people will continue to put out to

sea/economic problems are easily seen/no bread/they eat their one meal a day (spaghetti) without lights, without running water, without air conditioning/many professionals have given up their careers where they were paid with pesos to sell trinkets to foreign tourists

- Young people born after the revolution are totally disillusioned
- accused of selling rafts to cross the Florida straits
- "He has turned the desire of his people into a tool with which to pressure the United States to change its policy"
- trying to take advantage of the exodus of dissenters and once again is sending undesirables to American shores/will get rid of Cuban dissidents
- might try to slip in agents to cause riots at Guantanamo
- attempting to export his problems to the U.S./attempted to shift his problems to the U.S./sending his problems North/"Let them go, then its an American problem"/Castro's cynical attempt to solve his domestic problems by encouraging people to leave/has succeeded in making his problem Bill Clinton's problem/by giving the rafters the green light is getting rid of hundreds of enemies and potential security risks
- will not succeed in any attempt to dictate American immigration policy
- "Castro—immoral"
- became a tool of Soviet Union
- the Cold War ended three years ago, still Castro hangs on
- repressive government
- criticizes U.S. government for incarcerating Cubans in Guantanamo/accused United States of human rights abuses in its treatment of Cuban refugees on [Guantanamo]
- the black market is flourishing
- remains defiant/insists the army is more ready than ever to defend the island
- blamed the U.S. embargo for his problems/continues to blame the U.S. embargo for the hardships/demanded direct talks with Washington and blamed the United States embargo for the crisis/blamed the refugee crisis on the long-standing U.S. embargo/blamed the U.S. for the current refugee crisis/blamed the Clinton administration for the immigrants' nightmare/blaming the embargo for the plight of the Cuban people/blames the Americans, denies its policies are to blame/refugees are taking to the sea because of the economic hardships imposed by the thirty-one year trade ban, not because of government repression/blames the U.S. trade embargo for a long litany of economic problems/blames the United States for creating this crisis/"It's [the crisis] the consequence of the three-decade-long blockade"
- for thirty-five years he has been a thorn in America's pride/continues to play hardball with the White House/irritated Washington again/has harsh words for President Clinton—will be able to torment Washington to give in to his demands/holds a powerful hand this time; just by doing nothing he can bury the United States in unwanted refugee/rafters used as leverage to force the United States into talking

- called the [United States] immigration crackdown absurd
- called Guantanamo a concentration camp/denounced U.S. detention camps as concentration camps
- "Castro needs to be in consultation with his own folks"
- dialogue [with the United States] must wait for Fidel Castro to take some steps toward democratic reforms/economic reforms [enacted] are not enough/island's repressive government hasn't gone far enough toward reform
- delivered one of his harangues
- angry and animated
- "Cold-blooded attempt to maintain the Castro grip on Cuba and divert attention from his failed policies/encouraging the exodus to divert attention from Cuba's dire economic conditions/sooner or later he will have to change the way he is governing or export his problems to the United States [again]/hardships forcing people to leave are only going to get worse/ "Fidel Castro has to go"/as long as there is a way to escape the hunger and poverty they say is afflicting them, they will continue to go/Cuba's failed socialist system has created the problem/Castro's government is part of the problem/"As long as Castro refuses to give up a bankrupt system that is every day making Cubans more miserable, then we are always going to see Cubans trying to leave the island"/limited reforms are not enough/"The problem is Fidel Castro"/"The [Cuban] system is dead"
- condemned
- "More lives have been wasted and more lives have been lost by Fidel Castro than by any blockade that would be imposed on Cuba at this time"
- Washington will be to blame if the exodus picks up again
- uncertain whether Castro can hold up his side of the bargain and stop the refugee flow he unleashed two weeks ago
- dissent [in Cuba] is on the rise
- Castro played his last card in order to get the United States to change its policy and they didn't do it
- his regime was embarrassed by the fact that once the door was open, thousands of people risked their lives trying to flee
- "There are only 20,000 visas, what you have here are millions of people wanting to leave"

Descriptors Coded Neutral or Ambiguous
- has given refugees a green light to flee/ordered Cuban border guards not to fire on fleeing Cubans/police haven't interfered and look like they don't intend to bother/Coast Guard under orders not to interfere with anyone headed for the United States
- took power thirty-five years ago/in power for more than thirty years/the man who outlasted eight U.S. presidents
- wants to avoid drastic measures
- President

- is not to blame for the refugee crisis
- "There's a lot bad things here, but not enough to do that"/not everyone wants out
- has no idea how many refugees have left
- hopes the spotlight on the exodus forces some change in U.S.—Cuban relations
- some people openly denounce the Castro government, others defend the revolution
- claimed it was not his job to guard U.S. borders
- Cuba's maximum leader
- not on the ropes
- popular disgruntlement is not taking the form of overthrows of the government
- has never allowed refugees to come back/no indication whether Fidel Castro is prepared to take rafters back
- children and teenagers banned from taking part in the raft exodus/ordered Cuban Coast Guard to stop all unsafe boats, especially those carrying infants and children/Coast Guard ordered to detain unsafe rafts with children/ordered that children no longer be allowed to leave on rafts/trying to stop children or adolescents from boarding the rafts
- words of caution and praise for Fidel Castro [from Washington]
- listened, but did not agree to halt the current flow of refugees
- while some blame the repressive Castro government for prompting the flight, most blame severe economic hardships/main reason for exodus is economic deprivation and not political repression
- the greatest achievements [of the revolution] are health care, housing, and sports; the greatest failures are breakfast, lunch, and dinner
- even if the embargo were lifted, Cuba's problems won't be solved overnight. Much of the country's infrastructure will have to be rebuilt.
- the man in Havana who has the power to stop the refugees has to be convinced that it's worth his while to do so
- is no closer to solving his economic problems
- [agreement] captured Cuban headlines, pitched as a victory for Cuba

BALSEROS/RAFTERS

Descriptors Coded Positive
- coming despite a very dangerous journey/many are dying at sea/a dangerous journey to an uncertain future/willing to risk their lives on the open sea/continue to paddle over the treacherous waters of the Florida Straits/continue to defy death and detention/risk of death is one that Cubans are still prepared to take/risking their lives today in hopes of living better tomorrow/no one knows how many have died/most are miserable poor/"Who cares about bad weather, it's been bad here all our lives"/[woman] is desperate that she doesn't know whether her husband is dead or alive/"Crossing the Florida Straits in a raft is not a

game, it's as difficult as going over the Berlin Wall"/saying prayers for loved ones who fled by sea and whose fate in unknown/hundreds, maybe thousands, are lost at sea/entire families are risking their lives/"She's six years old—we've been at sea four days—four days without eating"

- "I'm not going to tell you I'm happy because I'm leaving behind an infinite number of people seeking the same freedom as I was"/"I'm leaving behind everyone"/husbands and wives, sons and mothers, must say goodbye
- they would rather die in prison here than be in Cuba/would rather be in an American jail than in Cuba/willing to run any risk to escape the island/could no longer endure conditions in Cuba/didn't want to live in Cuba anymore/lining the beaches, looking for a way out/hunger is fueling the exodus/"We have no choice but to leave. We don't eat, everything is lost, we have nothing"/fed up with the island's crippled economy/despair and desperation/have no other choice/continue to look to the sea as their only way out/"I don't want to live here [Cuba]"/ "No go back to Cuba—stay here"/poor, unemployed and have no immediate family to claim them/desperate to get out/claim to be casualties of Castro's Cuba/"I've been running away from misery so my daughter could be raised in a good place"/ "If we can't row out of here we're resigned to die of hunger. Its better to be in Guantanamo than here"/ "I have not job, every day the power is shut off, the gas is shut off, there's no kerosene—maybe out there its different"/if things don't get better economically, people will continue to put out to sea/wants out so that she can take better care of her child/sense of desperation
- locked up behind fences/not free
- dream of America hasn't soured yet
- hopes to live with a father he hasn't seen in fourteen years
- "Guantanamo is better than life under Castro"/if given a choice between Guantanamo and the Cuban mainland, they would rather stay here/most appeared delighted to be out of Cuba, even though they know they are headed for a refugee camp/"I will go anywhere to get out of Cuba"
- frantic to get word to relatives in Miami
- they believe in freedom; they trusted the United States
- have captured the world's attention and have underscored the economic hardships and frustrations that have caused them to leave everything behind
- agreement leaves them in limbo, no visas to the United States and no desire to go back to Cuba
- feeling of sadness and desperation

Descriptors Coded Negative
- sent a clear message that the United States would no longer bail them out

- not listening to Washington/few are heeding Washington's warnings/don't take Clinton seriously
- divorcing Cuban style—leaving women and children behind to start over in the U.S.
- *loco*/"They're crazy risking their lives on those rafts"
- "I don't want to stay in this concentration camp [Guantanamo]"
- growing hostility [at Guantanamo] could lead to a large violent demonstrations/threatening large-scale hunger strikes/turned violent/more defiant/rock throwing refugees slightly injured two U.S. Marines
- some rafters may have come from Castro's prisons
- the weaklings have left/an act of cowardice because they are abandoning their country

Descriptors Coded Neutral or Ambiguous

- hundreds prepared to leave/show no signs of staying on the island/continue to stream across the Straits of Florida/continue to look to the North/nothing persuades the Cubans to stay home/they keep coming/as long as there is a way to escape the hunger and poverty that the United States is inflicting on them, they will continue to go
- "We'll find ways to get into the United States"/trying to get to the United States anyhow/determined to get into the United States/"We'll row, we'll sail, whatever it takes"
- yesterday a privileged group, today off limits/many refugees are angry, they never expected to end up in Guantanamo, Cuba/angry over new system/Cubans and Haitians will be treated the same/"Unfair because we were at sea when the President made that decision"/ "It's not fair, it's not fair at all"/Have lost their automatic membership in Club America/unaware of change in U.S. policy
- some lost in the system
- some joyful just to have survived, some frustrated and angry/grateful to be here, but its not what they expected
- few are dying at sea
- have no idea that what awaits them is a return trip to Cuba/got on rafts believing that they enjoyed a special status/one more frustration for a people who have seen more than their share/brought to dry land, but not the promised land/"We are not cows, we are not prisoners, we are political refugees, we want to be free"/"We are political refugees, we risked our lives to be free"/"We are in a jail, in a prison, we don't have any democracy here"/"We don't want this, we want to go to the United States"/they feel they've been treated unfairly by our government and they're mad about it/"We have no chance to go to the U.S., we have no hope, this could be war"/"I will not go back to Cuba, never"/"We feel betrayed by the government of the United States"
- know they no longer have to go very far to be rescued
- must be discouraged [from leaving Cuba] because they are the raw material of the revolution

- terrible risks and change in U.S. policy have not been enough to stop the exodus/don't care what the United States says, anywhere is better than here
- looking for economic relief in the United States
- chances of winning asylum by arriving rafters is slim
- frustration is starting to show at Guantanamo
- only life they have [at Guantanamo] is the dreary one of a refugee
- floating in limbo—Cuba will not take them back, the United States will not let them in/there's no going back
- "I believe in God and I trust we will get to the United States"
- fear that Fidel Castro might try to stop them from leaving/many scrambling to get out now/many fear the open door will shut and are leaving now/don't care what comes out of the New York meetings, they just want out/negotiations are increasing Cubans' sense of urgency to get out fast/finding the urge to leave, hard to resist
- "If I were at the [New York] meetings, I'd grab the heads of those who were there and smash them together and end their stubbornness"

NOTES

1.   The Administration was indeed fortunate that the influential CANF, headed by the formidable Jorge Mas Canosa, reluctantly supported U.S. policy, claiming that short-term sacrifices had to be made to achieve the long-term goal of getting rid of Fidel Castro. Had the CANF opposed President Clinton's policy, things certainly would have been more difficult for him. As the crisis unfolded, with the support of the CANF, most of the opposition to the policy was voiced by nonelites, some on the streets in Cuba, some at sea, some in detention, and some on the streets in Miami.

2.   It became apparent watching the daily coverage that originated from Cuban beaches and at sea that as the crisis went on, the size and quality of the rafts that were taking refugees on their journeys increased significantly. Near the end of the crisis, many craft had motors and some were seen being trucked to the beaches. In the early days of the crisis they were being constructed on the beaches, more or less of pieces of scrap.

8

The Cuban Shoot-Down of "Brothers to the Rescue" Aircraft, 1996

Walter C. Soderlund

BACKGROUND

The seeming inability of the United States to respond creatively to changed Cuban circumstances, either in the talks ending the rafter crisis or in the months following, led to continued poor relations between the two countries, as outside of the area of immigration, there was no measurable improvement (Falk, 1997). On the immigration question, the terms agreed to in the September 1994 settlement to end the *balsero* crisis were further refined in May 1995 and incorporated into a formal immigration agreement, which allowed the immigration of 20,000 Cubans annually. In addition, Cubans interdicted at sea would be returned to Cuba unless exceptional circumstances could be demonstrated (Rieff, 1996; Domínguez, 1997).

While the *balsero* crisis was resolved without major incident, ironically it did lead directly to the dramatic events of February 1996 in which the Cuban Air Force shot down two small civilian aircraft flown by the Miami-based Cuban exile group, Brothers to the Rescue, killing four of its pilots. Brothers to the Rescue was formed in the context of the 1994 crisis to spot Cuban refugees in the Straits of Florida, drop water and supplies, and report their location to the U.S. Coast Guard for rescue. In carrying out these tasks the group performed admirable service.

After the end of the crisis and the formalization of immigration procedures between the United States and Cuba, the *balsero* channel of immigration dried up and Brothers to the Rescue became an organization in search of a new mission. That mission became flying over Cuban territory (Havana in particular), and dropping leaflets calling for the overthrow of Fidel Castro's government. These actions were not appreciated by Cuban authorities. By the time of the February 1996 shoot-down, Brothers to the Rescue flights over Cuba had resulted in formal protests from the Cuban government to the United States and hearings had been scheduled on whether the pilot's licence of the group's leader, José Basulto, should be revoked. Although the incident did not result in military hostilities between Cuba and the United States, in the hands of a more hard-line and impetuous U.S. leadership, it clearly could have. The actions taken to "punish Fidel" for his misdeeds (through the passage of the Helms-Burton legislation) targeted important U.S. trade partners, rather than the Cuban government directly. The extraterritorial reach of the Helms–Burton legislation created a new set of serious problems for the United States (see Lisio, 1996; LeoGrande, 1997; Roy, 1997; Smith 1997).

FINDINGS

News stories dealing with the aircraft shoot-down of February 24th, 1996, and events that followed appeared for about three weeks, beginning on February 25 and continuing until mid-March, when the Helms–Burton Bill, aimed at punishing the Castro government for the incident by "discouraging foreign investment" in Cuba, was passed by Congress and signed into law by President Clinton. The incident occurred in a presidential election year, effectively derailing what little progress had been made in Cuban–American relations during Clinton's first term, returning bilateral relations to the deep freeze, and setting in motion a new conflict between the United States and its major trading partners (chiefly Canada) over the extraterritorial application of the Helms-Burton legislation.

There were a total of twenty-eight news stories containing forty-six distinct news segments dealing with the aircraft shoot-down on the U.S. television networks. Coverage was concentrated in the week immediately following the start of the incident on February 24 (82 percent of stories) and focused largely on the shoot-down itself, the activities of the Brothers to the Rescue organization (their planned return to the site of the shoot-down to conduct a memorial service for their dead pilots), and how this might provoke a major military confrontation between the United States and Cuba. Once it was clear that a military confrontation was not likely to occur, media attention shifted to the efficacy of various U.S. strategies designed to punish Cuba, including the "embargo- tightening" provisions of the Helms-Burton legislation. Coverage, which was moderate at best, was more or less evenly divided among the networks: ABC ran eight stories, CBS ran ten, and NBC ran ten.

The language used to describe Bill Clinton and the U.S. government; Fidel Castro, his government and the Cuban Air Force; as well as José Basulto and the Brothers to the Rescue organization itself used by sources, reporters, and anchors as recorded, collated, and coded, is shown in the Appendix to Chapter 8.

Table 8.1 shows that, in a comparison with other crises studied, the volume of coverage was considerably less than might have been expected. Moreover, on other important indicators of media salience we do not see evidence of the shoot-down being treated as a major media event. For instance, only 25 percent of stories occupied the lead position; 75 percent ran in the first three positions, of these only 54 percent ran longer than three minutes, while 29 percent ran for thirty seconds or less. Video/film appeared in 71 percent of stories, half featured two or more news segments, and 39 percent of stories used a reporter in Cuba. President Clinton appeared on film in 18 percent of stories, while his Cuban rival, Fidel Castro, appeared in 25 percent.

Table 8.1
Story Characteristics N = 28

	Number		Percentage
Lead Story	7		25
1st Three Stories	21		75
Over 3 Minutes	15		54
Under 30 Seconds	8		29
Just Anchor Format	9		32
Use Of Experts	3		11
Reporter In Cuba	11		39
Two Or More News Segments	14		50
Film With Story	20		71
Film Of President Clinton	5		18
Film Of President Castro	7		25
Visual Violence	8		29
Tilt Favorable to U.S. Position on MiGs	10		37.5
Tilt Unfavorable To U.S. Position on MiGs	1		3.5
Tilt Favorable to U.S. Position on Trade	3		11
Tilt Unfavorable to U.S. Position on Trade	1		3.5
U.S. Involvement Index		3.35	

When we examine the evaluative components of the stories, we discover that U.S. journalistic coverage of the conflict tended to focus almost exclusively on the Cuban dimension of the story—the actual shoot-down—and concentrated on what the Cubans did, its possible implications, and how they should be punished for it. Very little coverage focused on the punishment that the United States had in mind for Cuba: The Cuban Liberty and Democratic Solidarity (Libertad) Act (better known as the Helms-Burton Bill, after its sponsors in the Senate and House), which was designed to target Canadian and other international businesses involved in trade and investment with Cuba. As is evident, most stories were favorably disposed towards the U.S. position on the downing of the aircraft (37.5 percent), and somewhat less so toward the notion that tightening the U.S. embargo against Cuba was an appropriate response (11 percent). Only one story was judged to be unfavorable on U.S. policy toward Castro ("not tough enough"), while another presented a sympathetic treatment of the Canadian position on Helms–Burton, and was coded unfavorable toward American policy.

Data in Table 8.2, show the number of times leading sources appeared on camera or were quoted in network news stories dealing with the incident.

Table 8.2
Number of Times Leading Sources Used (All Sources Used in Newscast)

News Source	Segment 1	Segment 2	Segment 3	Total
Bill Clinton and U. S. Government	21	8	0	29
Fidel Castro and Cuban Government	8	14	0	22
U.S. Congress	9	3	0	12
José Basulto and Brothers to the Rescue	9	1	0	10
Prominent Americans	3	3	0	6

Coverage was characterized by a rather restricted range of sources: official U.S. government sources: (the President, White House, State Department, and Pentagon), as well as members of Congress. Also heavily consulted in this crisis were "prominent Americans" (e.g., Pat Buchanan and Colin Powell). Fidel Castro and the Cuban government, and José Basulto and the Brothers to the Rescue organization also provided major input to stories. Foreign governments as well as representatives of various businesses and interest groups negatively affected by the legislation outside of the United States were virtually absent from reporting of the crisis. This provides another indicator that the non-Cuban dimension of the story was largely ignored by U.S. media.

Table 8.3
Percentage of Stories in Which Media Frames Are Used

Frame	Primary	Secondary	Tertiary	Total
Conflict containment	9	4	0	13
Violation of International Law	7	3	2	12
U.S. Foreign Policy Decision Making	3	3	5	11
Embargo Tightening	3	0	2	5
Restoration of Democracy	2	3	0	5
Extra Territoriality	1	0	0	1

Table 8.3 shows the frames employed by the networks in their coverage of the Brothers to the Rescue shoot-down and the events that it put into play. Two frames dominated coverage: (1) the need to contain the conflict so that tensions between Cuban-American exiles and Fidel Castro would not spin out of control and drag the United States into a military confrontation with Cuba; and (2) the violation of international law committed by Cuba in shooting down the two planes. Added to these were: U.S. foreign policy decision-making generally, and policy of tightening the embargo, which tended to focus on whether the various sanctions the United States imposed upon the Cuban government constituted severe enough punishment for their misdeed. The restoration of democracy frame centered on what was seen as a Cuban government that was becoming more repressive toward its citizens. In this context the excessive response in downing the two aircraft was explained as Castro's fear of Brothers to the

Rescue messages calling for the "liberation from tyranny." Discussed in only one story was the question of the "extraterritorial" application of the Helms–Burton legislation and its implications for U.S. foreign policy beyond Cuba.

There was general agreement that the Cuban action was an egregious violation of international law (in spite of some questions being raised as to whether the Brothers to the Rescue aircraft had actually penetrated Cuban airspace) and that a strong response by the United States was called for.[1] On this question, as one might have predicted (as the Republicans were in the process of selecting a challenger to confront President Clinton in the 1996 election), most contenders faulted the president for not taking actions against Cuba commensurate with the indignation of his rhetoric. As Brothers to the Rescue was planning a return by air and sea to the spot where its planes were shot down to pay respect to the four dead pilots, media framing of the incident quickly changed from the "cowardly act" itself, to how this planned memorial might get out of hand. This was not entirely fanciful speculation, as the Cuban government took an extremely nonrepentant stance toward the destruction of the Brothers to the Rescue aircraft, and claimed that if their territory were violated again, they would respond militarily as they had done before.

Here the Clinton administration drew a firm line, interestingly not only for the Cuban government, but for the Cuban-American exiles as well. In fact, both sides were warned to "behave themselves," with strict guidelines set down regarding acceptable behavior. Moreover, the U.S. Coast Guard was assigned to accompany the flotilla of small boats to make sure that they stayed in international waters and to protect them, should the Cubans do something provocative. As it turned out, bad weather and high seas kept the exiles and the Cubans far apart, and the memorial service was held without causing further incidents.

Following the dampening of a possible military crisis, the chief frame used for the remainder of the crisis on U.S. television news was that of tightening the embargo against Fidel. Significantly, in this presentation, Helms–Burton and other measures taken against Cuba were presented almost exclusively in terms of "punishing Castro." Although some passing mention was made that foreign investment in Cuba would be targeted, only one story (on ABC) provided in an in-depth treatment of the implications of extraterritoriality on countries that attempted to maintain trading relations with both the United States and Cuba, as well as the problems this created for the United States in its relations with major allies and trading partners.

The extraterritorial frame concentrated on two provisions of the Helms–Burton Bill: (1) barring executives and families of foreign companies doing business with Cuba from entering the United States (Title IV—Exclusion of Aliens), and (2) the possibility that foreign companies dealing in "confiscated properties" might be sued in U.S. courts by these properties' previous owners (Title III—Rights of Action) (Clagett, 1996).

Beginning with data in Table 8.4 we examine in detail how the various actors involved in the crisis and their positions were evaluated in media coverage.

Table 8.4
Text Evaluation of Major Participants

	U.S. MiGs (25 stories)	U.S. Trade (8 stories)	Cuba MiGs (26 stories)	Brothers MiGs (25 stories)
Favorable				
Number of Stories	10	3	1	7
Percentage	40	37.5	4	28
Neutral/Ambiguous				
Number of Stories	14	4	6	12
Percentage	56	50	23	46
Unfavorable				
Number of Stories	1	16	12	6
Percentage	4	12.5	73	24

First, there were two distinct dimensions to the crisis—the first dealing with the shoot-down of the aircraft, the second dealing with U.S. retaliation that targeted foreign business dealings with Cuba. Here news stories tended to be supportive of U.S. government positions on both these dimensions, but more supportive on the shoot-down (supportive in ten [40 percent] of twenty-five stories and negative in only one), than increased trade sanctions (supportive in three [37.5 percent] of eight stories and negative in only one). The actions of Cuba were condemned in nineteen (79 percent) of twenty-six stories, and only one presented an interpretation that was seen as favorable to Cuba's position. Brothers to the Rescue was the recipient of more or less equal positive and negative treatment—(seven [28 percent] of twenty-five stories positive, and six [24 percent] of twenty-five stories negative). Only one story dealt with the question of the extraterritorial application of trade sanctions (Helms-Burton), and it opposed the measures.

Table 8.5 presents the results of an analysis of the actual language used to describe Bill Clinton and the U.S. government; Fidel Castro, the Cuban government and military; and José Basulto and the Brothers to the Rescue organization. As mentioned, only descriptors deemed to be valenced (i.e., having a positive or negative value) are included in this analysis. Two items are of interest: the actual number of positive and negative descriptors gives an indication of the importance of each actor to network news programs in the two countries, and the actual percentage of positive and negative words and phrases provides an additional independent measure of actor evaluation.

With respect to the U.S. actors involved in the crisis, 62 percent of seventy-six evaluative words and phrases describing the United States were positive, with 38 percent negative. Negative descriptors focused largely on the U.S. government "not doing enough" to punish Castro; interestingly there was also some criticism that it had gone too far, and that the Cuban people (not Fidel Castro) would pay the price.

Fidel Castro and the Cuban authorities were the focus of the greatest amount of verbal attention on U.S. news programs (ninety-four descriptors), 85 percent negative versus 15 percent positive. Brothers to the Rescue, occasioned

Table 8.5
Percentage of Descriptors Reflecting Positively or Negatively on Major Actors

	Number of Descriptors	Percentage
Clinton/U.S. Government		
Positive	47	62
Negative	29	38
Total	76	100
Castro/Cuban Government		
Positive	14	15
Negative	80	85
Total	94	100
José Basulto/Brothers to the Rescue		
Positive	50	66
Negative	26	34
Total	76	100

the same amount of verbal commentary as did the U.S. government on television news (seventy-six valenced descriptors) and evaluation of the group tended to be quite favorable, with two-thirds of descriptors coded as positive.

CONCLUSIONS

In terms of their function to interpret the world to their audience, what can we conclude regarding the performance of U.S. network television news on the issue of the Brothers to the Rescue aircraft shoot-down?

Network television news essentially treated the shoot-down as one story with three component parts: the aircraft downing, the possibility of a military confrontation with Cuba, and the need to punish Castro through enhanced sanctions. That the third of these components (the Helms-Burton legislation) was a clear violation of international law and would create a new and different set of foreign policy problems for the United States involving its primary trading partner Canada, was virtually absent from U.S. coverage—only one story covered this aspect. While the networks were reasonably fair in airing information both supportive and opposed to U.S. policy positions, all measures of evaluation tilted in support of the U.S. government and Brothers to the Rescue and in opposition to the Cuban action and positions. Given the grim history of U.S.–Cuban relations since the 1959 revolution, this is hardly an unexpected finding.

Network news programs need to be faulted for not alerting the American people, to a far greater extent than they did, that the proposed strengthening of the anti-Castro embargo was about to spin out of control and negatively affect another sector of U.S. foreign relations—trade and investment with its major NAFTA partners, Canada and Mexico, both of whom had never participated in the U.S.-led embargo against Cuba since it had been imposed in the early 1960s. Thus, while U.S. media were on top of the possibility that the crisis might result in a military crisis between the United States and Cuba (this was the major frame in which the incident was presented), with respect to the predictable impact of the Helms-Burton sanctions on American-Canadian relations, it seemed as if they were fitted with a perfect set of blinders—they simply did not see it coming. Not foreseeing a problem, U.S. networks did little to warn the American people of the damage "getting at Fidel" through Helms-Burton was likely to do to the United States in terms of its international image (the "insensitive bully") and to its international reputation as a supporter of world-wide-free trade.

In the eyes of the U.S. government and media, the shoot-down was a decisive act. Following it, the Helms–Burton legislation that might not have gotten through Congress any other time (and if it had, would surely have been vetoed by President Clinton), not only was passed, but signed into law by the middle of March. While motivations underlying the Cuban action are somewhat speculative, its consequences are not. Castro is reported to have acknowledged that because of shoot-down, that "normal relations with the United States may never come in his lifetime"(CBS, 1996, March 2). Nothing that we have seen in the intervening years has indicated that he was wrong in this assessment.

APPENDIX 8.1

PRESIDENT CLINTON/U.S. GOVERNMENT

Descriptors Coded Positive

- "I condemn this action in the strongest possible terms"/expressed outrage at what Cuba did
- not ruling out a military response/doesn't mind Cuba knowing a military response is still an option
- will not limit itself to acting with the UN
- reaction from Washington was swift
- sent a clear message back to Cuba
- trying to craft a response that is firm but will not play into Castro's hands
- called for an emergency session of the UN Security Council
- seeking a full UN condemnation
- laid out a time line of events that challenged some of the claims of the government of Fidel Castro
- "this violation of international law will not go unanswered"
- talked tough/used stern language
- "a flagrant violation of international law"
- "it was wrong and the United States will not tolerate it"
- will compensate families/ will pay victims' families out of frozen Cuban assets
- time to tighten the embargo/will tighten the trade embargo/supporting Helms—Burton/Clinton
  and Congressional leaders agree to tighten the embargo against Cuba/squeezing Cuba with more punishment/hoped to punish the Castro regime/busy punishing Fidel Castro
- will suspend charter flights/halting charter flights
- will impose travel restrictions on Cuban diplomats/tightening restrictions on Cuban diplomats in the United States
- does not want to escalate the incident into an international crisis/wants to avoid a new showdown between Miami exile groups and the Cuban government/warned all parties to avoid a showdown/wants both sides to know what they're doing
- standing firm
- claims there were no warnings given to the aircraft
- declared a National Emergency to keep the peace in the Straits of Florida/declared a State of Emergency
- taking no chances
- hopes to intensify Cuba's shame
- had a message to Cuba and Cuban-Americans—stay away from each other

- increasingly concerned about the power of a small group of Cuban-Americans to provoke an international incident by violating Cuban airspace
- "In plain English, the United States will not tolerate unacceptable behavior by the Cuban Government"/ warned Cuba about causing trouble/ issued a stern warning to Cuba not to interfere with the planned protest
- seems to have both the facts and the law on its side
- goal is to make sure that no further confrontations at sea are possible
- State Department took Cuban warnings seriously
- ordered U.S. Coast Guard vessels to escort planes to the memorial site
- looking forward to smooth sailing based on public statements of Brothers to the Rescue
- and the government of Cuba
- monitored the flotilla/kept a close and watchful eye over today's mission
- took action against Cuba
- passed a bill tightening sanctions against Cuba

Descriptors Coded Negative
- "Wake up Bill"
- was warned something like this could happen
- acknowledged that there have been warnings [to the U.S. from Cuba]
- "this administration does not have a policy on Cuba"
- always trying to get close to Castro/moving the wrong way—coddling Castro
- criticized for relaxing travel and monetary restrictions against Cuba
- accused of lying
- "he laid an egg"
- his weak action did not match his tough rhetoric/his actions do not come near to what it takes to send Fidel Castro a stronger message
- Florida Democrats were not satisfied with his actions
- should have stopped Brothers to the Rescue flights
- decision to cut off charter flights stranded hundreds
- he should give the common people of Cuba a little more consideration/his actions against Cuba are unjust
- warning to exile groups should have been issued a long time ago
- "the Clinton administration did absolutely nothing until after the tragedy"
- distorted the episode
- has to the be the Americans' way or no way
- [Helms—Burton] violates international law
- "much prefer the American government to keep its laws to itself"

- "[Helms—Burton] will lead to total chaos in the international investment area"

Descriptors Coded Neutral or Ambiguous
- President
- a military response was unlikely/will not undertake military action/not talking about military action
- mystified as to why Cuba would shoot down civilian planes at a time when it seems to want better relations
- believes Cuba does not want to provoke another incident
- "as long as the Cuban response is reasonable, we will not intervene"
- under pressure to get tough with Castro
- refused to criticize Brothers to the Rescue
- investigating the legality of Brothers to the Rescue flights
- can't afford to look like he's letting Castro get away with murder
- Clinton administration's turn to be locked into a confrontation with Cuba
- considering a ban on Brothers to the Rescue flights
- conceded that two and possibly all three planes had violated Cuban airspace when shot
- warned Brothers to the Rescue that they must respect Cuban air space even though they do not like Fidel Castro
- FBI used Juan Pablo Roque as an informant
- tricky time for Clinton; he must stand firm against Castro and satisfy politically powerful exile groups, but must not give Republican presidential candidates an opening
- Canada is furious at the United States
- some in Congress want Clinton to be tougher on Castro; some want him to keep it under control
- may have to stop Brothers to the Rescue from flying back down to Cuba four days from now
- faces the ticklish problem of restraining exile groups in Florida from triggering another international incident
- had a blunt warning for Cuban exiles; any ship or plane entering Cuban waters or airspace would be subject to fine, imprisonment and seizure
- decided not to mention a possible ban on flights by Cuban exile groups
- [Clinton] has some flexibility to slow the impact of Helms—Burton
- [Helms—Burton] a major new challenge to foreign business

FIDEL CASTRO/CUBAN GOVERNMENT

Descriptors Coded Positive
- had seemed to be reaching out to Washington
- complained that the United States has done nothing about repeated violations of its airspace/had complained many times to the United

States about Brothers to the Rescue/provided evidence on Brothers to the Rescue activities to the U.S. government
- insists that all planes were violating their airspace/claim the incident occurred over Cuban territory/claim that Brothers to the Rescue pilots flew inside Cuba's twelve mile limit/produced evidence from downed planes found in international waters
- "It was real provocation. We have been patient, but there are limits"
- charges that two [other] small planes violated its airspace last weekend
- a clear case of provocation
- same thing that any other government would have done in a similar situation
- justified its actions/had the right to defend its waters
- may be willing to be more accommodating
- will act with utmost restraint to avoid any new incidents/promised to act with utmost restraint/trying to contain the incident—responding, but not too forcefully

Descriptors Coded Negative
- "an outrageous, unnecessary, bizarre and stupid act"
- a brutal dictator
- "explanations are neither plausible nor acceptable"
- plenty of time for Cuban pilots to do all the legal things
- "assassination on the high seas"
- put out a harsh warning to Brothers to the Rescue/"this is a warning to them and we hope they won't do it again"/sent a clear message to Brothers to the Rescue
- shot them down to teach them a lesson
- "a blatant violation of international law and norms of civilized society"/has no regard for international law/engaged in a blatant violation of international law/clearly violated international law
- "Down with Castro"
- shot down two civilian aircraft/shot down two light planes/shot down two unarmed civilian planes from America/two civilian planes were shot down by Cuban MiGs/its jets shot down two unarmed light planes/shot down two unarmed planes flown by Brothers to the Rescue/civilian planes were downed by Cuban fighters/its MiGs shot down two planes
- attacked two aircraft, downing them in international waters/downed planes were outside Cuban airspace/shot down planes in international waters
- the downing was not justified under any circumstances
- tyranny
- no justification for shooting down unarmed planes
- taking threats of peaceful opposition seriously/Castro fears internal opposition most

- cracked down on political dissidents/harassed and arrested members of protest groups/the real opposition to Castro is being put behind bars
- the Cuban Air Force was clearly waiting
- newest murders/killed four pilots a week ago
- his actions called cowardice
- dictatorship
- planted an intelligence agent in Brothers to the Rescue
- Cuban agent set a trap for Brothers to the Rescue
- attempts to deny freedom to the Cuban people
- hysterical
- "Castro is a murderer"/murdered people
- pilots were well aware they were attacking civilian, unarmed aircraft/knew aircraft were civilian and posed no threat
- Cuban pilots took joy in committing cold-blooded murder/acted in cold blood
- Cuban ground control authorized firing at aircraft six times, even though pilots described the location as outside Cuban airspace/issued the command to fire
- condemned internationally
- This is not cojones—this is cowardice"
- used animosity of the United States for severe restrictions on freedom in Cuba
- crackdown [on dissidents] drew international attention
- no apologies from the Cuban government issued
- "demonstrated a ready and reckless willingness to use excessive force"
- in July, a Cuban gunboat rammed a flotilla vessel
- repressive/a repressive regime
- "I'm so powerful that I can destroy U.S. aircraft and their pilots in the air and nothing happens to me—think about what will happen to you"
- he [Castro] raised the fear stakes in the game
- political tensions in Cuba are increasing
- "If Cuban exiles return, they should be shot down again"
- this is a message to the United States that Cuba is still a military power
- planes should only have been warned away

Descriptors Coded Neutral or Ambiguous
- Fidel Castro took full responsibility for downing the planes
- "We have the means to protect our airspace"
- seized power thirty five years ago
- claimed to have proof the plane was in Cuban airspace, but haven't shown it
- blamed the United States for organizing and financing human rights protests

- Cuban economy has gotten used to suffering under the U.S. trade embargo
- will protect itself again if provoked by terrorists/ready to do it all over again/will protect its airspace and sovereignty/will respond if provoked
- are not denying Juan Pablo Roque was a spy
- "We shot down a plane belonging to a terrorist organization in the U.S"
- vowed to keep its air force on high alert
- Castro regime
- Cuba outwardly remains calm
- timing of the shoot-down blamed on a right-wing faction in the Cuba government
- [aircraft downing] was an opportunity to say enough is enough
- are aware that they must live with the consequences of their action
- no anti-American demonstrations in Cuba
- Fidel spoke out for the first time since the shooting down of the two American planes
- "Cuba has no intention and no interest in making things worst with the United States"
- Fidel acknowledged that because of the shoot down, normal relations with the United States may never come in his lifetime
- ready to strike if its territory was crossed
- for the most part [Cubans on the street] ignored what was happening

JOSÉ BASULTO/BROTHERS TO THE RESCUE

Descriptors Coded Positive
- Miami-based rescue organization routinely flying over the Straits of Florida looking for rafters/group helping refugees fleeing Cuba/flying off the coast of Cuba for years helping Cuban boat people/Florida exile rescue group/began by flying humanitarian missions/acting on behalf of human life
- nonviolent/nonviolent organization
- insist their aircraft remained 12 mile off Cuba/were outside Cuban airspace
- two planes were shot down- one 5 miles, one 16 miles outside Cuban airspace
- its Cessnas were blown out of the sky by Cuban fighter jets
- anti-Castro group
- intended to raise the spirits of those opposing Castro
- "innocent of doing anything of a violent nature at that time or ever before"
- planning a memorial service where its planes were shot down/will send a plane and a flotilla of boats to the spot where its planes were shot down/planning a memorial service/want a proper memorial for the four downed pilots/planning a memorial service at sea for the four downed

pilots/want to conduct a memorial service for the four downed pilots/"We have to have a decent funeral for our pilots"/"I will exercise my right once again to be there"/would fly again to the scene/will return to the spot where its planes were blown out of the sky/planning to take two planes to where earlier planes were shot down/had the right to honor their dead comrades

- promising to play by the rules/have promised no problems/will conduct a peaceful and orderly memorial service/will not cross into Cuban airspace
- "purpose of the operation was to cast a message within the island"
- "We shall prevail"
- "We're going to continue our mission and the mission is not only to help rafters but to help a nation reach freedom through acts of civil disobedience"
- recommitted to foster democracy in Cuba
- support the struggle by all Cubans for a free and democratic Cuba
- a free Cuba is the only thing that would stop their search-and-rescue mission
- "We will resist the dictatorship—we will fight for our basic human rights"
- "I lost a Father but I know his death was not in vain—Helping Cuba, that's all he ever wanted to do"
- went nowhere near Cuba last weekend

Descriptors Coded Negative

- strayed from their mission and dropped pro-democracy leaflets over Havana/on at least two occasions dropped leaflets on Havana/dropped anti-Castro literature over the island/dropped anti-Castro leaflets over Havana/have violated Cuban airspace before/violated Cuban airspace before to drop anti-Castro leaflets over Havana
- one plane did briefly enter Cuban airspace/planes were in Cuban airspace/after being warned, allegedly came within five to six miles of the Cuban coast/Basulto's plane flew three miles inside Cuban airspace
- pirates
- their deaths should serve as a lesson to others
- engaged in a provocation for which they were shot down/engaged in a series of provocations/ conducted hundreds of missions near and over Cuba/flying in the teeth of repeated warnings by the Cubans to stay away/warned repeatedly by Cuba to stay out of its airspace were looking for trouble/"They harassed our air force, violated our airspace, dropped leaflets on our capital and engaged in other acts of provocation"
- one plane was well within Cuban airspace and intended to drop leaflets
- filed false flight plans
- has a history of provoking the Cuban government

- FAA considered revoking Basulto's pilot's license
- warned by FAA about the dangers of provoking Cuba
- an act bordering on conscious provocation
- "He [Basulto] seems to be a slow learner"
- terrorists/a terrorist organization/terrorist group trying to smuggle arms and explosives into Cuba
- not peaceful
- planned attacks on Cuban military, state security and Fidel Castro himself

Descriptors Coded Neutral or Ambiguous

- Cuban-American exile group/Cuban exiles/Cuban-American organization/Cuban exile group/exile group out of Florida/Miami-based group
- founder of the Cuban exile group, Brothers to the Rescue/founder of Brothers to the Rescue/leader of exile group
- "if we crossed the line, we did not know it and didn't intend to do so"
- not welcome in Cuba
- denounced accusations made by its former pilot [Juan Pablo Roque]
- talking military action
- still highly aroused/passions are running high/sparked outrage in Miami's exile community
- defiant
- U.S. Coast Guard will make sure the group stays out of Cuban territory
- will have no problems as long as they stay out of Cuban waters
- group responsible for the planes that were shot down

NOTE

1.   Whether the Cubans technically violated international law in shooting down these aircraft, under the circumstances in which it occurred, is by no means clear. There were a number of distinct factors involved in the shoot-down, and international law in the area was evolving. That the shoot-down violated the "spirit" of that evolving international law, however, appears beyond dispute (see Soderlund and Brown-John, 1999).

9

Conclusion

Walter C. Soderlund

At the time of the attempted coup in Trinidad and Tobago in late July and early August 1990, the Cold War was wheezing badly and looking quite pale. A little more than a year later, by the time of the Haitian coup in September 1991, the Cold War had expired, its grave had been dug, and the corpse was being prepared for burial. As John Kenneth White observed, "From the mid-twentieth century to 1991, war and near war gave Americans a fixed sense of who the enemy was and who we were" (White, 1997, p. 260). The demise of the Cold War changed this as it signalled the end of the 40-year-old ideological/ military/economic struggle between the United States and the USSR, leaving the United States as the one remaining superpower. In this new international configuration the United States was now referred to as the world's hegemonic power and there was considerable speculation among academics regarding what President Bush's New World Order might look like and what would drive U.S. foreign policy under it (see Blight and Weiss, 1992; Fascell, 1992–93; Casteñeda; 1993, Morales, 1994; Norris, 1995). The research reported in this book has attempted to analyze the foreign policy choices open to the United States in dealing with hemispheric conflict and crisis and to show how United States network television news interpreted these crises to the American people under the tempestuous circumstances that followed the Cold War.

That public perceptions of world events are influenced by mass media is indisputable. Perceptions of reality are shaped not only by what we experience directly in our daily lives, but by what we read, see, and hear in various mass communication channels. The further away an event is removed from us, the greater the relative impact of mass media vis-à-vis direct experience. As a consequence, for most international crises, we draw inferences and make judgments regarding what is happening, who is responsible, and what the likely impact will be for the United States, largely on the basis of what is reported in the mass media. Faraway events become "real" for us on the basis of what is reported, what is not reported, and the spin placed on that which is reported

(Smith, 1980). In this formula, it is important to point out that our reality does not include that which is not reported.

Most scholars agree that media provide the lenses through which mass publics view the world, but the question of who focuses these lenses remains:—media organizations or major political leaders, whether in the United States or elsewhere (Bennett, 1990; Alexseev and Bennett, 1995; Jakobsen, 1996; Mermin, 1997)? We do not believe that a fixed formula can answer this question. Prior research has indicated that in most cases of conflict definition, government officials take the pre-eminent role. However, much of the research on which this conclusion is based was done during the Cold War and the research reported in this volume shows that in a number of post–Cold War crises media organizations were given very little guidance from the U.S. government. In the absence of heavy government influence in setting the media agenda, media understandably appear to have more power to define situations independently (Livingston and Eachus, 1995). Specifically, it is possible for media to see events as unique occurrences growing out of their own historical and social contexts and capable of being resolved without the involvement of the United States. In these circumstances, framing applied to crises appears more consistent with journalists' own conception of what issues are involved, combined with a sensitivity to what kinds of news the public wishes to see and hear. Absent is any overriding view of the world or the dangers confronting the United States in the new order.

Regardless of whether the media are left on their own or are given direction through extensive elite political participation in the construction of news stories, the result is similar. Through the content and tone of crisis coverage, media have the unique capacity to define the issues and shape the images of the leaders involved, both in the United States and in the country where the crisis is occurring. This is an awesome responsibility and it is important that media be held accountable for their performance, and that ordinary citizens come to understand the process through which they receive critical information about our increasingly interdependent world.

In drawing conclusions from this study, which focuses on U.S. network television news coverage of seven post–Cold War crises in the Caribbean basin, we need to examine two distinct, but related dimensions: (1) the actual foreign policy responses of the U.S. government (under both the Bush and Clinton administrations) to these crises, and (2) the character of media coverage of them. In addition, in the relationship between these two dimensions, we are interested in examining the extent to which the former influenced the latter. In this discussion, Lance Bennett's theory of "indexing," which posits that media coverage of and positions taken on events by mass media are closely related to the volume and tone of commentary on the part of Washington-based politicians (Bennett, 1990), provides our major frame of reference.

U.S. FOREIGN POLICY—RELUCTANT HEGEMON

U.S. foreign policy in Caribbean Basin in the early years after the end of the Cold War can best be described as reactive and cautious (see Bryan, 1997). Given the possible hegemonic role of the United States, it is significant that none of the seven crises studied was initiated by the United States. Further at least three of the crises examined (Trinidad and Tobago, Haiti in 1991 and Chiapas) show unmistakably that the United States was following a strategy that at best can be described as risk avoidance with respect to direct involvement. Evidence confirming this strategy may be seen in the extreme reluctance of U.S. politicians and official spokespersons to provide anything but the most minimal responses regarding these crises on television news. In total, for these three crises, Presidents Bush and Clinton were used as sources six times (actually appearing on television news a total of five times); their administrations were used as sources nine times; and members of Congress were virtually absent as news sources. It is hard to imagine less adventurous responses from U.S. political leaders.

If one leaves aside the potential of a Libyan connection in the case of the Trinidad and Tobago crisis, a good case can be made that the coup occurring there should not have involved the United States. However, with respect to the Haitian coup and the Zapatista rebellion, such an argument is hard to sustain. The United States had been heavily involved in Haiti for most of the twentieth century, and was committed to developing democratic government there after the end of the Duvalier dictatorship in 1986. Given that the 1991 coup put a halt to this process, could the United States simply sit on the sidelines, allow the military to rule, and let events follow their own course? As events in Haiti between fall 1991 and 1994 demonstrate, the answer to this question is clearly "no", yet the U.S. response to the coup was characterized by verbal support and an embargo to bring about Aristide's return, but there was no commitment of U.S. military resources to accomplish this.

Chiapas also presented a huge challenge to the United States and its strategy of promoting democracy and justice in the Western Hemisphere through economic integration and free trade. NAFTA marked a major undertaking in this strategy and was the first attempt at integrating First World and Third World economies in a comprehensive free-trade agreement. Because Mexico borders on the United States, an insurrection occurring there would be seen as extremely important for no other reasons than those involving conventional security. Potentially at least, a great deal was at stake in Chiapas, yet the response of the United States to the Zapatista rebellion was clearly to ignore it and hope for the best. In short, if the U.S. had the slightest inclination to play a hegemonic role in the Caribbean Basin, there were ample reasons for it to have intervened in any of these three crises far more forcefully than it did.

The U.S. reaction to the Cuban shoot-down of the Brothers to the Rescue aircraft showed an intermediate intensity of response. It certainly could be argued that the Helms-Burton legislation was a significant response, although President Clinton and, after him George W. Bush, have opted to suspend the implementation of Title III (Rights of Action), the most objectionable provision of the legislation from the perspective of international law. However, given the violent nature of the attack against U.S. citizens by one of the most dedicated opponents of the United States, it would not be hard to imagine the United States using the incident to dispense with a long troublesome thorn in its side, especially because Cuba's Cold War protector was no longer in the picture. This did not happen, and the Clinton administration took serious measures to prevent further incidents that might lead to armed conflict between Cuba and the United States. In this matter, it is significant that conflict containment was the main interpretive frame seen in television news coverage of the shoot-down crisis.

Three Caribbean basin crises studied plainly did involve the United States in significant responses: Haiti in 1993 and 1994 and Cuba in 1994. In these cases, however, I would argue that the United States had little choice but to get involved, and that its involvement tended to be at the minimum level possible given the circumstances. In all instances the refugees fleeing Haiti and Cuba due to political repression and economic hardship ended up as problems (for U.S. Coast Guard, immigration, and social service providers) that were so significant that they could not be ignored. Even in these cases, we see a U.S. reluctance to respond decisively. In the Haitian crisis in October 1993, there was the very embarrassing withdrawal of a U.S. Navy vessel in the face of what most would argue was a minimal challenge posed by a poorly organized group of thugs. Although there is no doubt that in 1994 the United States was committed to a significant military invasion of Haiti, this clearly was a strategy of last resort; when presented at the last moment with the opportunity to negotiate the generals' withdrawal, this was the policy choice followed by the United States. Also, in Cuba in 1994 the United States did in fact do what it said it wouldn't do to resolve the crisis--negotiate with Fidel Castro; albeit, in the negotiations, the United States refused to discuss loosening or terminating of the trade embargo.

In general, these responses do not seem out of step with the thrust of U.S. foreign policy more broadly during the immediate post–Cold War period and are consistent with the description offered by Larry Berman and Emily Goldman of the first two years of Clinton's foreign policy as "characterized by vacillation, indecision, and the lack of a guiding principle or compass that might provide bearing for leaders and a direction for followers on a set of policies or a Clinton doctrine" (Berman and Goldman, 1996, p. 291). This harsh judgement is shared by George Edwards III:

> In 1992 Bill Clinton attacked George Bush for "a basic pattern of
> reactive, rudderless and erratic U.S. diplomacy." He claimed that
> Bush displayed "activism without vision, prudence without purpose
> and tactics without strategy." His remarks did not make much of an
> impression at the time, but the irony is that he now faces these same
> criticisms—and people are listening. (1996, p. 242)

Nor did Mr. Clinton's performance on the international scene appear to improve. Near the end of Clinton's presidency, John Chipman, Director of the London-based International Institute for Strategic Studies, concluded that "once the U.S. was thrust forward as the 'last superpower,' Mr. Clinton has shown no more grasp than his many critics of how to shape the international order…His approach to foreign policy has been mostly reactive; all too often action has been delayed until the breaking point, when disproportionate means were then thrown into the breach" (as quoted in Taylor, 2000). With the exception of the U.S.-led effort to expel Iraq from Kuwait in the Gulf War of late 1990/early 1991, the pattern of risk avoidance that we have seen demonstrated by the United States in the Caribbean Basin would appear similar to the less-than-forceful U.S. foreign policy responses to crises occurring in the former Yugoslavia and Africa in the same period.[1]

PATTERNS OF MEDIA FRAMING

If a cautious, risk-avoidance approach is an accurate characterization of U.S. foreign policy in the early post–Cold War period, how did U.S. television network news report these crises to the American people? And were there any identifiable patterns in how the crises were framed?

Our first observation is that following Bennett's theory of indexing, there is a near perfect Spearman Rank Order Correlation (+.964) between our measure of U.S. involvement and volume of coverage based on number of television new stories a crisis generated.[2] Moreover, if we create a "media attention" index[3] based on the five separate measures of media interest shown in Table 9.1, we calculate a Spearman Rank Order Correlation of +.857. Clearly, as U.S. interests became more involved in a crisis, television news coverage increased dramatically (Bennett, 1990).

In explaining this relationship we need to point out that political elites hold unique power to define whether a particular crisis poses a threat to the United States; and they do this through mass media. Importantly, in the cases of the Trinidad and Tobago coup and the Zapatista rebellion, U.S. political elites, largely through their silence, indicated that these events did not affect U.S. national security issues to any significant extent. Also, the way that political elites commented on the Cuban shoot-down of the Brothers to the Rescue aircraft sought to minimize the incident as a military threat to the United States, stressing instead that it was a cowardly act of a dictator out of touch with both his people and international law. In fact, only in the case of the projected U.S. invasion of Haiti in 1994 do we see evidence of political leaders using television news in a coordinated way to mobilize the American people behind a policy of engagement. It must be pointed out, however, that counter elites were at least equally effective in presenting their case for U.S. non-involvement.

Also of interest in assessing the role of mass media is the evaluation or spin that their coverage gave to U.S. foreign policy. Data in Table 9.2 are again arranged according to intensity of U.S. involvement (1.25 to 4.5) On this dimension, we find that network television news on the whole tended to give positive evaluations to the cautious direction followed by the Bush and Clinton administrations in the Caribbean Basin. The Spearman Rank Order Correlation between intensity of U.S. involvement and percentage differences between positive and negative evaluations (PD) was calculated at +.411 (Ma and

Table 9.1
Relationship Between U.S. Involvement and Media Attention

Crisis	U.S Involvement Index	Number of Stories	Leads	Top 3 Placements	Long Stories	Anchor/ Reporter Format	Multiple News Segments	Total
Chiapas	1.25	16	.06	.19	0	.62	0	1.41
Trinidad and Tobago	1.4	15	.47	.67	0	.67	0	1.81
Haiti, 1991	2.1	20	.05	.25	0	.50	0	1.25
Cuba, 1996	3.35	28	.25	.75	.54	.68	.50	2.72
Haiti, 1993	3.5	63	.35	.66	.31	.73	.31	2.36
Cuba, 1994	4.0	80	.35	.61	.61	.91	.58	3.06
Haiti, 1994	4.5	93	.53	.76	.61	.90	.43	3.23

Hildebrandt, 1993). The correlation here is not nearly as high as those seen above between U.S. involvement and volume of coverage and the media attention index, but keeping in mind all the exigencies involved in the different crises, on balance we see a moderate but discernable tendency toward media support for the low-profile role its leaders chose for the United States in the early post–Cold War world.

Table 9.2
Relationship Between U.S. Involvement and Media Attention

Crisis	U.S Involvement Index	Percent Positive	Percent Negative	Percentage Difference
Chiapas	1.25	6	13	-07
Trinidad and Tobago	1.4	60	0	+60
Haiti, 1991	2.1	55	10	+45
Cuba, 1996	3.35	38	4	+34
Haiti, 1993	3.5	10	45	-35
Cuba, 1994	4.0	9	24	-15
Haiti, 1994	4.5	22	28	-05

In specific comparisons regarding framing, keeping in mind that they all involved domestic political conflict, we will treat the two coups and the Chiapas insurgency as one group of crises; and the three refugee/dictatorial governments crises, all directly involving the United States as the recipient of the refugees, as a second group. The Brothers to the Rescue shoot-down was a discrete act of military violence that does not fit cleanly into either category.

COUPS AND INSURRECTIONS

The major characteristic of media coverage of the domestic conflict group of crises is that of minimal coverage: fifteen stories on the Trinidad and Tobago coup, twenty on the Haitian coup, and sixteen on the Zapatista rebellion. In addition to these meagre numbers, this group of crises scores lowest overall on the media attention index.

A second distinguishing feature of this group is that U.S. government officials were used very sparingly as sources. Those U.S. sources that did not appear at all are perhaps as important as those who appeared infrequently. In this regard, that members of Congress, from whom opposition to administration policy is expected to flow, were scarcely seen or heard on network television news is indicative that little partisan gain was seen in opposing the minimal-risk strategies being followed by the Bush and Clinton administrations.

However, not on every dimension of television news coverage are these crises similar. When we compare the extent to which the key personalities associated with the initiation of violence are given media attention, major differences in treatment become apparent. This is most noticeable in the extensive media attention given Abu Bakr, and the virtual dismissal of Subcomandante Marcos. Media treatment of Raoul Cédras, the Haitian coup maker, occupies an intermediate position. He was used very sparingly in coverage of the coup. However, as the Haitian crisis moved to the restoration phases, media attention to him increased in 1993 and especially in 1994, when he rivalled Presidents Clinton and Aristide in on-screen appearances.

We find both similarities and differences in media framing of these crises. Violence and the need for the United States to craft appropriate foreign policy response are frames common to all three events. Violence in the Trinidad and Tobago coup was presented as episodic and formed an important component of the hostage crisis frame that dominated in media coverage. Reports include violence that took place in launching the coup, the supposed wiring of hostages to explosives, the shooting of the Prime Minister, and the burning and looting of Port of Spain. Likewise, in the Chiapas rebellion, violence, presented as an episodic outburst, predominated in framing. In this case, violence focused almost exclusively on the efforts of the Mexican army to dislodge the rebel Zapatistas. While the violent acts of the Zapatistas in capturing the towns they occupied briefly were mentioned in commentary, all of the important visual content tended to show the Zapatistas as victims of violence, rather than the perpetrators of it. In contrast, violence in the Haitian coup was primarily thematic and tied into both the restoration of democracy and societal instability frames. Violence appeared in text as well as in visuals and focused on the killing of Aristide supporters by the army and police, both in carrying out the coup and in their consolidation of control in its aftermath. Dead bodies left on the street dominated violent visual content. The episodic portrayal of violence in Trinidad and Tobago and Mexico is consistent with the nonreactive tone of U.S. foreign policy. In Haiti, the situation is more complex. On the one hand, violence tied into the restoration of democracy frame would be consistent with strong U.S. efforts to restore President Aristide. On the other hand, linking violence to societal instability conveyed the distinct impression that, regardless of who controlled the Haitian government, pacifying Haitian society would be no easy task. With this pessimistic spin, the U.S. policy of a response limited to a trade embargo appeared in a favorable light.

Other than the violence frame juxtaposed to the discussion of post–Cold War foreign policymaking, we fail to find any dominant thread replacing the Cold War as a frame in the group of crises related to domestic conflict and violence. Instead, we find that largely idiosyncratic factors surrounding the events themselves tended to dictate the frames that were used to interpret them. In Trinidad and Tobago the uncertainty regarding the outcome for the hostages and the bizarre character of Abu Bakr and his organization drove television news coverage. In Haiti the need to restore President Aristide was central; however, this was presented in a way that would not involve the U.S. directly. In Chiapas, while violence linked to issues of long-standing aboriginal abuse drove coverage, the rebellion was linked neither to NAFTA nor to the need for an U.S. response to it.

GENERALS AND REFUGEES

How conflict is constructed, both by the governments that craft the policies to deal with it and by the media that report on and analyze it for mass publics, has been our primary focus; in cases involving Haiti and Cuba in 1994 we have the opportunity for a unique comparison. Both crises involve a very similar set of elements: (1) dictatorial governments out of favor with the United States (to the extent that there were programs of economic sanctions in place to remove them); (2) worsening economic conditions leading to greater numbers of refugees streaming from the Caribbean toward U.S. shores; and (3) the potential for negative domestic political fallout from the refugee dimension that would be likely to ensue either from action taken by the United States to resolve the problem or from continued inaction.

These similarities not withstanding, the Haitian and Cuban crises were handled in significantly different ways by the Clinton administration. Further, it is evident from an examination of media coverage of these events, that although television news reporting was quite hostile to President Clinton's foreign policy performance (in general, as well as specifically toward the two Caribbean countries), the way television network news actually framed the situations served to give Clinton an unexpected bonus. That coverage neither challenged, nor called attention to, the fundamentally different ways that two similar situations (taking place literally next door to each other) were being handled, suggested to the American public the compartmentalization of policies to deal with them. This gave President Clinton far more flexibility in his responses than a more rigorous comparative analysis, highlighting the linkages and contradictions, would have allowed.

Extensive media coverage characterized all three of these crises U.S. government spokespersons and members of Congress were used extensively as sources. Moreover, considerable use was made of the people actually involved in the crises—Haitians on the street and Cuban rafters—as well as political figures from both countries involved.

In coverage of Haiti in 1993 and 1994, media framing focused on the negative impact of the generals, not only on the human rights of people in Haiti, but on the cause of democracy in the Western Hemisphere more generally. While this construction could have been linked to the domestic U.S. goal of ending the flow of Haitian refugees into the country, importantly, such a connection was not made in any sustained way. This is an interesting omission; if he had made such a link, President Clinton would have made his task of selling the need for a military intervention to the American people much easier by establishing the connection to a well-understood national interest (see Mandelbaum, 1996; Edwards III, 1996; DiPrizio, 2000).

On the other hand, media framing of Cuban crisis focused on the plight of desperate people fleeing poverty, who seemingly were caught between the conflicting wills of two governments—U.S. and Cuban. In this framing, although the Cuban government, due to its restrictive economic policies, was held at least partially responsible for the problem, the U.S. government, both through the trade embargo and the change in immigration policy that detained interdicted refugees to Guantanamo Bay, was portrayed as the more significant contributing agent to the crisis. While this construction was overtly critical of the United States, it also was compatible with the U.S. policy of addressing the crisis solely in terms of ending the flow of refugees and of not needing to deal with the so-called "root causes" of human suffering, either by terminating the embargo or moving against an undemocratic and repressive regime. These differences in framing—in Haiti, human rights abuses and restoration of democracy and in Cuba, human interest concerns related to refugees—are underscored by the visuals that accompanied stories: refugees at sea-- Haiti 3 percent, Cuba 89 percent; refugees in detention—Haiti 4 percent, Cuba 53.5 percent; dead bodies—Haiti 36 percent, Cuba 1 percent.

Divergent framing in media coverage is especially evident as two of the crises were taking place virtually at the same time in summer and early fall 1994. On August 19, President Clinton ended the so-called "double standard" that existed in U.S. foreign policy with respect to the treatment of Cuban and Haitian refugees, but he left unmentioned, and media left largely untouched, the emerging double standard in the treatment of the Cuban and Haitian governments. In the case of Haiti, a major U.S. military invasion was about to be launched to unseat the generals, while for Cuba, and the Castro government, the most the United States was prepared to do was to leave in place an embargo that had failed for mare than thirty years to dislodge the Cuban dictator from power.

That U.S. television news failed to seize upon this discrepancy is especially significant, given the generally hostile stance the U.S. media adopted toward Clinton's overall foreign policy performance, and their pointed criticisms of the specific policies advanced to deal with both the Cuban and Haitian crises. In spite of clear negative media evaluations of U.S. positions on both crises, television news did interpret each crisis more or less in the way advanced by the U.S. government. Moreover, media never raised in any sustained way the contradictions inherent in the way the two similar situations were being dealt with and defined.

Overall trends in U.S. foreign policy in the Caribbean Basin and media framing of that policy appear to confirm that "as the years have passed since the collapse of the Soviet Empire, it is obvious that the U.S. government planned for every Cold War contingency but one: victory" (White, 1997, p. 254). Neither the Bush nor the Clinton administrations appeared to have been guided by any over-arching principles in dealing with foreign relations. Moreover, Presidential Decision Directive 25 (PDD25), drafted in the apprehensive environment after the death of 18 U.S. Army Rangers in a Somalian peace-enforcement operation in fall 1993, placed many restrictive conditions on the commitment of American troops and "made it clear that peacekeeping operations would not be central to the new administration's policy on the use of force" (DiPrizio, 2000, p. 4). At least in part as a consequence of the lack of firm government direction in responding to post–Cold War violence, no dominant pattern in post–Cold War media framing emerged, save that the world was a violent place, and that in some fashion U.S. foreign policy would have to at least pay some attention to, if not deal with, that violence.

The policy vacuum at the governmental level gave media considerably more power to define what was happening in the world, interpret how this affected the United States, and offer suggestions on what needed to be done. In spite of this opportunity, U.S. television news organizations did not take it upon themselves to offer any solutions to the violence springing up in various places in the Western Hemisphere; in this sense there was no evidence of Cohen's "the press as policy maker role" (Cohen, 1963, pp. 39–45). Television news producers tended to set the level of attention given a crisis to the extent of official Washington's involvement; and in the tone of that coverage, appeared to be more supportive of limited engagement on the part of the United States than of U.S. interventions to resolve them. In short, neither the U.S. government nor the country's most important media outlets appeared eager to accept the role of "hegemon" thrust upon the United States at the end of the Cold War. The United States approached crises very circumspectly, even those occurring in the part of the world where it had first cut its teeth as an imperial power in the early decades of the twentieth century. Arguably destabilizing events in the Caribbean would have a greater impact on the United States than would be the case if they had happened in Europe, Asia, or Africa. Even so, U.S. responses to crisis events occurring there were, if possible, muted, and if forced by circumstances to become involved, responses undertaken by the United States tended to be at the minimum level necessary.

With the obvious exception of the 1989 invasion of Panama to dispose of General Manuel Noriega in the dying days of the Cold War, there is precious little evidence that the United States indulged in "neo-Monroeism" with respect to its Caribbean neighbors. In spite of fears of "military paternalism" and "neo-imperialism" (Blight and Weiss, 1992; Morales, 1994), in the absence of a well-defined foreign threat, there was little to mobilize an active interest in the region in the decade after the end of the Cold War.

The positive response pattern of U.S. media to this policy of restraint should not necessarily be interpreted negatively. Much of the criticism of U.S. media during the Cold War centered precisely on the "too close" relationship between media and the government (see Herman and Brodhead, 1984; Parenti, 1986; Herman and Chomsky, 1988). In the circumstances surrounding the end of the Cold War, it may be that in the absence of government guidance, media interpretations of complex world events may turn out to be far richer than was characteristic of coverage during the Cold War. If this is to be the case, the nation's mass media need to take far greater advantage of their freedom from government direction than was evident in their coverage of the crises studied in this book.

NOTES

1.   Michael Mandelbaum argues that there was indeed a Clinton vision of foreign policy centered on attempting to ameliorate social and economic hardships within borders of countries peripheral to U.S. national interests (see Mandelbaum, 1996). Our analysis would indicate that, at least with respect to Haiti, had not the Clinton administration been pressured by domestic political concerns (chiefly refugees fleeing the island to the United

States), the deplorable domestic conditions in Haiti would not have resulted in the 1994 U.S. invasion/occupation (see DiPrizio, 2000).

2.   The formula used to calculate the Spearman Rank Order Correlation is

$$r_s = 1 - \frac{6 \sum_{i=1}^{N} D_i^2}{N\left(N^2 - 1\right)}$$

3.   The Media Attention Index combines the percentages each crisis generated on five indicators of media interest: Percentage of lead stories, percentage of stories run in the first three positions in the newscast; percentage of stories longer than three minutes in length, percentage of stories in the anchor/reporter format, and the percentage of stories with two or more news segments. The potential range of the index would be zero to five. The actual range of scores ran from 1.25 to 3.23.

References

Abbott, E. (1988). *Haiti: An Insider's History of the Rise and Fall of the Duvaliers.* New York: Simon and Schuster.

Ackerman, H. (1996). "The Balsero Phenomenon, 1991–1994." *Cuban Studies,* 26, 160–200.

Ackerman, H., and Clark, J. (1995). *The Cuban Balseros: Voyage of Uncertainty.* Miami, FL: Policy Center of the Cuban American National Council.

Alexseev, A., and Bennett, W.L. (1995). "For Whom the Gates Open: News Reporting and Government Source Patterns in the United States, Great Britain, and Russia." *Political Communication,* 12, 395–412.

Alger, D. (1989). *The Media and Politics.* Englewood Cliffs, NJ: Prentice-Hall.

Allison, G., and Zelikow, P. (1999). *The Essence of Decision: Explaining the Cuban Missile Crisis.* 2nd. ed. Addison Wesley Longman.

Anderson, M. (1998). "'What's to Be Done with 'Em?' Images of Mexican Cultural Backwardness in the United States Press, 1913–1915." *Mexican Studies/Estudios Mexicanos,* 14, 23–71.

Aristide, J-B. (1990). *In the Parish of the Poor: Writings from Haiti.* Amy Wilentz (trans. and ed.) Maryknoll, New York: Orbis.

Barkin, S. (1989). "Coping with the Duality of Television News." *American Behavioral Scientist,* 33, 153–156.

Beer, D. (2001). *The Partnership of Peacebuilding: A Case Study of Justice Development in Haiti.* Unpublished Master's Thesis, Department of Political Science, University of Windsor, Ontario, Canada.

Bellegarde-Smith, P. (1990). *Haiti: The Breached Citadel.* Boulder, CO: Westview Press.

Benjamin, M. (1995). "Interview: Subcomandante Marcos." In E. Katzenberger (ed.) *First World, Ha Ha Ha! The Zapatista Challenge.* San Francisco: City Lights Books.

Bennett, W.L. (1988). *News: The Politics of Illusion.* 2nd. ed. New York: Longman.

Bennett, W.L. (1990). "Toward a Theory of Press-State Relations in the United States." *Journal of Communication,* 40, 103–125.

Berman, L., and Goldman, E. (1996). "Clinton's Foreign Policy at Midterm." In C. Campbell and B. Rockman, (eds.), *The Clinton Presidency: First Appraisals.* Chatham, NJ: Chatham House Publishers.

Best, L. (1990, September). "Wiser than Gulliver." *Trinidad and Tobago Review,* 12, 1; A-D.

Blalock, H. (1972). *Social Statistics.* 2nd. (ed.) New York: MacGraw-Hill.

Blight, J., and Weiss, T. (1992). "Must the Grass Suffer? Thoughts on Third World Conflicts after the Cold War." *The Third World Quarterly,* 18, 63–73.

Bohning, D. (1998, July 11). "Power Struggle in Leaderless Haiti Takes Toll on Fledgling Democracy." *The Miami Herald,* 19-A.

Bosworth, B., Collins, S., and Lustig, N., (eds.) (1997). *Coming Together? Mexico-United States Relations.* Washington, DC: Brookings Institution.

Bryan, A. (1997). "The New Clinton Administration and the Caribbean: Trade, Security and Regional Politics." *Journal of Interamerican Studies and World Affairs,* 39, 101–120.

Burbach, R. (1994). "Roots of the Postmodern Rebellion in Chiapas." *New Left Review,* 205, 113–124.

Castañeda, J. (1993). *Utopia Unarmed: The Latin American Left After the Cold War.* New York: Alfred A. Knopf.

CBS "Evening News." (1996, March 2).

Chopra, J. (1998). "Introducing Peace-Maintenance." *Global Governance,* 4, 1–18.

Chrétien, R. (1997). "Some Views from a Close Friend." Address to the Carnegie Foundation Seminar, *Face to Face.*

Clagett, B. (1996). "Title III of the Helms-Burton Act Is Consistent with International Law." *The American Journal of International Law,* 90, 434–440.

Clark, J., Lasaga, J., and Reque, S. (1981). *The Mariel Boatlift: An Assessment and Prospect.* Washington, DC: Council for Inter-American Security.

Cleaver, H. (1998). "The Zapatistas and the Electronic Struggle." In J. Holloway and E. Peláez, (eds.), *Zapatista! Reinventing Revolution in Mexico.* London: Pluto Press, 81–103.

Cohen, B. (1963). *Press and Foreign Policy.* Princeton NJ: Princeton University Press.

Collier, G., with Quaratiello, E. (1994). *Basta! Land and the Zapatista Rebellion in Chiapas.* Oakland, CA: The Institute for Food and Development Policy.

Collihan, K., and Danopoulos, C. (1993). "Coup d'Etat Attempt in Trinidad: Its Causes and Failure." *Armed Forces and Society,* 19, 315–329.

Conger, L. (1994). "Mexico: Zapatista Thunder." *Current History,* 93, 115–120.

Constable, P. (1992–93). "Dateline Haiti: Caribbean Stalemate." *Foreign Policy,* 89, 175–190.

Daily Express. (1990). *Trinidad Under Siege: The Muslimeen Uprising, 6 Days of Terror.* Port of Spain, Trinidad: Trinidad Express Newspapers Ltd.

Danner, M. (1993a, November 4). "Haiti on the Verge." *The New York Review of Books,* 40, 25–30.

Danner, M. (1993b, November 18). "The Prophet." *The New York Review of Books,* 40, 27–36.

Danner, M. (1993c, December 2). "The Fall of the Prophet." *The New York Review of Books,* 40, 45–53.

Deosaran, R. (1993). *A Society Under Siege: A Study of Political Confusion and Legal Mysticism.* St. Augustine, Trinidad: McAl Psychological Research Centre, University of the West Indies.

DiPrizio, R. (2000). "Post–Cold War Humanitarian Interventions: What Motivated the Bush and Clinton Administrations?" Paper presented to the Annual Meeting of the International Studies Association–North East, Albany, NY.

Domínguez, J., and Hernandez, R. (1989). *U.S.-Cuban Relations in the 1990s.* Boulder, CO: Westview Press.

Domínguez, J. (1989). *To Make a World Safe for Revolution: Cuba's Foreign Policy.* Cambridge, MA: Harvard University Press.

Domínguez, J. (1997). "U.S.–Cuban Relations: From the Cold War to the Colder War." *Journal of Interamerican Studies and World Affairs,* 39, 49–75.

Donnelly, J. (1999, December 21). "Waiting for Aristide," *The Globe and Mail,* R-3

Doyle, K. (1994). "Hollow Diplomacy in Haiti." *World Policy Journal,* 6, 50–59.

Edwards III, G. (1996). "Frustration and Folly: Bill Clinton and the Public Presidency." In C. Campbell and B. Rockman, (eds.), *The Clinton Presidency: First Appraisals.* Chatham, NJ: Chatham House Publishers, 234–261.

Entman, R. (1991). "Framing US Coverage of International News: Contrasts in Narratives of the KAL and Iran Air Incidents." *Journal of Communication,* 41, 6–28.

Entman, R. (1993). "Framing: Towards Clarification of a Fractured Paradigm." *Journal of Communication,* 43, 51–58.

Evans-Pritchard, A. (1993, November, 29). "Getting to Know the General." *National Review, 45,* 24–26.

Falcoff, M. (1994). "Cuba and the United States: Back to the Beginning." *World Affairs,* 156, 111–133.

Falk, P. (1986). *Cuban Foreign Policy: Caribbean Tempest.* Lexington, MA: Lexington Books.

Falk, P. (1997). "The US–Cuba Agenda: Opportunity or Stalemate." *Journal of Interamerican Studies and World Affairs,* 39, 153–162.

Farmer, P. (1994). *The Uses of Haiti.* Monroe, ME: Common Courage Press.

Farmer, P. 1995). "The Significance of Haiti." In D. McFadyen and P. La Ramée, (eds.), *Haiti:Dangerous Crossroads.* Boston: South End Press, 41–45.

Farrell, T. (1993). "In Whose Interest? Nationalization and Bargaining with the Petroleum Multinationals: The Trinidad and Tobago Experience." In B. Ince, A. Bryan, H. Addo and R. Ramsaran, (eds.), *Issues in Caribbean International Relations.* Lanham, MD: University Press of America.

Fascell, D. (1992–93). "Prospects of United States-Latin American Relations in the New World Order." *North-South,* 2, 11–13.

Fatton, R. (1997). "The Rise, Fall, and Resurrection of President Aristide." In R. Rotberg (ed.), *Haiti Renewed: Political and Economic Prospects.* Washington, DC: The Brookings Institution.

Fauriol, G. (1988). "The Duvaliers and Haiti." *Orbis,* 32, 587–607.

Floyd, J.C. (1996). "A Theology of Insurrection? Religion and Politics in Mexico." *Journal of International Affairs,* 50, 142–165.

Furlonge-Kelly, V. (1991). *The Silent Victory.* Port of Spain, Trinidad: Golden Eagle Enterprises, Ltd.

Gamson, W. (1989). "News as Framing." *American Behavioral Scientist,* 33, 157–161.

Gibbons, E. (1999). *Sanctions in Haiti: Human Rights and Democracy Under Assault.* Washington, DC: Praeger/CSIS The Washington Papers.

Gibson, C. (1966). *Spain in America.* New York: Harper and Row.

Giffard, C.A. and Rivenburgh, N. (2000). "News Agencies, National Images, and Global Events." *Journalism & Mass Communication Quarterly,* 77, 8–21.

Gitlin, T. (1980). *The Whole World is Watching: Mass Media in the Making and Unmaking of the New Left.* Berkeley, CA: University of California Press.

Gleijeses, P. (1991). *Shattered Hope: The Guatemalan Revolution and the United States.* Princeton, NJ: Princeton University Press.

Gonzalez, D. (2002, July 30). "8 Years After Invasion, Haiti Squalor Worsens." *The New York Times,* p. A1.

Gordon, M. (1994, July 8). "Panama refuses to take Haitians." *The New York Times,* A-1.

Gorham, R. (1992). "Canada-Cuba Relations: A Brief Overview." In M. Erisman and J. Kirk, (eds.), *Cuban Foreign Policy Confronts a New International Order.* Boulder, CO: Lynne Rienner.

Grant, L. (1990). "Forward: The Way We Were." In *Trinidad Under Siege.* Port of Spain, Trinidad: Trinidad Express Newspapers Ltd., 3–6.

Greenhouse, S. (1994, March 30). "Aristide Cool to U.S. Shift in Haiti Policy." *The New York Times,* A-11.

Grenier, Y. (2000). "Our Dictatorship: Canada's Trilateral Relations with Castro's Cuba." In M. Molot and F. Osler Hamson, (eds.). *Canada Among Nations 2000: Vanishing Borders.* Don Mills, ON: Oxford University Press, 247–273.

Griffith, I. (1993). *The Quest for Security in the Caribbean: Problems and Promises in Subordinate States.* Armonk, New York: M.E. Sharpe.

Gunn, G. (1990). "Will Castro Fall?" *Foreign Policy,* 79, 132–150.

Haiti. (1987). *Constitution de la République d'Haiti.* Port-au-Prince. Ministère de L'Information et de la Coordination.

Halleck, D. (1994). "Zapatistas On-line." *NACLA Report on the Americas,* 28, 30–32.

Hanson, E. (1995). "Guest Editor's Introduction: International News After the Cold War: Continuity or Change?" *Political Communication,* 12, 351–355.

Harvey, N. (1998). *The Chiapas Rebellion: The Struggle for Land and Democracy.* Durham, NC: Duke University Press.

Hector, C. (1988). "Haiti: A Nation in Crisis." *Peace and Security,* 3, 6–7.

Herman, E., and Broadhead, F. (1984). *Demonstration Elections: U.S.-Staged Elections in the Dominican Republic, Vietnam and El Salvador.* Boston: South End Press.

Herman, E. (1985). "Diversity in the News: 'Marginalizing' the Opposition," *Journal of Communication,* 35, 135–146.

Herman, E., and Chomsky, N. (1988). *Manufacturing Consent: The Political Economy of the Mass Media.* New York: Pantheon Books.

Hogan, J. (1994, May 6). "Haiti's Bishops Turn Their Backs," *Commonweal,* 121, 22–24.

Holsti, O. (1969). *Content Analysis for the Social Sciences and Humanities.* Reading, MA: Addison-Wesley.

Horlacher, F. (1990). "The Language of Late Nineteenth-Century Expansionism." In S. Ricard, (ed.), *An American Empire: Expansionist Cultures and Policies, 1881-1917.* Aix-en-Provence: Université de Provence, 31–49.

Hugeux, V. (1994. October 27). "Titid II, prophète sous l'influence." *L'Express,* 2259, 33–35.

Huntington, S. (1993). "The Clash of Civilizations?" *Foreign Affairs,* 72, 22–49.

Ince, B. (1983). "Leadership and Foreign Policy Decision-Making in a Small State: Trinidad and Tobago's Decision to Enter the OAS." In B. Ince, A. Bryan, H. Addo, and R. Ramsaran, (eds.), *Issues in Caribbean International Relations.* Lanham, MD: University Press of America, 265–295.

Iorio, S., and Huxman, S. (1996). "Media Coverage of Political Issues and the Framing of Personal Concerns." *Journal of Communication,* 46, 97–115.

Ives, K. (1995a). "The Lavalas Alliance Propels Aristide to Power." in D. McFadyen and P. LaRamée, (eds.), *Haiti: Dangerous Crossroads.* Boston, MA: South End Press, Boston, MA: South End Press, 41–45.

Ives, K. (1995b). "Unmaking of a President." In D. McFadyen, and P. LaRamée, (eds.), *Haiti: Dangerous Crossroads,* 65–87.

Ives, K. (1995c). "Haiti's Second U. S. Occupation." In D. McFadyen, and P. LaRamée, (eds.), *Haiti: Dangerous Crossroads,* 107–118.

Iyengar, S., and Kinder, D. (1987). *News That Matters: Agenda-Setting and Priming in a Television Age.* Chicago: University of Chicago Press.

Iyengar, S. (1991). *Who Is Responsible: How Television Frames Political Issues.* Chicago: University of Chicago Press.

Jakobsen, P. (1996). "National Interest, Humanitarianism or CNN: What Triggers UN Peace Enforcement after the Cold War?" *Journal of Peace Research,* 33, 205–215.

Kagay, M. (1994, September 21). "Occupation Lifts Clinton's Standing in Poll, But Many Americans Are Sceptical." *The New York Times,* A-16.

Kaplan, M. (1983). "American Policy Toward the Caribbean Region: One Aspect of American Global Policy." In B. Ince, A. Bryan, H. Addo, and R. Ramsaran, eds. *Issues in Caribbean International Relations.* Lanham, MD. University Press of America, 51–60.

Kegley, C., and Wittkopf, E. (1991). *American Foreign Policy: Pattern and Process.* 4th ed. New York: St. Martin's Press.

LaFeber, W. (1963). *The New Empire: An Interpretation of American Expansion, 1860–1898.* Ithaca, NY: Cornell University Press.

LaFeber, W. (1983). *Inevitable Revolutions: The United States and Central America.* New York: W.W. Norton.

LaFeber, W. (1989). *The American Age: United States Foreign Policy at Home and Abroad since 1750.* New York: W.W. Norton and Company.

Larson, W. (1990). "Television and U.S. Foreign Policy: The Case of the Iran Hostage' Crisis." In D. Graber, (ed.), *Media Power in Politics.* 2nd ed. Washington: CQ Press, 301–312.

Larzelere, A. (1988). *The 1980 Cuban Boatlift: Castro's Ploy–America's Dilemma.* Washington, DC: National Defense University Press.

LeoGrande, W. (1997). "Enemies Evermore: U.S. Policy Towards Cuba After Helms-Burton." *Journal of Latin American Studies,* 29, 211–221.

Lisio, S. (1996). "Helms–Burton and the Point of Diminishing Returns." *International Affairs,* 39, 77–108.

Livingston, S., and Eachus, T. (1995). "Humanitarian Crises and U.S. Foreign Policy: Somalia and the CNN Effect Reconsidered." *Political Communication,* 12, 413–429.

Livingston, S. (1996). "Suffering in Silence: Media Coverage of War and Famine in the Sudan." In R. Rotberg, and T. Weiss, (eds.), *From Massacres to Genocide: The Media, Public Policy and Humanitarian Crises.* Washington, DC: The Brookings Institution, 68–89.

Ma, J., and Hildebrandt, K. (1993). "Canadian Press Coverage of the Ethnic Chinese Community: A Content Analysis of the *Toronto Star* and the *Vancouver Sun.*" *Canadian Journal of Communication,* 40, 479–496.

Maingot, A. (1986–87). "Haiti: Problems of a Transition to Democracy in an Authoritarian Soft State." *Journal of Interamerican Studies and World Affairs,* 28, 75–102.

Mandelbaum, M. (1996). "Foreign Policy as Social Work." *Foreign Affairs,* 75, 16–32.

Manwaring, M., Schulz, D., Maguire, R., Hakim, P., and Horn, A. (1997). *The Challenge of Haiti's Future.* Carlisle Barracks, PA: Strategic Studies Institute, U.S. Army War College.

Marajh, C., and Robinson, L. (1990). "Robinson Set Free." In *Trinidad Under Siege.* Port of Spain, Trinidad: The Trinidad Express Newspapers Ltd. 78.

Martin, I. (1995). "Haiti: Mangled Multilateralism." *Foreign Policy,* 95, 72–89.

Matthews, M. (1990, September). "The Long Hot Session." *Trinidad and Tobago Review,* 12, 12–13.

Maynard, D. (1990). "Fourteen Hours of Sheer Anarchy and Madness." In *Trinidad Under Siege.* Port of Spain, Trinidad: The Trinidad Express Newspapers Ltd.

McCombs, M., and Shaw, D. (1972). "The Agenda-Setting Function of Mass Media." *Public Opinion Quarterly,* 36, 176–187.

McCombs, M., and Shaw, D. (1993). "The Evolution of Agenda-Setting Research: Twenty-Five Years in the Marketplace of Ideas." *Journal of Communication,* 43, 58–67.

McFadyen, D., and LaRamée, P. (1995). *Haiti: Dangerous Crossroads.* Boston: South End Press.

Mermin, J. (1997). "Television News and American Intervention in Somalia: The Myth of a Media-Driven Foreign Policy." *Political Science Quarterly,* 112, 385–403.

Mesa-Lago, C. (1993). *Cuba After the Cold War.* Pittsburgh, PA: University of Pittsburgh Press.

Millis, W. (1931). *The Martial Spirit. A Study of Our War with Spain.* New York: Houghton Mifflin

Mintz, S. (1995). "Can Haiti Change? Foreign Affairs, 74, 73–86.

Monfils, B. (1995). "Crisis in the Caribbean: A Narrative Communication Analysis of Newspaper Coverage of the 1990 Muslimeen Insurrection in Trinidad." Paper presented at the Convention of the Speech Communication Association of Puerto Rico, San Juan, PR.

Morales, W. (1994). "US intervention and the New World Order: lessons from Cold War and post–Cold War Cases." Third World Quarterly, 15, 77–101.

Morgan, H.W. (1965). America's Road to Empire: The War with Spain and Overseas Expansion. New York: Wiley.

Morley, M., and McGillion, C. (1997). "'Disobedient' Generals and the Politics of Redemocratization: The Clinton Administration and Haiti." Political Science Quarterly, 112, 363–384.

Nairn, A. (1994a, October 3). "The Eagle Is Landing." *The Nation,* 344–348.

Nairn, A. (1994b, October 24). "Our Man in FRAPH: Behind Haiti's Paramilitaries." *The Nation,* 458–461.

Nash, J. (1995). "The Reassertion of Indigenous Identity: Mayan Responses to State Intervention in Chiapas." *Latin American Research Review,* 30, 7–41.

Nazario, O. (1996). "Overcoming Political Isolation and Responding to International Pressures: Cuba's New Independent Foreign Policy." *Cuban Studies,* 26, 75–96.

Nelson, R., and Soderlund, W. (1992). "Press Definitions of Reality during Elections in Haiti." *Media Development,* 39, 46–49.

Niblack, P. (1995). *The United Nations Mission in Haiti: Trip Report.* Santa Monica, CA: Rand Corporation.

Nicholls, D. (1996). *From Dessalines to Duvalier: Race, Colour and National Independence in Haiti.* New Brunswick, NJ: Rutgers University Press.

Norris, P. (1995). "The Restless Searchlight: Network News Framing of the Post–Cold War World." *Political Communication,* 12, 357–370.

Oppenheimer, A. (1992). *Castro's Final Hour: The Secret Story Behind the Coming Downfall of Communist Cuba.* New York: Simon and Shuster.

Orenstein, C. (1995). "Haiti in the Mainstream Press." In D. McFadyen, and P. LaRamée, (eds.), *Haiti: Dangerous Crossroads.* Boston, South End Press, 103–105.

Packer, G. (1993, Summer). "Choke Hold on Haiti." *Dissent,* 40, 297–308.

Paletz, D., and Entman, R. (1981). *Media, Power, Politics.* New York: The Free Press.

Pantin, R. (1990). "The Days of Wrath." In *Trinidad Under Siege.* Port of Spain, Trinidad: The Trinidad Express Newspapers Ltd., 37.

Para, M. (1995). "The Politics of Representation: The Literature of the Revolution and the Zapatista Uprising in Chiapas." *Journal of Latin American Cultural Studies,* 4, 65–71.

Parenti, M. (1986). *Inventing Reality.* New York: St. Martin's Press.

Pastor, R. (1997). "A Popular Democratic Revolution in a Predemocratic Society." In R. Rotberg, (ed.), *Haiti Renewed: Political and Economic Prospects.* Washington, DC: The Brookings Institution Press, 118–135.

Pérez, L. (1998). *The War of 1898: The United States and Cuba in History and Historiography.* Chapel Hill, NC: University of North Carolina Press.

Perusse, R. (1995). *Haitian Democracy Restored, 1991–1995.* Lanham, MD: University Press of America.

Portes, A., and Bach, R. (1985). *Latin Journey: Cuban and Mexican Immigrants in the United States.* Berkeley, CA: University of California Press.

Poyo, G. (1989). *"With All, and for the Good of All": The Emergence of Popular Nationalism in the Cuban Communities of the United States, 1848–1898.* Durham, NC: Duke University Press.

Pride, R. (1995). "How Activists and Media Frame Social Problems: Critical Events Versus Performance Trends for Schools." *Political Communication,* 12, 5–26.

Reding, A. (1994). "Chiapas Is Mexico: The Imperative of Political Reform." *World Policy Journal,* 6, 11–25.

Rieff, D. (1995). "From Exiles to Immigrants." *Foreign Affairs,* 74, 76–89.

Rieff, D. (1996). "Cuba Refrozen." *Foreign Affairs,* 75, 62–76.

Rioux J-S., and Van Belle, D. (2001). "L'influence des médias sur l'allocation d'aide bilatérale cedilla française, 1986–1995." Paper presented at the Annual Meeting of the Canadian Political Science Association, Quebec City, CA.

Rippy, J. F. (1926). *The United States and Mexico.* New York: Alfred A. Knopf.

Robinson, P. (2000). "The Policy-Media Interaction Model: Measuring Media Power During Humanitarian Crisis." *Journal of Peace Research,* 37, pp. 613-633.

Rogers, E., and Dearing, J. (1988). "Agenda-Setting Research: Where Has It Been, Where Is It Going?" In J. Anderson, (ed.), *Communication Yearbook,* Vol. 11. Beverley Hills, CA: Sage Publications, 555–594.

Ross, J. (1995). *Rebellion from the Roots: Indian Uprising in Chiapas.* Monroe, ME: Common Courage Press.

Rota, J., and McLaughlin, E. (1999). "The Coverage of Mexico by Leading American News Media." Paper presented at the 16th Annual Intercultural Communication Conference, Miami, FL.

Rotberg, R., and Weiss, T. (1996). *From Massacres to Genocide: The Media, Public Policy; and Humanitarian Intervention.* Washington, DC: The Brookings Institution.

Roy, J. (1997). "The Helms–Burton Law: Development, Consequences, and Legacy for Inter- American and European–U.S. Relations." *Journal of Interamerican Studies and World Affairs,* 39, 77–108.

Ryan, S. (1991). *The Muslimeen Grab for Power: Race, Religion and Revolution in Trinidad and Tobago.* Port of Spain, Trinidad: Imprint Caribbean, Ltd.

Schlesinger, S., and Kinzer, S. (1983). *Bitter Fruit: The Untold Story of the American Coup in Guatemala.* New York: Anchor Press.

Schulz, D. (1993). "Can Castro Survive?" *Journal of Interamerican Studies and World Affairs,* 35, 89–117.

Schulz, D. (1997). "Political Culture, Political Change, and Etiology of Violence." In R. Rotberg, (ed.), *Haiti Renewed: Political and Economic Prospects.* Washington, DC: The Brookings Institution Press, 93–117.

Shacochis, B. (1999). *The Immaculate Invasion.* New York, Viking Press.

Shattuck, J. (1966). "Human Rights and Humanitarian Crises: Polity-Making and the Media." In R. Rotberg, and T. Weiss, (eds.), *From Massacres to Genocide.* Washington, DC: The Brookings Institution, 169–178.

Shiras, P. (1996). "Big Problems, Small Print: Guide to the Complexity of Humanitarian Emergencies." In R. Rotberg and T. Weiss, (eds.), *From Massacres to Genocide: The Media, Public Policy and Humanitarian Intervention.* Washington, DC: The Brookings Institution, 93–114.

Smith, A. (1980). The Geopolitics of Information: How Western Culture Dominates the World. New York: Oxford University Press.

Smith, W. (1992). *The Russians Aren't Coming: New Soviet Policy in Latin America.* Gainesville, FL: University of Florida Press.

Smith, W. (1997, June). "The Helms–Burton Act: A Loose Canon?" *International Policy Report,* 1–10.

Soderlund, W. (1970). "An Analysis of the Guerrilla Insurgency and Coup d'Etat as Techniques of Indirect Aggression." *International Studies Quarterly,* 9, 335–360.

Soderlund, W., Wagenberg, R., and Pemberton, I. (1994). "Cheerleader or Critic? Television News Coverage in Canada and the United States of the U.S. Invasion of Panama." *Canadian Journal of Political Science,* 27, 581–604.

Soderlund, W., Wagenberg, R., and Surlin, S. (1998). "The Impact of the End of the Cold War on Canadian and American TV News Coverage of Cuba: Image Consistency or Image Change?" *Canadian Journal of Communication,* 23, 217–231.

Soderlund, W. (2001). *Media Definitions of Cold War Reality: The Caribbean Basin, 1953–1992.* Toronto: Canadian Scholars' Press Inc.

Soderlund, W., and Brown–John, C.L. (1999). "Cuban MiGs, Helms–Burton and International Law." Paper presented to the Speech Communication Association of Puerto Rico, San Juan, PR.

Stephen, L. (1995). "The Zapatista Army of National Liberation and the National Democratic Convention." *Latin American Perspectives,* 22, 88–99.

Stinchcombe, A. (1994). "Class Conflict and Diplomacy: Haitian Isolation in the 19th-Century World System." *Sociological Perspectives,* 37, 1–23.

Stotzky, I. (1997). *Silencing the Guns in Haiti: The Promise of Deliberative Democracy.* Chicago: University of Chicago Press.

Tannenbaum, F. (1966) [1933]. *Peace by Revolution: Mexico After 1910.* New York: Columbia University Press.

Taylor, P. (2000, May 5). "U.S. struggles to wield power, strategic study says." *National Post,* A15.

Terry, J. (1990, September). "Shall We Dance with Teddy Roosevelt." *Trinidad and Tobago Review, 12,* 30.

Thomas, H. (1971). *Cuba: The Pursuit of Freedom.* New York: Harper & Row.

Treverton, G. (1989). "Cuba in U.S. Security Perspective." In J. Domínguez and R. Hernandez, (eds.)., *U.S.–Cuban Relations in the 1990s.* Boulder, CO: Westview, 63–83.

Vanderbush, W. and Haney, P. (1999). "Policy toward Cuba in the Clinton Administration." *Political Science Quarterly,* 114, 387-408.

von Hippel, K. (1995). "Democratisation as Foreign Policy: The Case of Haiti." *The World Today,* 11–14.

Waters, M. (1992). "Introduction." In F. Castro, and E. Guevara *To Speak the Truth: Why Washington's "Cold War" Against Cuba Doesn't End.* M. Waters, (ed.). New York: Pathfinder Press.

Weber, C. (1995). "Dissimulating Intervention: A Reading of the U.S.-led Intervention into Haiti." *Alternatives,* 20, 265–277.

White, J. (1997). *Still Seeing Red: How the Cold War Shapes the New American Politics.* Boulder, CO: Westview Press.

Wiarda, H. (1989). "Cuba and U.S. Foreign Policy in Latin America: The Changing Realities." In J. Domínguez, and R. Hernandez, (eds.). *US.–Cuban Relations in the 1990s.* Boulder, CO: Westview Press, 155–178.

Womack, J. (1968). *Zapata and the Mexican Revolution.* New York: Random House.

Author Index

Subject Index

About the Editor and Contributors

WALTER C. SODERLUND (Professor Emeritus) received his Ph.D. in Political Science from the University of Michigan in 1970 and has taught courses in international relations and mass media at the University of Windsor from 1968 until his retirement in 2002. He has maintained a long-standing research interest in international communication, especially in the context of Latin America and the Caribbean. He is the coeditor of *Mass Media and the Caribbean* (1990); coauthor of *Media Canada* (1996); and author of *Media Definitions of Cold War Reality* (2001).

E. DONALD BRIGGS (Professor Emeritus) received his Ph.D. from the University of London in 1961 and taught international relations at the University of Windsor from 1963 until his retirement in 1999. Primarily interested in international relations theory, his research interests were widely cast. He was the coauthor of *Media and Election in Canada* (1984) as well as numerous journal articles. He is currently involved in a research project focused on peacekeeping in Africa in the post–Cold War era.

RALPH C. NELSON (Professor Emeritus) holds a Ph.D. in philosophy from the University of Notre Dame and taught both philosophy and political science at the University of Windsor until his retirement in 1993. One of his major research interests is democratic theory, and the uncertain path of Haiti toward democratic governance has occupied his attention since the end of the Duvalier dictatorship in 1986. Among other works, he is co-author of *Canadian Confederation: A Decision-Making Analysis* (1979).